"Jack Cashill has researched, organ...
of this intrigue in an outstanding and readable style. He has provided the needed resolution to finally end the TWA 800 conspiracy. It is—by far—the most thorough, insightful, and believable accounting of that tragedy."

—**VERNON GROSE**, former NTSB board member
and CNN commentator on TWA 800

"In this extraordinary book, Jack Cashill—America's greatest investigative reporter—provides new and overwhelming evidence that the official explanation [of TWA 800] from the Clintons couldn't possibly be true, and that something is very, very wrong at both the FBI and the CIA."

—**HERBERT E. MEYER**, former National Intelligence
Council vice chairman

"Jack Cashill has done it again. He is one of the great investigative journalists in America, at a time that it has become a lost art. In his new book, *TWA 800: Behind the Cover-Up and Conspiracy*, he walks us through one of the most important and revealing stories of the last twenty years.... He also presents new evidence and fresh perspectives, linking the cover-up to today's presidential race."

—**ROGER ARONOFF**, editor of Accuracy in Media and producer of the
award-winning documentary *TWA 800: The Search for the Truth*

"Jack Cashill has worked tirelessly for almost twenty years to bring the truth of what really happened to TWA Flight 800 to the public, and most of all, to the families who lost loved ones on that flight. Because I lost my son, Yon Rojany, that fateful night of July 17, 1996—and never believed the government line about a spark in the center fuel tank—I am forever indebted to Jack. This book is a compelling read laying out the facts of what really happened. It is a book you won't be able to put down. Thank you, Jack!"

—**LISA MICHELSON**, family member of TWA 800 victim

TWA 800

TWA 800

Behind the Cover-Up and Conspiracy

JACK CASHILL

REGNERY
HISTORY
Washington, D.C.

Regnery History™ is a trademark of Salem Communications Holding Corporation
Regnery® is a registered trademark and its colophon is a trademark of Salem Communications Holding Corporation

First trade paperback edition published 2023

Cataloging-in-Publication data on file with the Library of Congress

ISBN: 978-1-68451-455-7
Library of Congress Control Number: 2016004757

Published in the United States by
Regnery History, an Imprint of
Regnery Publishing
A Division of Salem Media Group
Washington, D.C.
www.Regnery.com

Manufactured in the United States of America

10 9 8 7 6 5 4 3 2 1

Books are available in quantity for promotional or premium use. For information on discounts and terms, please visit our website: www.Regnery.com.

To James and Elizabeth Sanders

CONTENTS

At 8:19 p.m. on July 17, 1996, TWA Flight 800 left JFK Airport bound for Paris. At 8:31 p.m. the plane was destroyed ten miles off the popular South Shore of Long Island. The FBI would interview more than 250 people who saw an object streaking toward the plane.

Chapter: ONE

THE BREACH

But you also had systemically a wall that was in place between the criminal side and the intelligence side. What's in a criminal case doesn't cross over that line. Ironclad regulations, so that even people in the criminal division and the intelligence divisions of the FBI couldn't talk to each other, let alone talk to us or us talk to them.[1]

—*Director of Central Intelligence, George Tenet, before the 9/11 Commission, March 24, 2004*

"**J**ack Cashill?"

I took the call in my Kansas City office on my landline. I still had one. It was the spring of 2009.

"You got 'im."

"This is witness number seventy-three. Do you know who I am?"

I did indeed. She was arguably the single most important eyewitness to the destruction of TWA Flight 800 off the coast of Long Island thirteen years earlier. During those years her identity eluded the many independent researchers into the crash, myself included. As she told me, physicist Tom Stalcup, among the more dedicated of those researchers, had recently tracked her down. Before that contact, she had no idea how crucial was her testimony. Once she learned, she wanted to learn more and called me, since I had co-authored a book on TWA 800 with James Sanders called *First Strike*.

"Do you remember what I told the FBI?" she asked.

"I certainly do." I could almost recite it. "Upside down Nike swoosh, correct?"

"That's me."

On July 17, 1996, Sandy—not her real name—was visiting friends on Long Island. They were relatives of her fiancé who was working in New York City. That evening Sandy and her two friends drove to a beach near the Moriches Inlet on the South Shore of Long Island. Just a few minutes after sunset, the FBI would report, "She observed an aircraft climbing in the sky, traveling from her right to her left." This would have been from the west, JFK airport in New York City, towards the east, eventually Paris, the original destination of the ill-fated 747 with 230 souls on board.

The sun was setting behind her. "While keeping her eyes on the aircraft," the FBI report continued, "she observed a 'red streak' moving up from the ground toward the aircraft at an approximately 45 degree angle. The 'red streak' was leaving a light gray colored smoke trail. The 'red streak' went passed [sic] the right side and above the aircraft before arcing back toward the aircraft's right wing."

According to the FBI, Sandy described the arc's shape "as resembling an upside down NIKE swoosh logo." The smoke trail, light gray in color, widened as it approached the aircraft. Agent Lee Butler interviewed Sandy at her North Carolina home three days after the disaster and wrote down Sandy's account on a "302," the standard FBI report form. "She never took her eyes off the aircraft during this time," the 302 continued. "At the instant the smoke trail ended at the aircraft's right wing, she heard a loud sharp noise which sounded like a firecracker had just exploded at her feet. She then observed a fire at the aircraft followed by one or two secondary explosions which had a deeper sound. She then observed the front of the aircraft separate from the back. She then observed burning pieces of debris falling from the aircraft."

Weeks before the FBI and the National Transportation Safety Board (NTSB) were able to piece together the break-up sequence of the aircraft, Sandy had nailed it. She was the perfect eyewitness. She worked in the travel industry. She had a long-standing interest in aviation. She tracked the plane and the "flare" as separate objects. She read no more into the explosion than what she could observe. At the Moriches Inlet, she was as close to the actual site of the explosion as any other witness, less than ten miles away. And she was not grandstanding. Just the opposite. Her friends and her fiancé were dead set against her cooperating with the FBI. The following day agent Mary Doran called and asked Sandy to talk to her friends. Doran wanted their accounts as well. Sandy balked. As she told Doran, her friends were "really upset" she had given their names to the FBI. "They did not want to have any involvement whatsoever with the FBI," she added. Sandy's fiancé sided with his relatives, so much so that she feared he would break off the engagement if the FBI contacted them.[2]

Sandy would marry her fiancé. At the time she called me, he was being treated for cancer in a hospital about an hour up the road from my Kansas City office. Had her husband been healthy, she would not have dared to follow up. He wanted her to have nothing to do with the case, but now there was a story she felt the need to share.

It involved her second interview. As reported on an FBI 302, agents Steven Bongardt and Theodore Otto visited Sandy at her North Carolina home on April 29, 1997, and produced a report more detailed than Agent Butler's from July 1996. Sandy covered much of the same territory, but her account was not as precise as it had been during the first interview nine months earlier. In that earlier interview, she claimed the object hit the right wing. This time "she could not recall which of the wings" was struck. Nor did she repeat her claim that the object came "up from the ground." In this second account, she only claimed to have seen the object in mid-flight.

Unlike Agent Butler, Bongardt and Otto asked her what kind of object she had observed. "She replied that she believed she witnessed a missile," the agents reported, "which had been fired from a boat which was located somewhere on the Atlantic Ocean." By this time the idea that a missile struck TWA 800 had been shuttled off to the netherworld of the conspiracy theorist. A month earlier, the CIA and the FBI concurred that a sighting like hers was an optical illusion. The agents did not include the "missile" detail to make Sandy look astute. They included it to make her look flighty. They also suggested a reason why her initial account might be unreliable. Although denying she was "inebriated" at the time of the crash, Sandy did admit that "she had consumed two (2) 'Long Island Ice Tea' cocktails" earlier that evening. This admission rendered her initial account suspect.[3]

At the time, the FBI did not make audio recordings of interviews. A secretary simply took the handwritten 302s and typed them up. Sandy had only recently read the two separate 302s. She was still fuming when I talked to her. She had real problems with that second one.

"I don't even know what a 'Long Island Ice Tea' is," she told me.

"Could it have been another drink?" I asked.

"No," she told me. "I don't drink, not at all. And there's something else you don't know, something stranger."

"Tell me."

"There was no second interview. They made it all up."

"There's something you may not know." I added. "You're not the only witness they did that to."

As Sandy was learning, she was one of more than 700 witnesses to the crash or its aftermath that the FBI interviewed. The fact that her two friends refused to be interviewed suggests that there were many more who saw the incident but refused to cooperate. By the National Transportation Safety Board's count she was one of 258 eyewitnesses who saw a rising streak of light and one of fifty-six who traced that light to the ground or the horizon.[4] She had no idea there were so many. Few people did. Of the fifty-six, the *New York Times*, which more or less owned the story, interviewed exactly none after the first two days of the investigation and those in the first two days only cursorily.

While Sandy and her friends were enjoying the summer evening at the Moriches Inlet, Bill and Hillary Clinton were working the rope line at the Women's Leadership Forum of the Democratic National Committee. At 8:35 p.m., four minutes after TWA 800 was blown out of the sky, a motorcade whisked the Clintons to the White House. They arrived at

8:45 p.m. and made their way to the family residence.[5] Soon after they arrived, Clinton's chief of staff Leon Panetta called the president with the grim news out of Long Island.[6]

By 9 p.m. the White House was abuzz with talk of the disaster. In his bestselling 2004 memoir, *Against All Enemies*, Richard Clarke provided the most detailed account of that evening. At the time, Clarke served as chairman of the Coordinating Security Group (CSG) on terrorism. Within thirty minutes of the plane's crash, wrote Clarke, he had called a meeting of the CSG in the White House Situation Room. This involved the FBI, the CIA, the Federal Aviation Administration (FAA), the departments of State and Defense, the Pentagon, and the Coast Guard.[7] "The investigation [looked] at almost every possibility including a state actor," said Panetta. From the beginning, no one considered this an ordinary plane crash.

For reasons unknown but easily imagined, the president chose not to join Clarke and the other anxious officials in the Situation Room, located in the White House's basement. Instead, as Retired Air Force Lieutenant Colonel Robert "Buzz" Patterson confirmed, the Clintons spent the evening on the second floor in the family residence. Patterson believes there was another person with the Clintons, Sandy Berger, the deputy national security advisor. At the time, Patterson carried the nuclear football for the president, which kept him in close proximity. That night, he too was in the White House, but he was not involved in any relevant discussions.[8]

That same night, Captain Ray Ott and his crew on a Navy surveillance plane, the P-3 Orion, were flying almost directly above the 747 when it exploded. After circling for a half hour and shooting video of the debris field, the plane quit the scene and headed south two hundred miles on a routine sub-hunting exercise. No entity in the military arsenal was as capable of hunting down any suspected terrorists as the P-3, but Ott had orders to do otherwise.[9]

For the next six hours the Clintons gathered information and evaluated possible responses. The response Clarke dreaded most went by the cryptic name, the "Eisenhower option." According to Clarke, Clinton argued for a "massive attack" against Iran if American interests were to be attacked again as they had been in June when terrorists blew up the Khobar Towers complex in Saudi Arabia, killing nineteen American servicemen. "Clearly," Panetta would later tell CNN, "if we had determined that this was a foreign act or a terrorist [sic] similar to what had happened to 9/11 that President Clinton would not have hesitated to take action."[10] So charged was the atmosphere following TWA 800's destruction that Clarke called this moment in history, "The Almost War, 1996."

This was exactly the kind of crisis the president feared most. He had even given it a generic name, "Greg Norman." Clinton and golfer Greg Norman were buddies. A few months earlier, in April 1996, Norman took a six-stroke lead into the final round of the Masters and blew it. Clinton worried that his campaign might suffer a similar fate. He told press aide Mike McCurry, "That's going to be the new *theme* for the campaign, that we're not going to allow ourselves to be Greg Normanized."[11] He and Hillary had spent the last sixteen months scrambling out of the crater left by the disastrous 1994 mid-term elections. Now with a lead in the polls seemingly as solid as Norman's at the Masters, Clinton would leave nothing to chance. "We could have a major crisis go bad on us," he worried.[12] "Greg Norman," he reminded his staff over and over. "Greg Norman."[13]

By 3 a.m. the Clintons had settled on a strategy, one even bolder than it might have seemed to those not in the know. At that fabled hour—the one Hillary would mythologize in her run against Barack Obama—Bill called Berger's boss, National Security Advisor Tony Lake, with the following message: "Dust off the contingency plans."[14] For the time being, the president, in private at least, would blame terrorists for the attack, Iran the chief suspect among them.

The apolitical Lake may not have known any more than this. Only a handful of people did. Evidence strongly suggests that a trusted source in the U.S. Navy received orders to secure the plane's black boxes and to silence his colleagues. The Department of Justice got the word to have the FBI take the investigation over from the National Transportation Safety Board, the NTSB. Although arguably illegal, this move was made publicly. Less public but even more suspect was the intervention of the CIA. Very quietly, as a treasure trove of recently unearthed CIA documents confirm, the CIA was allowed to breach the storied "wall" that prevented the nation's intelligence arm from collaborating with its prosecutorial arm. The agency involved itself on day one of the investigation and ultimately seized control. Ironically, the same Justice Department official who authorized the wall in 1995 was one of the select few chosen to oversee its violation.

Although the phrase has been much abused, there is none better than "cover-up" to describe what followed. Like many initiatives the Clinton White House choreographed, this one was highly improvisational. Before it was through, the TWA 800 investigation would make several sharp course corrections. To be sure, the great majority of those working the investigation had little or no idea it was being misdirected. Some who did harbor suspicions bravely resisted the misdirection, but they had almost nowhere to turn with their protests. Had there been a vigilant media to hear these individuals, or even a mature Internet to share their objections, the truth would have surfaced. To make sure it did not, the CIA, the FBI, and the White House largely avoided the subject of aviation terror for the next five years. As the nation learned in the aftermath of 9/11, the "wall" that was breached all too easily to protect the secrets of TWA 800 held much too firmly when it came to the secrets of our enemies.

Chapter: TWO

CONSPIRACY THEORIST

I never intended to become a conspiracy theorist. In the fall of 2000, when I first dipped my toe into the murky headwaters of the TWA 800 intrigue, I thought myself something of a skeptic, the Socratic nitpicker who rained on the paranoid parades of others. At the time, I was working as an independent writer and producer, mostly in advertising. A variety of new technologies had allowed me to quit the agency world ten years earlier. By the year 2000 I was also doing a fair amount of writing unrelated to advertising. I contributed the odd piece to the *Washington Post*, the *Wall Street Journal*, *Fortune*, and the *Weekly Standard*. Locally, I wrote occasionally for the *Kansas City Star* and regularly for the regional business magazine, *Ingram's*. That year too I had my first and only novel published, a moderately successful, dystopian political fantasy called *2006: The Chautauqua Rising*. In writing the novel I discovered how useful the Internet could be. Over time I came to appreciate it much more than did the FBI or the *New York Times*. For the curious citizen, the Internet was an equalizer.

I anticipated none of this on that September evening when I headed off to a local country club to hear a presentation by James Sanders. A veteran cop turned investigative reporter, Sanders had authored the 1997 book, *The Downing of TWA Flight 800*, and paid a high price for doing so. As he explained, fifty-three TWA employees were on board that doomed aircraft, most of them deadheading back to Paris. His wife, Elizabeth Sanders, had served as a trainer for TWA flight attendants. She knew many of those who had died on the plane, attendants and pilots both, and attended more memorial services than she had ever hoped to.

At one of those services she encountered a friend named Terry Stacey, a 747 pilot and manager. Stacey had been working at the investigation site in Calverton on Long Island and harbored deep suspicions about the direction of the investigation. Knowing that James Sanders was an investigative reporter with a couple books to his credit, Stacey asked Elizabeth to introduce them. Her role in what followed would not go much deeper, but for the authorities that was deep enough.

Elizabeth's life began to unravel in March 1997 when California's Riverside *Press-Enterprise* published a front-page article headlined, "New Data Show Missile May Have Nailed TWA 800."[1] The story described in some detail Sanders's inquiry into the TWA 800 investigation over the preceding five months. A still unknown individual working at Calverton had removed a pinch of seatback material from the plane and sent it to Sanders by Federal Express for testing. That person was Stacey. For the FBI this was a problem much greater than a pinch of foam rubber might suggest. If that pinch had escaped the hangar, who knew what else had?

Once the story broke in the *Press-Enterprise*, the Clinton Justice Department (DOJ) had little choice but to hunt down the conspirators. The Sanderses were not hard to find. Two DOJ prosecutors told them if they did not reveal their source within the investigation, both would become grand jury targets themselves. Lest she be forced to give up Stacey, Elizabeth went into hiding for the next eight months in an Oregon trailer park. That exile almost cost Elizabeth her sanity. James refused to cooperate.

The FBI honchos pursued the removal of the TWA 800 evidence with more passion than they pursued the evidence itself. Soon enough, agents soon found their way to Stacey, arresting him and the Sanderses. "Conspiracy theorist and wife charged with theft of parts from airplane,"[2] the FBI announced much too proudly on the New York office's website. Despite Sanders's two previous books, the DOJ decided that was not enough output to merit standing as a "journalist." Denied that standing, the Sanderses were tried as thieves, Elizabeth the Bonnie to James's Clyde. To save his considerable pension, Stacey pled guilty to a misdemeanor. The Sanderses went to trial in a Long Island federal court and were convicted of conspiracy to steal airplane parts.

This was the story James told to a large crowd at the country club. Not until I recalled that Kansas City was the ancestral home of TWA did the size and intensity of the audience make sense to me. The company had shifted its hub to St. Louis some years back, but its overhaul base remained in Kansas City, as did many of its retired employees. Almost to a person, the TWA people in the room appeared to endorse Sanders's argument that TWA 800 had, in fact, been shot down. This surprised me. At the time, I thought this theory among the more improbable then in circulation. Admittedly, though, I had paid little attention to the investigation. I could not recall, for instance, where I was when I first heard about the plane's demise.

Being on the board of the group that invited the Sanderses, I went to dinner with them afterwards at an Italian restaurant on Kansas City's Country Club Plaza. We sat at a long table, and I found myself at the end of it seated next to Elizabeth. We had a chance to talk. As she related, when she and James first met, he was a police officer and accident investigator in Orange County, California, and she a Polynesian dance instructor. Of Filipino descent, she looked the part. She was sweet, soft-spoken, and agelessly pretty.

Looking for a more substantial job, Elizabeth signed on with TWA, first as a flight attendant and then as a senior trainer. Losing her job pained Elizabeth more than being arrested or convicted. She loved her work and thought of her colleagues as family. This, I gleaned, was not an unusual sentiment among TWA employees. By evening's end, I had begun to reassess Sanders's missile theory. I figured if agents of the government were willing to arrest someone like Elizabeth Sanders for conspiracy, they might, in fact, have had something to hide. Hoping to probe a little deeper, I asked the Sanderses if they could meet me the next morning for breakfast, and they agreed.

Later that night I went online to research TWA Flight 800—and quickly sobered up. The debate had apparently been settled. Three years earlier, in November 1997, the FBI essentially closed its criminal investigation into the disaster. At a press conference that day, the FBI declared emphatically, "No evidence has been found that would indicate that a criminal act was the cause of the tragedy of Flight 800."[3] For its part, the NTSB wrapped up its investigation in August 2000, a month before the Sanderses' appearance in Kansas City. At the final NTSB hearing, Bernard Loeb, the agency's director of the Office of Aviation Safety, said confidently, "The physical evidence indicated indisputably that a missile did not strike the airplane."[4] Neither the FBI nor the NTSB was sure exactly what electrical source sparked an explosion in the plane's center fuel tank (also known as a "center wing tank"), but each agency vigorously rejected the idea that a bomb or missile might have been responsible. Words like "no evidence" and "indisputably" left little room for argument.

Knowing how hard the media rode "conspiracy theorists," I had no interest in becoming one. At the time, it was hard for me to imagine that the FBI and the NTSB would have colluded to conceal the true cause of so public an event in so visible a place. Journalists, I could see, were equally dismissive of so unlikely an intrigue. At least three years earlier, the mainstream media had written off as cranks and kooks anyone who challenged the official explanation. So, for the most part, had the conservative media. The fear of being called a conspiracy theorist paralyzed the respectable right. Although not one to worry about respectability, agenda-setting radio host Rush Limbaugh had another issue. Jim

Kallstrom, the head of the FBI investigation, was a friend. "I don't know of anybody with more honesty or integrity," said Limbaugh of Kallstrom.[5] If anyone of consequence on the right or left felt otherwise about TWA 800, that person was keeping quiet about it.

My idea was to do a video documentary, one that would make a case this complex at least reasonably comprehensible. At breakfast that next morning, I shared my idea and my reservations with the Sanderses. They liked the idea and understood my skepticism. To address it, they invited me to their home in Florida to review the data they had collected. Before heading south, I explored the literature on this particular disaster. There was a ton of it, much of it technical and some of it impenetrable. I could see why the complexity of any given plane crash could intimidate journalists. With so much information to absorb, the temptation was to trust the experts and yield to their authority. In the four years following TWA 800's destruction, the media had done just that.

By this time, two mainstream books had been written on TWA Flight 800. In 1999, Random House published Pat Milton's *In the Blink of an Eye*. Three years earlier, Milton led the Associated Press's coverage of the disaster. According to Milton, the book "resulted from the willingness of the FBI to open itself up to a journalist."[6] Kallstrom trusted her, and she rewarded his trust with something like adulation. The *New York Times* reviewer commended Milton for avoiding "the pitfalls of conspiracy mongering,"[7] high praise from the *Times*. HarperCollins followed in early 2000 with a book from CNN's Christine Negroni called *Deadly Departure*. The book's subtitle pretty well summed up Negroni's thesis: "Why the Experts Failed to Prevent the TWA Flight 800 Disaster and How It Could Happen Again." Not surprisingly, Negroni left CNN soon after the book came out to work for a high-end personal injury law firm that specialized in suing airlines and aircraft manufacturers.

I read these books before going to Florida. They almost made me rethink my trip. At the time, I had little up-close insight into the way the national media worked. I had to assume that two reporters with great contacts working for top-flight media outlets had a pretty good grasp on the facts. Each apparently knew enough to have a book accepted by a major publisher, and a book is not a solitary adventure. A successful one requires a collaboration of sorts among author, agent, publisher, editor, attorneys, and reviewers. All parties seemed to line up behind both books, especially *Deadly Departure*, a *New York Times* "Notable Book of the Year." Sanders, by contrast, was an off-brand reporter and convicted felon living in a low-end Florida apartment complex hard by a smelly canal from which alligators occasionally emerged to eat neighborhood dogs. I owed him a visit, but I expected little.

I underestimated the Sanderses. During our few days together, James impressed me with his relentless, good-spirited energy. In his mid-fifties when we met, he called to mind the cops I grew up around back in Newark, New Jersey—my father, my uncle, several of my cousins. He saw the world as it was and did not flinch from its occasional injustice. As I came to appreciate, he was as much a bulldog as his nemesis Kallstrom. They shared a first name, were of roughly the same age, the same medium height, the same stocky build, the same cop pugnacity. The difference was that Kallstrom, head of the FBI's New York City office, controlled all the levers of power, and Sanders controlled none, not even his ability to come and go. He still needed permission from his probation officer to travel. This power disparity fazed Sanders not at all. The truth emboldened him, just as he believed it enfeebled Kallstrom.

Three intense days with James and Elizabeth in March 2001 left me convinced they had a much better handle on the facts of the case than did Milton, Negroni, or the *New York Times* newsroom. Two things persuaded me. One was the willingness of the Sanderses to confront the evidence and follow where it led. They hid nothing. They fudged nothing. They offered no improbable rationales. Kallstrom, I came to see, could not do the same.

The Sanderses' integrity was just the half of it. For all their good intentions, I would not have embarked on this excellent adventure had they not shown me one particular swath of evidence: the eyewitness testimony. I could scarcely believe there was so much of it, and that it was so consistent and so credible. As something of a news junkie, I had to scold myself for being so unknowing. There was an untold story here, a big one. After three days and a contemplative flight home, I started imaging how I would look in a tin-foil hat.

Chapter: THREE

THE
BEST PEOPLE

I n the early 1990s, my producing partner Michael Wunsch and I decided to canoe down an industrial river in the midst of Kansas City and record our adventure. We funded the subsequent documentary ourselves. KCPT, the regional PBS station, picked it up, and the airing of *Blue River Blues* attracted the attention of a local foundation as we hoped it might. The foundation commissioned us to create a history of Kansas City and transformed us in the process from commercial video makers to documentarians.

By the decade's end, I had produced at least half a dozen additional long form videos, several for KCPT, a few for cable networks, a couple for ourselves, each with a different funding formula. After meeting with the Sanderses, I convinced Wunsch that their story had enough merit to risk my time and his studio overhead on an hour-long documentary. My goal was to make the video as simple and straightforward as possible. In a story as visual as this one, a video could have an impact print could not.

Fortunately, the networks and their affiliates had lost their monopoly on video imagery. The technology that broke the network stranglehold was not the Internet, but the underestimated videocassette recorder. The VCR allowed producers to create products that went straight to consumers unfiltered by the networks' anxious lawyers and activist suits. Our plan was to recuperate our costs through direct sales of our video to the individual consumer. We had no illusions that a network would want in.

A little naïve at the time, I found it hard to believe that broadcasters would leave so powerfully visual a story on the table for shoestring producers like us to take up. But leave it they did. On the up side, we had an open field. On the down side, the networks had produced few visuals for us to use in constructing the documentary. Although CNN named the TWA 800 tragedy the number one domestic news story of 1996[1]—Clinton's reelection was number two—the various TV stations shot very little footage beyond the wreckage recovery. Much more helpful was Accuracy in Media, a D.C.-based watchdog group founded by the tireless Reed Irvine in 1969 and still managed by him more than thirty years later. Irvine and his associates tracked down eyewitnesses, recruited technical experts, videotaped conferences, and routinely dug up stuff the major media tried to bury.

Thanks to the various sunshine laws, the U.S. government proved surprisingly helpful. Once the NTSB wrapped up its case in August 2000, we had access to a mother lode of data, much of it visual. This included an animation of the crash created by the CIA, NTSB animations, hours and hours of video from the NTSB hearing, all seven hundred or so of the FBI witness interviews, scores of eyewitness drawings, and a vast library of charts and photos and technical data.

In a totalitarian country, authorities can suppress information at will. In America, the media have to collaborate in that suppression. During the Clinton era, the White House did a superb job convincing the media to do just that. This was not a new phenomenon. More than fifty years earlier, former communist Whittaker Chambers discovered how seamlessly self-censorship worked. At the time, Chambers was a reluctant witness to the treason of his former friend and comrade, Alger Hiss. A highly respected Harvard Law grad, Hiss had insinuated himself into the upper reaches of the State Department. Despite the enormity of the evidence against him, establishment worthies refused to believe this popular Democrat was a Soviet agent. "It was, not invariably, but in general, the 'best people' who were for Alger Hiss and who were prepared to go to any length to protect and defend him," wrote Chambers in his 1952 masterwork, *Witness.* "It was the enlightened and the powerful, the clamorous proponents of the open mind and the common man, who snapped their minds shut in a pro-Hiss psychosis, of a kind which, in an individual patient, means the simple failure of the ability to distinguish between reality and unreality, and, in a nation, is a warning of the end."[2]

So it was with TWA Flight 800. Minds snapped shut early on in spite of the evidence. The fact that TWA 800 went down during the reelection campaign of a popular Democrat contributed mightily to the ensuing psychosis. This was less a media conspiracy than a collective pathology, as unwitting as it was unhealthy. The "best people" of the late 1990s could no more acknowledge their susceptibility to groupthink than the "best people" of the late 1940s could theirs. So locked were they into their delusions they mocked those who did not share them.

They directed much of their mockery at Internet users. Still in its embryonic state in July 1996—the *New York Times* went online that same year—the Internet challenged the traditional arbiters of information in ways as unwelcome as they were unprecedented. Most critically, the Internet reduced the information imbalance between "the best people" and what Chambers called "the great body of the nation." He referred here to those ordinary Americans who, unlike their betters, kept their minds open, "waiting for the returns to come in." Thanks to the Internet, those everyday citizens had much quicker and more complete access to the "returns" than they ever had before.

The "best people," with the *New York Times* in the lead, pushed back hard. On November 24, 1996, for instance, just four months after the crash and a year before the FBI closed its investigation, the *Times* ran an all-too-typical article headlined "Pierre, Is That a Masonic Flag on the Moon?"[3] In the first sentence reporter George Johnson singled out the ostensible target, the Internet with its "throbbing, fevered brain." Johnson directed his contempt, however, at those ordinary Americans whose Internet use threatened the *Times'* hegemony on the news. "Electrified by the Internet," Johnson complained, "suspicions about the crash of T.W.A. Flight 800 were almost instantly transmuted into convictions that it was the result of friendly fire."

On the tenth anniversary of the crash in 2006, CNN's Jeffery Reid nicely captured the anti-Internet bias still prevalent in America's newsrooms. Reid explained how ten years earlier a "slew of sinister conspiracy theories" diverted investigators' attention from the accepted cause of the disaster, a center fuel tank explosion, "most likely" caused by a spark in its vapor-filled center tank. "So prevalent were these theories," Reid added, "that the term 'Pierre Salinger Syndrome'—the belief that everything on the Internet is true—entered the lexicon."[4]

In the real world, no one suffered from Pierre Salinger syndrome, least of all Pierre Salinger. As press secretary to President John F. Kennedy, Salinger helped create and sustain the Camelot mythology in which he himself—a quotable, cigar-chomping citizen of the world—played an integral part. Salinger was nothing if not connected. He stood just feet from Robert Kennedy when the senator was shot. He served briefly as a U.S. Senator from California. And in the years that followed, he made a nice career for himself as a journalist and international public relations executive. In 1996, his name still opened doors on both sides of the Atlantic, but he overestimated his clout.

About a month after the TWA 800 disaster, retired United Airline pilot and accident investigator Dick Russell received a phone call from Jim Holtsclaw, a friend of his who served as a deputy regional director for the Air Transport Association (ATA).[5] Although Holtsclaw worked out of Los Angeles, he had been in Washington for a regular monthly ATA meeting soon after the TWA 800 disaster. In Washington, a friend alerted Holtsclaw that the air traffic controllers in New York sensed something amiss. The friend put Holtsclaw in touch with one of them. "I'll send the radar tape," the controller told him. "You decide what you are seeing."[6]

Holtsclaw knew something about radar. He graduated from the U.S. Air Force Air Traffic Control School and the FAA Air Traffic School, served as LAX Control Tower manager and ATC manager with American Airlines before moving on to the Air Transport Association. As he would later testify under oath, he had received a copy of the radar tape recorded at the New York Terminal Radar Approach Control (TRACON). It showed, in Holtsclaw's words, "a primary target at the speed of approximately 1200 knots converging with TWA 800, during the climb out phase of TWA 800."[7]

"Target" was controller-speak for "unknown object." That first night a missile strike seemed the obvious cause of the plane's demise. MSNBC, on the air for just two days, had secured an amateur video showing an object approaching the plane. Russell saw the video several times before it was pulled. Although the government and the media would scramble to change the storyline, CNN was still reporting on July 19 that "radar records reviewed by military officials showed a mystery blip in the vicinity of the TWA flight path."[8]

Those officials had reason to be concerned. CNN's Negroni provided the most detailed account of this radar data in her book *Deadly Departure*. This account has added value in that it represents what attorneys call an "admission against interest." Negroni's primary source was Ron Schleede, then a deputy director of aviation safety at the NTSB. On the morning after the crash, July 18, an FAA official showed him a radar plot that got his complete attention. "Holy Christ, it looks bad," he said at the time. He told Negroni, "It showed this track that suggested something fast made a turn and took the airplane." This was the same track that alarmed Holtsclaw and the air traffic controller who tipped him off. That same morning, said Schleede, "The FAA was working with people at the top secret level. They were in a crisis room with intelligence people and everybody else."[9]

During their phone conversation, Russell wrote down what Holtsclaw had to tell him verbatim.[10] Russell had no trouble believing it. He had been suspicious since Pentagon spokesman Ken Bacon first announced the crash. Russell had been around long enough to know that civilian plane crashes were not the natural bailiwick of the Defense Department. Russell e-mailed Holtsclaw's highly specific message to eleven confidantes who shared his interest in air safety. The gist of the e-mail was that "TWA Flight 800 was shot down by a U.S. Navy guided missile ship which was in area W-105." Wrote Russell, "It has been a cover-up from the word go."[11] Although recipients had vowed to keep the information among them, one of them posted the information on the Internet, and it somehow found its way through French intelligence and on to Pierre Salinger.

At the time, Salinger was working in Paris where the interest in TWA 800 remained high. Thirty-six French citizens died in the crash. Salinger called Russell about the rumors and visited him in Florida soon afterwards. In addition to the information Russell and his colleagues had been sharing, Salinger had with him several government dispatches that reinforced the theory that the U.S. Navy accidentally shot down the 747. As to Salinger's motives, Russell believes that he seriously disliked the Clintons. He remained a loyal enough Democrat, however, to sit on his information until it lost its political punch. He broke his silence at an aviation conference in the French resort city of Cannes two days after the November 4 presidential election. There, Salinger told the assembled executives that he had "very important details that show the plane was brought down by a U.S. Navy missile." He added the obvious: "If the news came out that an American naval ship shot down that plane it would be something that would make the public very very unhappy and could have an effect on the election."[12]

American authorities did not care what role Salinger had played in Camelot. They were quick to swat him out of the Kennedy pantheon. The FBI, the White House, the Navy all took a shot. Salinger was unready for the assault. The documents he had were sketchy, and his knowledge base was shallow. The media found the subject irresistible.

In the month of November 1996 alone, the *New York Times* ran four articles with headlines that mocked Salinger. George Johnson was particularly merciless. "It was all linked to Whitewater," Johnson wrote, "unless the missile was meant for a visiting U.F.O.?" Johnson's reference to "Whitewater" was not uncommon. He made slighting allusions as well to Waco, Ruby Ridge, Arkansas state troopers, Vincent Foster, and other sources of amusement in Clinton-era newsrooms. What Johnson was attempting to do, and he was hardly unique in so doing, was to paint TWA 800 as one wacky anti-Clinton conspiracy out of many. What he did not do—no one at the *Times* did after the first two days—was speak to any of the 258 FBI witnesses to a likely missile strike.

At the time, I must confess to having enjoyed the attacks on Salinger. It was not that I trusted the Clintons. I did not, but like many Americans, I trusted the U.S. Navy or certainly wanted to. Salinger's accusations seemed not just wrongheaded. To me, they seemed borderline treasonous.

THE
VIDEO

We called our documentary *Silenced*. It opened with a relevant quote from Thomas Jefferson: "If a nation expects to be ignorant and free in a state of civilization, it expects what never was and never will be."[1] The problem we faced, the problem Whittaker Chambers faced, was a problem even our founders faced. This was a problem rooted deep in human nature: the temptation to *not* know, to remain ignorant even in the face of evil—especially in the face of evil. As I was learning, the magnitude of the TWA 800 deception helped protect it. Skeptical as I was of the administration's good intentions, even I had a hard time believing that its minions could execute such spectacular legerdemain. Skepticism made sense. We made *Silenced* to help overcome it. An honest recounting of known facts might not stir the best people from their slumber, but it just might rouse the "great body of the nation" to ask questions.

Here is what we knew for sure in the spring of 2001 and shared in *Silenced*.[2] At 8:19 p.m., on a pleasantly cool evening, TWA Flight 800 left JFK Airport in New York with 230 people on board bound for Paris. The 747 headed east in fair skies along the affluent south coast of Long Island. Twelve minutes into this so-far uneventful flight, witnesses along the coast began to notice inexplicable phenomena in the sky. Mike Wire, working on a Westhampton bridge, watched as a flaming streak of light rose up from behind a beach house and zigzagged south-southeast away from shore. Senior Navy NCO Dwight Brumley saw another streak from his window seat thousands of feet above TWA 800 on US Air Flight 217. This second streak rose up towards his plane before leveling off and heading north towards Long Island on a course perpendicular to TWA 800's. Engineer Paul Angelides tracked the southbound streak from his Westhampton deck and then watched in awe as the northbound streak rose off the horizon.

At 8:31 p.m., Wire, Brumley, Angelides and hundreds of others, perhaps thousands, watched helplessly as TWA 800 exploded in mid-air. Air National Guard pilot Major Fritz Meyer had little doubt what caused the plane to explode. "It was definitely a rocket motor," he said. "What I saw explode was definitely ordnance. I have enough experience. I saw one, two, three, four explosions before the fireball." No one was in a better position to see. Meyer was in a helicopter over the Long Island shore facing southbound.

"The plane broke jaggedly in the sky," said witness Lisa Perry. "The nose is continuing to go forward; the left wing is gliding off in its own direction, drifting in an arc gracefully down; the right wing and passenger window are doing the same in their direction out to the right; and the tail with its fireball leaps up and then promptly falls into the water below."

In the course of *Silenced*, we told in brief the story of James and Elizabeth Sanders. We delved into the radar data, the physical evidence, the debris field, the rocket residue, the flight data recorder, the cockpit voice recorder, the characteristics of Jet A fuel, and other technical information. Without question, the most compelling part of the video was the eyewitness testimony. No network had ever interviewed Mike Wire, Lisa Perry, Paul Angelides, Dwight Brumley, or Major Fritz Meyer. Ten years after the disaster, CNN's Internet-basher Jeffrey Reid did not even know they existed. Those who watched *Silenced* were finally able to compare the credibility of the witnesses to that of the government officials tasked with discrediting them. To the dispassionate observer, it was no contest. The witnesses knew what they saw. Despite all the incentives not to, they continued to plead their case and go public with their dissent. We paid no one for his or her testimony.

To make its "no physical evidence" alibi stick, the administration somehow had to trivialize the witness testimony. Recently discovered CIA memos show the CIA got the assignment immediately after the crash. The agency's quiet work behind the scenes culminated in the public premiere of an animated video in November 1997. The FBI showed the video during a news conference announcing the suspension of its criminal probe. Although the networks would never air the video again, we got hold of a copy and included relevant sections of it in *Silenced*.

"The following program was produced by the Central Intelligence Agency." So began the narration of what has come to be called the zoom climb video. The narrator explained that there were three major theories as to what destroyed TWA 800: bomb, missile, or mechanical failure. What concerned investigators, however, were reports "from dozens of eyewitnesses" who had allegedly seen objects in the sky before the explosion. "Was it a missile?" asked the narrator. "Did foreign terrorists destroy the aircraft?" Of course not. "What the witnesses saw," the narrator reassured the media, "was a Boeing 747 in various stages of crippled flight." After some thoroughly confusing misdirection about sound analysis, the narrator weighed in with his money quote, underlined on screen in case someone might miss the point, "The Eyewitnesses Did Not See a Missile."

As to what the witnesses did see, the CIA and other agencies involved could never get their stories quite straight. This was evident on the very day of the video's premiere and would become problematic as the investigation ground on. The narrator talked of "a trailing cascade of flames" falling to the horizon, and the video showed as much. The FBI claimed this was the image that confused the witnesses. "What some people thought was a missile hitting the plane was actually burning, leaking fuel from the jet after the front part had already broken off,"[3] reported CNN, paraphrasing the FBI.

The CIA narrator, however, said something quite different. "Just after the aircraft exploded," he insisted, "it pitched up abruptly and climbed several thousand feet from its last recorded altitude of about 13,800 feet to a maximum altitude of about 17,000 feet." The animation showed the plane doing just that. As the narrator explained, when the nose of the plane broke off, the sudden loss of mass caused the plane to turn up and climb. This rocketing, noseless 747 was what witnesses "repeatedly described as an ascending white light resembling a flare or firework."

As we noted in *Silenced*, the CIA explanation mystified not only the eyewitnesses, but also the aviation experts. Among those we interviewed on camera was Dick Russell's friend and mentor, Ray Lahr. A retired United Airlines pilot, Lahr enlisted in the U.S. Navy right out of high school in 1943. He was still in training when the war ended, but he elected to get his commission and remain in the reserves. In 1953, he began his career as a pilot with United Airlines and remained with the company until his retirement in 1985. While still with United, he pursued advanced studies at UCLA in gravity, a field that Lahr describes as "the love of my life." In addition, he worked with the Airline Pilots Association (ALPA) as an accident investigator. Given his background, no one in America was better positioned to critique the CIA zoom climb than Lahr.

Lahr is an American original. He has since become a good friend. At the time of our interview he was seventy-five years old. With his close-cropped dark hair and compact, athletic build, he looked twenty years younger. He still does. "All the pilots that I've spoken to think it's ridiculous," Lahr said of the zoom climb. He argued that when the nose left the aircraft, the center of gravity moved "aft," to the rear of the plane. "The tail section fell backward," witness Lisa Perry told the FBI.[4] Lahr described the phenomenon as "putting two people on one side of teeter totter." He added, "The plane would not have any opportunity to climb." It would be so out of balance, he argued, that it "would immediately stall and fall out of the sky."

The most formidable of the zoom climb's critics to appear in *Silenced* was Bill Donaldson. As a twenty-five-year Navy carrier pilot, Donaldson flew more than seventy strike missions over North Vietnam and Laos. Retired at the time of TWA 800's destruction, Donaldson wrote a letter to the *Wall Street Journal* critical of the investigation in 1997. That letter led to the formation of a high-level group of TWA 800 dissenters known as the Associated Retired Aviation Professionals, which he headed.

In high school, Donaldson had been an all-state football player, and in his mid-fifties, he still looked the part. When he spoke, people listened. The fact that he had investigated a dozen aviation accidents during his tenure with the Navy added to his natural air of authority. Tragically, while we were putting together our video, Donaldson was suffering from a fatal brain tumor. He died at fifty-six, just weeks before 9/11. Although I had never met Donaldson, I spoke with him about the crash and watched clips of his public presentations that we included in *Silenced*. "Once it goes beyond twenty degrees nose up," said Donaldson of the aircraft in one dramatic show-and-tell, "it can't fly anymore because these wings are no longer into the wind. They can't produce lift." There was, in fact, a certain force that caused the plane to fall out of sky, Donaldson deadpanned. "It's called gravity."

Chapter: FIVE

THE MAN ON THE BRIDGE

The CIA analysts never interviewed Mike Wire, the fellow who saw the incident from a bridge in Westhampton. One would think they might have, given that they built their animation around his perspective. We interviewed Wire, and we did so on the bridge in question. This no-nonsense, six-foot, seven-inch millwright told us and showed us what he told the FBI five years earlier. In *Silenced*, we created our own animation of what he had actually seen.

On that fateful evening, Wire was working late with several engineers and electricians to open a new bridge on Beach Lane. It now spans the Quantuck Canal that separates the mainland from the pricey spit of a beach beyond. Wire's job put him in the windowless switchgear room at the base of the bridge. Needing a breather, he surfaced at about 8:30 and leaned out casually over the rail with his eye on the dunes and beach houses beyond. From this vantage point, he saw—and felt—events unfold.

Soon after the event, Wire returned to his Richboro, Pennsylvania, home. Alerted to what Wire had seen by a co-worker, FBI agent Daniel Kilcullen called Wire on July 23. The brief conversation convinced Kilcullen that Wire deserved an interview. On July 29, agent Andrew Lash showed up *chez* Wire, and Wire told his story. At the time, he had no idea that hundreds of others had seen what he had seen. After his interview, Wire returned to work and gave the incident little thought. He did not pay much attention to the news accounts until November 18, 1997, the day the FBI wrapped up its investigation. After seeing an abbreviated version of the CIA video on the news, he presumed it to be "some temporary scheme to pacify the public."[1] He did not learn of his starring role in the complete video until AIM's Reed Irvine found him in the spring of 2000. An Army vet, Wire was about to get a fresh look at the way the government worked.

Wire was an "excellent eyewitness," claimed the narrator of the CIA video. He watched a white light travel upwards. "It zigzagged" as it rose. And at the apex of its travel, it "arched over and disappeared." In the video, while the narrator was saying these words, the viewer was watching a flaming TWA 800 zoom up and arch over. "So the white light the eyewitness described," concluded the narrator, "probably was the aircraft briefly ascending and arching over after it exploded, rather than a missile attacking the aircraft."

By the time we interviewed Wire in the spring of 2001, we had access to some eye-opening documents. One was Wire's original FBI 302 from July 29, 1996. In it, FBI agent Lash reported faithfully, if a bit sloppily, what Wire told him.

Wire saw a white light that was traveling skyward from the ground at approximately a 40 degree angle. Wire described the white light as a light that sparkled and thought it was some type of fireworks. Wire stated that the white light "zig zagged" as it traveled upwards, and at the apex of its travel the white light "arched over" and disappeared from Wire's view.... Wire stated the white light traveled outwards from the beach in a south-southeasterly direction.

Seconds after the light disappeared, Wire reported seeing "an orange light that appeared to be a fireball." The fireball fell from the sky at approximately a thirty-degree angle and "left a fire trail burning behind it." Only "after" the fireball descended behind the houses on the beach, did Wire hear the first of four explosions. The first was the loudest, and it shook the bridge sufficiently that the other workers came running out of the switchgear room to see what was going on.

One highly useful document clarifies how Wire found himself center stage in this drama.[2] I refer here to the word-for-word transcript of a meeting between the NTSB's witness group and the CIA analysts responsible for the video. To read the document is to understand the thoroughly corrupting role the CIA played in the investigation. The meeting took place in the fifth floor boardroom of the NTSB offices in Washington. Representing the CIA were the unnamed deputy director of the Office of Transnational Issues (OTI) and the two analysts who did the work on the video, also unnamed. "Analyst 1" was almost assuredly Randolph Tauss, a senior weapons analyst in the Directorate of Intelligence who would later take credit for his efforts on the case. At the table for the NTSB were managers Bernard Loeb and David Mayer as well as five industry members of the NTSB witness group.

The two members of that group who offered any real challenge to the CIA were J. Dennis Rodrigues, an air safety accident investigator for Boeing, and Bob Young, director of Flight Safety for TWA. One of the objections I have heard as to why there could not have been a cover-up goes something like this: "Are you telling me that the hundreds of people who worked on this investigation conspired to corrupt it?" No, that is not the way conspiracies unfold. After the crash, thousands of workers made a great, good faith effort to redeem the bodies, retrieve the wreckage, and search for answers. Few of those, however, were allowed to see beyond their immediate assignments. And fewer still had access to the big picture. On April 30, 1999, Rodrigues and Young got a glimpse of that picture. With no support from their superiors—Mayer, in fact, had been quietly working with the CIA—they pursued the truth in an environment rich with intimidation. To date their efforts have come to naught, but they did succeed in exposing a major plot twist in the CIA's knowing rewrite of aviation history.

The NTSB made the report public in April 2000, a year after the meeting and four months before the final NTSB hearing in August. There was a Pulitzer waiting for the journalist who read it, dissected it, and pursued it. As far as I can tell, no one seems to have bothered. In my experience, and more on this later, journalists rarely explore material if they fear—or their superiors fear—the implications of their research. For ideological reasons, that fear factor seems to intensify in presidential election years. For all the power of the Internet, independent investigators cannot get agency honchos to answer their phone calls. To this day, only the major media have this power. Indeed, were it not for the *Washington Post*, the word "Watergate" would have little meaning beyond D.C.'s real estate community.

This gathering was held in April 1999. Incredibly, it had taken the NTSB a year and a half to set up a meeting with the CIA analysts who were doing a job that its own staffers should have been doing from day one of the investigation. It was decided early in the two-hour meeting to allow the NTSB reps to set the agenda. Analyst 1 answered almost all of their questions. As the analyst explained, the FBI originally provided the CIA with thirty or forty witness summaries, ostensibly to help determine whether there was any evidence of terrorism. Over the next ten months, the FBI provided the CIA with more than two hundred additional 302s.

To say the least, the 302s lacked precision. The FBI agents had little, if any, aviation experience. And unless accompanied by representatives from Suffolk County or the Defense Intelligence Agency, they had no instruments with which to gauge position. The CIA analysts had no relevant experience either. Nor did they interview any of the eyewitnesses. Working with about one-third of the 302s, the analysts somehow concluded that the witnesses had deceived themselves into thinking they saw something that they hadn't. They came to this conclusion, said Analyst 1, "late on December 30, 1996." As shall be seen, these analysts used gratuitously specific details for a reason.

The NTSB's Young had questions. "CIA Analyst #1, we've had access to 755 witness statements versus your 244." The analyst could only answer, "Right." He offered no explanation. More troubling than this disparity was the fact the NTSB witness group did not get to see the eyewitness summaries until more than two years after the CIA had. "We only read these in the last few months," said Rodrigues, "long after the video came out."

Young and Rodrigues sensed that the die had been cast. Although legally charged with responsibility for domestic airline crashes, the NTSB had yielded its authority to the FBI, and the FBI passed it on to the CIA. Their superiors allowed this to happen. The meeting that they and their more responsible colleagues had been demanding for months, if not years, was something of a dumb show. Still, they persisted. "The video shows, or the video in effect says," asked Rodrigues skeptically, "that what the eyewitnesses saw was the crippled airplane, after the nose comes off, climbing." Said Analyst 1 in response, "That is something that a few eyewitnesses saw. The guy on the bridge saw that." Rodrigues sighed in frustration, "If it's only one or two of them, it's not representative of all of them." Seemingly cornered, Analyst 1 improvised a response, "Let me say something else about this eyewitness [Wire] because I think this is interesting":

> He was an important eyewitness to us. *And we asked the FBI to talk to him again, and they did.* In his original description, he thought he had seen a firework and that perhaps that firework had originated on the beach behind the house. We went to that location and realized that if he was only seeing the airplane, that he would not see a light appear from behind the rooftop of that house. The light would actually appear in the sky. It's high enough in the sky that that would have to happen.

When he was reinterviewed, he said that is indeed what happened. The light did appear in the sky. Now, when the FBI told us that, we got even more comfortable with our theory. He also described, he was asked to describe how high in the sky above the house he thought that light appeared, and he said it was as if—if you imagine a flag pole on top of the house it would be as if it were on the top or the tip of the flag pole. [Emphasis added.]

If nothing else, one has to admire the CIA analysts' nerve. They built their animation around Wire's perspective in Westhampton, but in building it they took total liberty with his original testimony. In his July 1996 FBI 302, Wire reported a "40 degree" climb. In the CIA, animation, however, the noseless TWA 800 climbs at a seventy-degree angle or more. Wire spoke of an object zigzagging "outward from the beach." The animation shows an object ascending briefly in a two-dimensional plane far from shore. Of most importance, Wire claimed that the object ascended "skyward from the ground." The CIA analysts could not live with this. In their animation, the object first appears about twenty degrees above the horizon almost exactly where TWA 800 would have been when blown out of the sky. If nervy, the analysts were often careless. In the animation, the narrator echoes Wire's claim that the object "zigzagged" as it rose even while the object on screen ascends without hint of a wiggle.

The astute reader may know where this is heading. As with Witness 73, there was no second interview. The FBI talked to Wire on July 29, 1996, and never talked to him again. Analyst 1, who artfully adlibbed his way through the two-hour meeting, may well have concocted this interview on the fly. With Witness 73 at least there was a second 302 in the NTSB docket. For Wire there was none. The NTSB sustained this charade in its final August 2000 report. The report specifically referenced the July 29, 1996, in-person interview, and then spoke of how Wire changed his story in "subsequent interviews," plural, with no date or agency attached to any of them.[3]

In the years since, I have gotten to know Mike and his wife Joan well. He is a stalwart guy and a great patriot. He worked extensively in lower Manhattan on wreckage removal after the World Trade Center attack and suffered severe health problems as a result. He accepted that risk as part of his responsibility. But he couldn't accept the passivity of the media in the face of so transparent a fraud.

The man-on-the-bridge ruse was not the only one Young and Rodrigues exposed during their much-delayed interview with the CIA analysts. They had issues with sound as well as sight, particularly Wire's claim that a sound wave shook this seventy-ton bridge eleven miles from TWA 800. "The problem I'm having a little bit," Rodrigues asked the analysts, "is that the center tank explosion is categorized as a low order explosion." Unwilling to defend the notion that a low-order explosion at that distance—or any distance—could have shaken the bridge, Analyst 1 argued instead that an explosion of a missile warhead was "not nearly loud enough to do that sort of thing."

Although Young and Rodrigues were willing to challenge the CIA analysts, they seemed unwilling to offer the obvious alternative thesis, namely that a missile or missiles had generated a sonic boom. In late January 2016, for instance, residents up and down the coasts of Long Island and New Jersey reported what they thought was an earthquake only to be told that "Naval aircraft testing over the Atlantic Ocean" had caused a series of sonic booms.[4] If there were missiles involved in the 2016 test, authorities were mum. Young was not prepared to talk about missiles either. He offered defensively, "I don't see how we can get a center tank to make that sound." When no one picked up this train of thought, Young's superiors, Loeb and Mayer, allowed the conversation to drift away.

A third issue involved Eastwind Airlines pilot, David McClaine. On the night in question, McClaine was flying from Boston to Trenton, New Jersey. He had just descended to 16,000 feet when he watched TWA 800 explode right in front of him. Later that night, when he returned home to the Charlotte area, he wrote a report of what he had seen and submitted it to Eastwind Airlines. The next day, July 18, a female FBI agent interviewed him at his home for about an hour. Another agent called him at home later that evening and confirmed the details of the interview. "I don't think they had any aviation experience," McClaine would later tell the NTSB.[5] Much later.

NTSB witness group members did not interview McClaine until March 25, 1999, nearly three years after the disaster and a month before their interview with the CIA. This was shocking, appalling really. Until that time, NTSB group members had not seen the incident report McClaine submitted to his employer late on July 17, had not seen the FBI 302 on McClaine, and were unaware that he had already given several media interviews explaining what he had seen. In October 1997, David Hendrix, who helped break the Sanderses' story for the Riverside *Press-Enterprise*, reported in some detail what McClaine had witnessed a month before the CIA premiered its notorious video.[6] Had official Washington been aware of McClaine's testimony before the premiere of the video, the FBI might have hesitated to show it.

In this instance, as in so many others, it is hard to tell where incompetence left off, and intrigue began. Again, only Young and Rodrigues tried to straighten out the record. McClaine obliged them. As always, he was open and forthcoming. While descending into Trenton, he had his eye on TWA 800 for some five minutes. "Boy, did he have a pair of landing lights," he told his interrogators. It was their brightness that attracted his attention. He saw no missile approach the plane, but as he explained, "The fuselage and the wing could have blocked that out." Besides, he occasionally looked at his instrument panel and away from TWA 800. When the Eastwind plane reached 16,000 feet, McClaine flipped on his landing lights to alert the TWA 800 captain to his proximity. Just at that moment, the 747 exploded right in his face. "It all ended right there," said McClaine. "And everything went down."

"Was there any flaming object that climbed to your altitude, 16 [thousand feet] or more?" asked Rodrigues. "Not that I could see," answered McClaine. "You didn't see any structure or anything else zoom up 1,000, 1,500, 3,000 feet?" asked Young. "No," said McClaine unequivocally. When asked about the CIA video, McClaine volunteered,

"I didn't see [TWA 800] pitch up, no. Everything ended right there at the explosion, as far as I'm concerned." With the wings and nose blown off, he could not imagine the aircraft "pushing against the wind" and zooming upwards. "I didn't see that happen." Young knew it could not have happened. Said he, "We'd be cutting new trails in aerodynamics if we could do that." No one in the room dissented. Even before their interview a month later with the CIA analysts, the NTSB witness group members all knew their zoom climb scenario was a crock.

During that April 1999 CIA interview, Young recounted the interview with McClaine in some detail. "If [TWA 800] had ascended," said Young, "certainly he would have been concerned because it would have ascended right through his altitude." In his response, Analyst 1 unthinkingly referred to the CIA's "analysis of the 302 information." He and his partner had read McClaine's 302 before they made the video. They knew what he had seen. Analyst 1 tried to squirm out of this logical black hole, but Young kept coming back to it.

"He never saw any ascension," said Young. Analyst 1 stalled for time. "It was my understanding, based on the 302 information we had," he bluffed, "that the pilot never reported seeing the plane. He only saw a light." At this point, the newly appointed head of NTSB witness group, David Mayer, intervened to protect the CIA thesis. Unknown to the other members of the witness group, the crafty Mayer had been "working closely" with the lead CIA analyst for the previous sixteen months. CIA head George Tenet admitted as much to the NTSB's Jim Hall in a March 1999 letter.

There was much going on that investigators working with the NTSB did not know about, and the CIA preferred to keep it that way. In that same letter to Hall, Tenet expressed his wish "that the briefing will be in a closed session, that no transcript will be made of CIA's presentation and that appropriate safeguards will be made to protect any extraneous CIA and FBI interests."[7] Before the NTSB closed its case and even after, Mayer would go to great lengths to protect "CIA and FBI interests." In this kind of environment, national interests did not stand a chance.

Inexplicably, in 2008, the CIA's Randolph Tauss went public with an authorized explanation for the agency's involvement.[8] According to Tauss, the FBI immediately requested CIA assistance given "the possibility that international terrorists may havę been involved." Tauss claimed the agency responded to the FBI's request for help less than twenty-four hours after the plane's destruction and cited Executive Order 12333 as justification. A clause in that order authorizes the CIA to "conduct counterintelligence activities outside the United States and, without assuming or performing any internal security functions, conduct counterintelligence activities within the United States in coordination with the FBI."[9] When President Ronald Reagan signed this order in 1981, he likely did not think "counterintelligence" would include the making of cartoons to discredit citizen testimony.

There is something fishy about all of this. In the FBI's case-closing press conference from November 1997, Kallstrom said the FBI "looked throughout the government" to find the experts best able to answer the question, "What did the eyewitnesses see?"[10] Kallstrom appears to have echoed a talking point on this subject prepared for him by the CIA immediately before this press conference. The relevant CIA memo reads as follows, "The FBI requested CIA technical assistance in analyzing more than 200 eyewitness reports to determine what those eyewitnesses saw."[11]

In fact, however, the people with the "best expertise" were on the ground in Long Island helping the FBI interview eyewitnesses in the first weeks of the investigation. These were the representatives from the Missile and Space Intelligence Center (MSIC) in Alabama, a subset of the Defense Intelligence Agency. Missiles were their business. Counterintelligence was the CIA's. The shift in the CIA's mission from hunting "international terrorists" to providing "technical assistance" on witness observations took place fully off camera. The fact that the FBI fed the CIA the witness statements so slowly and incompletely suggests the agency's help was not welcome. Once empowered, however, the CIA analysts bullied the MSIC reps and the FBI into accepting the CIA's counterfeit thesis. "We found the talent we were looking for in the CIA," said Kallstrom in closing the criminal investigation. By that time, he was too compromised to say otherwise.

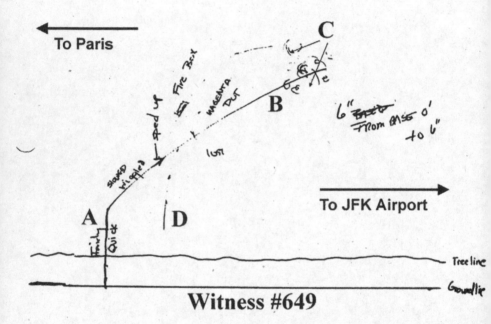

To Paris

C

Fire Box

Magenta
Duf

B

sped up

slowed (ripped)

lost

6" from Base 0'
to 6"

A

To JFK Airport

D

Fairly
Quick

Tree line

Groundlie

Witness #649

Witness 649, Joseph Delgado, was one of many witnesses to provide the FBI with a detailed drawing. He saw the missile rise from behind a tree line and make "a dramatic correction" to strike TWA 800. The missile trajectory he saw closely resembled one captured on video five days earlier during an apparent missile test. *Federal Bureau of Investigation*

Chapter: SIX

INTELLIGENCE MEDAL OF MERIT

Quietly, after the media lost interest in TWA 800, the CIA awarded Randolph Tauss its Intelligence Medal of Merit, an award given "for performance of especially meritorious service or for achievement conspicuously above normal duties."[1] In a perverse way, Tauss deserved it. More through chutzpah than hard evidence, he and his colleagues managed to convince all relevant parties that nearly three hundred good citizens—pilots, surfers, fishermen, boaters, National Guard officers—could not tell up from down.

To communicate the depth of the CIA's deception, I have condensed the 302s of the most observant of the witnesses. The FBI gathered this information in the first few weeks of the investigation and shared many of the best 302s with the CIA. The Suffolk County Police, the MSIC reps, and the FBI re-interviewed several of these people. The nearly seven hundred other witnesses did not see something different from what these people saw. They saw something less, usually just a final spectacular explosion and/or the descent of the wreckage into the sea. I beg the reader's patience if this exercise seems a bit repetitive. It is important to understand just how much solid, consistent testimony the authorities chose to distort or ignore.

Five days after TWA 800's destruction, Witness 82 told two Suffolk County PD detectives that she was sitting at Smith's Point Beach when she "saw a flare shoot from the water" and fly upwards in a "concave arc."[2] As the woman reported, the flare had a pink flame that turned orange as it ascended and was followed by a "thin black smoke trail." She watched the object for about five seconds before "it turned into a large ball of orange fire." She did not see the fireball fall to the surface or "hear any sound."

Witness 88 was fishing with friends in Moriches Inlet facing south out over the ocean.[3] Before he saw anything, he heard an explosion. He then saw to the southeast what looked like a "firework ascending." The object left "a wispy white smoke trail." At the peak of its ascent, the object, now flaming red at its tip, arced from the east to the west. He then saw an airplane come into the field of view. The bright red object "ran into the airplane and upon doing so both exploded into a huge plume of flame." He believed the object hit the plane near the cockpit area. The plume of flame separated into two and "spiraled to the ground." He heard no further sounds. Witness 88 shared this information with the New York State Police ten days after the crash. No one else appears to have interviewed him, but the report was included in the FBI docket.

Witness 129 was fishing with a friend off a jetty in the Moriches Inlet, when he saw to his southeast a "flare rising upwards."[4] He followed it for about five seconds as it lifted from his eye level and curved southeast and slightly downward. He then saw a small flash, followed by a large explosion. A huge fireball then fell to the oceans in two pieces. Five to ten seconds after the wreckage hit the water, he heard "a thunder or rumbling." Two FBI agents interviewed Witness 129 on July 19, 1996.

Later that day, they interviewed him again, this time accompanied by a MSIC analyst.

Witness 144, Ann DeCaro by name, was walking around the track at Mastic Beach High School with a friend when she noticed a plane, traveling west to east, the direction TWA 800 was heading.[5] She then "saw an object to the right with a bright orange glow with a white streak behind it." She described the streak as "taking off like a rocket." After losing sight of it for a moment, she saw a bright orange fireball, which broke into two pieces and "fell straight down." She told the FBI she heard no sound nor felt any thunder and was one of the few witnesses to insist she saw a "missile."

At Bayshore, Long Island, Witness 145 was looking out the window of a friend's house when she "saw a plane and noticed an object spiraling towards the plane."[6] She described the object as having "a glow at the end of it and a grey/white smoke trail." She watched "the object hit the plane" but was not sure where. She did, however, "hear a loud noise" just as the object hit the plane. The plane then split in two and dropped to the water. A few seconds later, she told the FBI, "she heard another explosion." A week later, the Suffolk County Police took GPS readings of her sighting.

Witness 159 was leaving a restaurant in Quogue when "two claps of thunder" drew his attention.[7] Looking to his southwest, he "observed an orange/white glow diminishing in size as it moved away from him." He described it as "rising skyward." At top of its trajectory, he saw a whitish glow, heard "more thunder" and saw an orange ball of flames drop toward the ocean. The Suffolk County Police re-interviewed him.

Witness 166, a veteran of the Polish Army with missile experience, was at a park in Lindenhurst with his wife when he "noticed something ascending...like white, yellow fire, trailed by black smoke."[8] He heard a "shhh" sound. The object arched slightly at top. He then observed an explosion. Said the FBI agent, "After hearing news of the crash, he concluded he had seen a missile."

Witness 174, a retired naval officer, was looking out the window of his beachfront home in Rowayton, when he "saw a skyrocket type object streak up into the night sky from behind Sheffield Island."[9] A few seconds later, "after the skyrocket contrail disappeared," he saw "a large orange fireball." Although the two FBI agents interviewing Witness 174 neglected to ask about sound, they did ask "whether he may have actually seen something going down instead of up." Four weeks after the crash, the agents had likely gotten the hint to discourage missile talk. The naval officer did not oblige them. He "insisted that his skyrocket went up."

Witness 221 was sitting on the beach in Fire Island with his wife watching the surf come in. He saw a commercial jet fly by, surely TWA 800, and then "saw a streak of light travel up from the water into the sky. [He] described the streak of light as though it was like a rocket or shooting star only going upward."[10] He then heard a "low rumbling sound" and saw a flash of light but was not sure whether sound or light came first.

Witness 233 was looking out the open window of her parked car at Patchogue Bay when she "noticed a flare off into the distance, rising off into the air."[11] She described it as "moving steadily straight up" and as being "reddish orange with a short reddish-orange smoke trail." Like many of the other witnesses, she saw something "brightly pulse." Two seconds later, "she observed a large object seemingly stopping its forward momentum while igniting into a fireball." The fireball broke into two pieces and floated downward. As the FBI agent duly noted, this witness "could not recall hearing any sound related to the incident."

Witness 241, while walking around the track at Westhampton High School, "observed a bright white light arching into the sky."[12] At its apex, she observed "that the light appeared to fizzle out, then moments later, a huge explosion occurred." The FBI agent reported that she "did not hear any sound or explosion."

Witness 243 was crabbing with about twenty other people on the dock at Forge River Marina in Mastic when a young boy alerted him and the others to what appeared to be "a flare flying up into the air."[13] Two days after the crash Witness 243 told the FBI, "The flying object was relatively slow in flying up and took four or five seconds before hitting the airplane. The smoke, which trailed this object, was whitish in color and the band of smoke was narrow." The resulting explosion "made no noise."

Witness 260 and a friend were fishing at the Moriches Inlet when he saw an apparent flare rise into the sky south-southeast of his position. The witness told an FBI agent he "watched the flare move upward in the sky to a point where the flare seemed to lose energy and arc and begin to descend."[14] The witness then "observed a fireball somewhat above where he saw the last flare." The agent recorded no information about sound.

Witness 275 was walking to her car in East Quogue. She looked up and "observed an orange colored 'arc' moving upward from behind the trees southwest of her home."[15] The arc continued to travel upward and "ended in a large explosion." Once again, the FBI agent made no reference to sound.

Witness 280, sitting in his jeep with the top down in Riverhead, "saw a red dot traveling from west to east, parallel to the horizon."[16] Three or four seconds later he saw a "bright orange explosion." He told the FBI, "It was like the red object pushed whatever it hit forward, causing it to explode, and dive downward." The witness added that he "never heard any sounds."

Witness 282, a master sergeant with the New York Air National Guard, had just parachuted into his base at Gabreski Airport as part of an exercise. He was on the ground, looking south, "when he saw what looked like a flare at about 2500 to 3,000 feet traveling from west to east. The object was orange with a pink center. It also had a very faint grayish white plume."[17] The flare then "erupted into a fireball and the fireball fell straight down and broke into two." Although the witness was interviewed by an NYPD detective and an FBI agent, neither appeared to inquire about sound.

Witness 305 was looking out a restaurant window in Sayville when she saw a "thin stream of orange flame, but no smoke, which traveled for about three seconds...until it disappeared over the horizon."[18] To her, it looked like a "firework" that came "straight up out of the water."

This was immediately followed by "a huge explosion." The witness told the FBI agent she "did not hear a sound."

Witness 324 was standing on the outside deck of the Westhampton Yacht Squadron when someone yelled, "Look!"[19] He turned and "observed a red flare arching in the sky and descending downward. As it descended downward, "he heard a 'thump' and then there was a sudden burst of flames." This large body of flames split in two and descended.

Witness 326 was driving westward along the Sunrise Highway when he "saw a red glowing object ascending from the tree tops."[20] The object arced from the west to the east and suddenly "burst into a larger red glowing ball." He told the FBI agents he "did not hear any sounds at all."

Witness 332, an air traffic controller at Gabreski Airport, "saw a flash of light" that he initially thought was a flare or fireworks.[21] He told the FBI, "He heard no noise." He then saw a fireball that "fell straight down" in three pieces.

Witness 358 was fishing off a boat in Moriches Inlet with friends when he saw a "flare like object for eight to ten seconds at which time it turned into a bright yellowish orange glow."[22] This glow then turned into a wide flame that fell towards the ocean in two pieces. The FBI agents do not appear to have inquired about sound.

Witness 364, who had once served as the Marine Corps crew chief of a helicopter squadron, was sitting on the dock of the Bellport Yacht Club with a female friend. Looking to the southeast, he "noticed an object rising vertically."[23] It had a red glow and "rose from the east to the west on a steep angle." The object took about thirty seconds to reach its zenith, then arced downwards for ten seconds, and sped off on a flat, horizontal course for about fifteen seconds. Just as he told his friend to look, the witness saw a small red explosion, followed by a "tremendous" bright white second explosion, which evolved into an orange-yellow ball that fell in two pieces to the sea. "He realized he had seen two different things," reported the FBI, "namely the rising 'object,' and the subsequent explosions." After learning of TWA 800's destruction, "He came to the personal conclusion that what he had seen was a missile hitting the airplane." If this witness heard anything, the FBI did not report it. During the interview, the Suffolk County PD used GPS to plot the object's trajectory.

Witnesses 385 and 386, a couple with their young children, were boating in the Moriches Inlet. They told the FBI that a bright orange-red glow "seemed like it came off the horizon and rose slowly, weaving as it continued upward."[24] It traveled diagonally at a seventy-degree angle going in a westerly direction and left a white smoke trail in its wake. It then disappeared, and a "large oval ball of fire" appeared just above where the object was last sighted. The two heard no sound as they watched as "the ball of fire came straight down," breaking eventually into two pieces.

Witnesses 394 and 395, another couple, were standing on a platform behind Westhampton when they "saw a red dot in the sky."[25] The fellow saw "stream of white or grey smoke prior to seeing red dot." It looked like a flare and was moving from west to east. It soon exploded and "came down like a curtain of flame." The female witness told the FBI they heard the sound of four explosions in rapid succession beginning about ten seconds after they saw the first one.

The FBI interviewed Witnesses 409 and 607, a man and wife, in July 1997. It was his second FBI interview, her first.[26] Two agents from the Bureau of Alcohol, Tobacco and Firearms (ATF) also interviewed the couple three days after the crash. The ATF interview and the first FBI interview in January 1997 dealt mostly with what the husband and his son saw at the crash site to which they repaired by boat after the explosion. The second FBI interview covered what they saw before the explosion. At the time, the couple and their son were standing on a dock at Great Gun Beach on what they described as a "clear, chilly night." They were looking out on to the water when the wife said, "Watch this, we're going to see fireworks." Her husband then "saw a light greyish streak/line ascending into the sky over the ocean." It was southeast of their location and moving from east to west. The streak disappeared, and he saw a "bright white light" in the sky where the streak had ended. A second explosion followed, bright orange in color. The flaming debris broke into two pieces and fell to the sea. The couple "never heard an explosion."

In July 1996, Witness 484 told the FBI she was sitting on a neighbor's dock in Shirley when she saw "a streak rising into the sky at an angle curving a little to the west."[27] She then saw an explosion that sounded like a "loud firework." In July 1997, this witness gave a more detailed account to the FBI. The ascending object reminded her of "a lighted match head, blue and orange in color...brighter at its head and faded toward its tail." She watched it for roughly ten seconds "traveling in an arc from her lower right to her upper left." The object disappeared for a moment, and soon after she witnessed a large explosion, the mass of which separated into two flaming pieces that fell to the sea. In this interview she claimed to have heard no sounds emanating from the event. As was the norm with these second interviews, the FBI questioned her about her eyesight and her drinking and concluded, "She was not under the influence of any substance on July 17, 1996." As was the norm as well, the FBI relied on the witness's gesticulations with her arms and thumbs to plot the object's trajectory.

Witness 491 was fishing with some buddies off a dock in Center Moriches when he "observed a red light moving up into the air."[28] It was moving in an "irregular type arc" in a southeasterly direction. He followed this "red flare" for an estimated thirty seconds and felt it "was trying to follow something." The flare then suddenly "turned into a huge ball of flame and fell in two pieces." Interviewed in July 1996 by the FBI and a New York State Police investigator, the witness made no comment about sound.

Witness 496, while standing on the dock in East Moriches, saw what appeared to be a flare ascending in the sky. In July 1996, she told the FBI the object was already in mid-air when she saw it.[29] The flare had an orange tail and traveled from south to southwest. About ten seconds after she first saw the object she observed an explosion. She first realized "a plane had exploded when she saw the plane break into two pieces as it fell straight to the ground." Two days after the first interview she returned to the site and helped the Suffolk County Police plot the course of what she had seen. A year later, in July 1997, the FBI interviewed Witness 496 once again. Her story did not change but for one caveat. She allegedly told the agents, "At no time while she was witnessing the event did she identify the object as an aircraft." The first 302 reported otherwise. The witness also addressed the issue of sound, which did not come up in the first interview. As she told the agents, she reportedly heard a "loud boom" five seconds after the falling plane wreckage descended below the tree line.

Witness 497 got double tapped by the FBI as well. In July 1996, he told the FBI he was sitting in his car facing south at Moriches Bay when he saw "a red flare begin its ascent above the horizon line."[30] It flew "straight up" for three seconds or so and terminated in a "bright white explosion." He heard a "boom," and after watching the flaming wreckage fall to the sea, he heard four more booms. In June 1997, the FBI interviewed him once more. This time he admitted having a couple of beers. The agents reported an additional and unlikely caveat, namely that his sight was fixed on the horizon, and he was confident the object did not originate at the water line.

Witness 536 was on Ponquogue Beach with a friend and her children when she saw a "huge flare that came up from the water."[31] There was "grey smoke and white smoke" behind the flare and a "bright orange glow" at the leading edge of the smoke. After the explosion, she heard a "deep, boom-boom-boom-boom-boom sound" that shook the ground. In a second FBI interview in July 1997, she reiterated her story, but the agents added, in what may have been a misprint, that at the time of the incident the witness "was under the influence of alcohol or drugs."

Witness 550, working on a charter boat off Fire Island, was interviewed by the FBI and ATF on July 19, 1996, and by the FBI, MSIC, and Suffolk County Police Department a day later.[32] The witness "saw a plane coming from west to east and then what looked like a 'smaller' plane coming from the northeast on a dead course heading towards the nose of the larger plane." He heard a "crackling sound" when the two planes "crunched up," then a "poof" followed by a "whooshing sound." As he saw it, "The larger plane blew up and became a big fireball which then broke into four pieces."

Witness 558 was on fire duty for the Air National Guard at Gabreski Airport. As he told the FBI five days after the crash, "He noticed a red flare or roman candle ascending [above] the tree line," gaining altitude and bearing in a southeasterly direction.[33] He watched the flare ascend for as long as thirty seconds, lost it for a split second, and then observed "a large fireball erupt in the sky" before becoming "a ball of fire which separated into two equally sized balls dropping from the sky with no audible sound." The FBI interviewed him again a day later, and his story remained the same.

Witness 560 was still another of those citizens who enjoyed a second visit from the FBI.[34] In her first interview in July 1996, she told the two agents she was sitting in her car overlooking Northwest Bay in East Hampton when she noticed a fine white line extending upwards in the sky in a north-northwesterly direction. As the trail extended upwards and began to arc, the trail began to dissipate. The thin line then turned "bright white" and then became "a bright red/orange ball of fire" that cascaded down towards the sea. She heard no relevant sounds. In her second FBI interview in June 1997, the agents had her relating a more confusing tale. It concluded with the claim that "she did not see anything traveling in an upward direction."

The FBI interviewed Witness 570 a second time as well. In July 1996, he told the agent he had been swimming at water hole in Speonk when "he observed a reddish/orange flare ascending in the sky."[35] The apparent flare "was followed by a white vapor trail." He then observed an explosion in the sky from which "two large balls of fire" fell to the earth. In June 1997, he repeated his story to the agents in more detail. Although largely consistent with his first interview, the agents made a point of the fact that the flare-like object "made a sharp turn downward as if it were dropping out of the sky." The witness also noted "a deep sound like thunder" after the wreckage fell from the sky.

Witness 640 was standing in the surf at Smith Point Park when "his eye caught a jet plane, off to his left, and moving eastward."[36] At the same time, the witness saw "off to his right, a 'green flash' rising up, and going toward the plane." The flash was far out in the ocean and moving east as was the plane. A week after the crash, he took the FBI to the spot and showed them where he had seen what he had seen. He did not, however, track the object to the point of collision or hear anything.

In the first few weeks of the investigation, the FBI still seemed intent on gathering information about what appeared to be a missile attack. Agents were instructed to ask witnesses questions about the "missile launch point," "the color of the smoke trail," and "the impact point"— at least these were some of the questions forwarded to the Florida agents interviewing Witness 32, Dwight Brumley.[37] They never did ask Brumley these questions, but that had likely more to do with incompetence than ill intention.

On July 21, 1996, two FBI agents along with representatives from the New York State Police, the Coast Guard, the Defense Intelligence Agency and the Suffolk County Police escorted Witness 648 a mile or so out into the ocean south of the Moriches Inlet.[38] Their goal was to get perspective on what the witness and his two fishing buddies had seen four days earlier. According to the FBI, the witness kept continuously in his sights "a faint yellow star-type object" that moved in an east to west direction—the opposite direction TWA 800 was flying—before "it banked and turned downward toward the water." Its glow grew more intense, producing a mushroom of white smoke and "a rushing roar-type sound." At that instant, the witness "observed a plane which separated into two flaming parts," one the fuselage, the other a wing, and both crashed into the water. Sufficiently alarmed, he called a "May Day" into the Coast Guard.

Of all the witnesses, none provided the FBI with a more precise illustration of what he had seen than Witness 649. In *Silenced*, we animated his illustration to show the sequence of events from his perspective. Although we did not know his name at the time, Joseph Delgado, a public school administrator in Suffolk County, has since gone public. The CIA's Tauss described the "most useful reports" as those that "referenced identifiable landmarks." Delgado did just that, starting with his initial phone interview a day after the disaster.

"His point of reference on the Mill Road tree line was a telephone pole next to the yellow fire hydrant," the FBI reported.[39] The reader

would do well to keep this reference in mind. It will come in to play soon
enough. The following day, July 19, two FBI agents visited Delgado at
his home with his wife present. As he told the agents, he had just finished
exercising on the track at Westhampton High School and was walking
to his vehicle when he observed "an object ascending from behind the
trees." He described the bright white light object as "elongated." More
specifically, it had a reddish pink aura around it and a grey tail. It
ascended vertically, moving in a "squiggly" pattern, and arced off to the
right in a southwesterly direction.

Had he not been tracking "object number one," Delgado would not
likely have seen "object number two," which "glittered" with the reflec-
tion of the sun. That first object, said Delgado, "appeared like it was
going to slightly miss object number two unless it made a dramatic correction." This, it apparently did. Although he failed to see the actual
contact, he saw a "white puff," out of which emerged two objects "that
arched upward from the initial impact trailing smoke." These then
turned into large rectangular balls of fire that descended at an angle
down past the tree line. Delgado heard nothing, but he was sufficiently
concerned to drive to the beach where he thought the collision might
have taken place. According to the FBI report, when Delgado heard later
about the destruction of TWA 800, "He realized he had observed the
entire occurrence." Unlike most witnesses, Delgado brought the agents
to the site, and they noted again that the "point of reference was a telephone pole next to a yellow fire hydrant located on Mill Road."

The authorities took Delgado's account seriously. The next day, July
20, three FBI agents, three investigators from the Suffolk County Marine
Bureau (SCMB), a Suffolk County police officer, and two MSIC analysts
visited the site. There, the SCMB personnel, using a GPS 45 Personal
Navigator and a hand-bearing magnetic compass, tracked the paths of
objects one and two. Delgado's was one of eleven witness reports that
the SCMB plotted in the first two weeks after the incident. Although
talk of missiles had been discouraged from day one, investigators, even
those not fully in the loop, had to know that a missile or missiles had
destroyed TWA 800. Indeed, they were tasked with asking questions

such as, "What did it look [like] when it impacted the aircraft? Small, single burst of fire/sparks or multiple bursts?"

The authorities were not through with Delgado. On May 8, 1997, two agents from the FBI and a representative from the Naval Air Warfare Center in China Lake, California, interviewed Delgado at his Long island school. According to FBI notes, the China Lake rep was introduced to Delgado simply as "a member of the Department of Defense." Delgado repeated his account without any seeming change other than the addition of a second "puff" after the collision and the use of the word "firebox" to describe what fell from the sky. He told his interrogators he was confident he had seen a missile strike but having heard nothing in the ten months since the incident to confirm his suspicions, he was beginning to doubt himself.

The FBI agents ran a little game on Delgado. They showed him a drawing of the incident produced by Tauss's office in the CIA and, lest he be intimidated, told him another witness had drawn it. Delgado knew what he saw, and this was not it. He told the agents the drawing was "missing the entire first part"—that is, the ascent of the missile—and he made appropriate modifications. This interview took place six weeks after the CIA's Deputy Director of Intelligence had sent the following memorandum to the FBI's Kallstrom:

> Our analysis demonstrates that the eyewitness sightings of greatest concern to us—the ones originally interpreted to be of a possible missile attack—took place after the first of several explosions aboard the aircraft...combined with the total absence of physical evidence of a missile attack, [this] leads CIA analysts to conclude that no such attack occurred.[40]

In his 2008 report, Tauss described how the CIA came to this conclusion.[41] He larded the report with enough techno-gobbledygook to mesmerize the media into inaction, but the "crucial" element at the heart of his analysis was "the fact that the explosion was extraordinarily loud." Tauss's report left the distinct impression that sound was more important than sight. One problem, he conceded, was that the sightings were "remarkably detailed" and "surprisingly consistent." This much was true. Another problem, one that he evaded, was the wild inconsistency in the sounds witnesses reported hearing, if they heard any sounds at all.

Still, as Tauss noted, "a few eyewitness reports proved particularly useful." Among the "most valuable" was a fellow in a beachfront condominium. According to Tauss, even though he saw nothing before the plane exploded, "His report of loud sounds just after the fireballs hit the water made it possible to calculate the elapsed time from when the plane first exploded to when it hit the water." He was referring here to Witness 83. According to his FBI 302, this witness told the agents that five to ten seconds after the plane's wreckage met the horizon, he "heard an extremely loud explosion that shook his house." Knowing where the plane was when it exploded and where Witness 83 was located, Tauss was able "to calculate how long it took sound to travel from the explosion to the observer (49 seconds)." Incredibly, Tauss used this forty-nine second differential as the basis of his "sound-propagation analysis" to establish that "eyewitnesses who appeared to have seen a missile 'streak up' and cause the plane to explode could not have seen such an occurrence."

I say "incredibly" because the "man in the condominium" was Paul Angelides, the forensic engineer who appeared in *Silenced*. As he tried to do with Delgado's drawing, Tauss edited out of Angelides's account what he witnessed before the explosion. According to his FBI 302, Angelides had seen a "red flare" followed by "a thin white smoke trail."[42] He tracked this object for three or four seconds before the plane exploded. According to Tauss, however, Angelides's "observations began well after Flight 800 first exploded." Truth, as they say, is the first casualty of war. Tauss had no such excuse. This was peacetime. The shameless CIA analyst followed his passage on Angelides with a sentence that begins, "Another excellent eyewitness on the land…" That witness was Mike Wire, the man on the bridge.

Not even knowing the role he played in the creation of the CIA zoom climb video, Angelides was appalled when he first viewed it. "That bore no resemblance whatsoever to what I saw," he told us. In fact, he was so disgusted he called the FBI and insisted they come back and talk to him. His request was ignored. Wire was none too pleased either. Said he of the zoom climb video, "When I saw the scenario I thought it was strange because it was nothing like what I observed." The plainspoken Meyer may have summarized the CIA scenario best: "It was totally ludicrous."

Tauss singled out a third *Silenced* witness for analysis. This was Witness 32, Dwight Brumley, the senior Navy NCO, who was a passenger on board US Air Flight 217. After watching a small plane fly underneath 217, Brumley, according to the FBI, "observed a light which appeared to be a 'flare' and looked like the shooting of an unexploded firework into the air." The object was moving from right to left. US Air 217 was heading northeast to Providence. "Right to left" from Brumley's perspective meant roughly parallel to the path of 217 but on a slightly more northerly course. This was more or less perpendicular to the path of TWA 800. The flare-like object appeared to peak and head downward. Just then, Brumley saw a small explosion, followed by a large one, which turned into a "fireball" that fell from the sky. He estimated that this incident took place three thousand to four thousand feet below US Air 217.

This version of events did not work for Tauss. In his report, he claimed that Brumley's flare-like object first appeared just where TWA 800 was when it exploded. More troubling, he claimed the object was heading not north but east, the same direction in which TWA 800 was traveling. This lie enabled Tauss to claim that Brumley's flare "almost certainly was Flight 800 just after it exploded, not a missile." The CIA video showed this sequence as Tauss described it. Brumley was not amused. "The flight sequence shows TWA 800 in crippled flight crossing my field of view from left to right and ahead of US Air 217," he swore in an affidavit. "This is not correct. At no time did I see a burning TWA 800 crossing my field of view. If anyone claims I did they are very much mistaken."[43]

What Brumley found surprising—disturbing really—was that no one from the CIA or the NTSB talked to him before contorting his testimony to fit the CIA scenario. A twenty-five-year Navy vet, Brumley had trained in electronic warfare and participated in various missile-firing exercises. Given his knowledge base and his perspective on the disaster, he thought he might warrant more than a forty-five-minute interview by two FBI agents who knew little about aviation. "One of the biggest questions I have," said Brumley after the investigation closed, "is why I was never contacted 'officially' by somebody with aviation experience."[44] The only people who did talk to him after the initial interview were independent researchers like Commander Donaldson.

Like so many other witnesses, Brumley heard no sound. Indeed, only those who had not read the witness summaries—or who were complicit in the CIA's disinformation campaign—could have taken the notion of "sound propagation analysis" seriously. In seven of the forty witness accounts summarized previously, the interviewing agents did not even bother to ask about what the witnesses heard. In another nineteen, the witnesses heard nothing at all. In only fourteen of the forty summaries did a witness admit to hearing a sound, and in only three of those did the witness report hearing, more or less, what Angelides heard. A few reported hearing a sound as the objects collided. Witness 550 described a "crackling sound" when the two objects "crunched up." He then heard a "poof" followed by a "whooshing sound." Several heard what Mike Wire had heard, as Witness 536 described it: an earth shaking "deep, boom-boom-boom-boom-boom sound." Almost assuredly, an object breaking the sound barrier caused a sonic boom, but Tauss never entertained the possibility.

The CIA's elevation of these random aural accounts over the highly consistent visual ones had nothing to do with science and everything to do with politics. In fact, thirty-nine of these forty witnesses saw a red or orange or pink flare-like object ascending. Sixteen of the forty specified that the object was trailed by a white or grey smoke trail. Many described it as arcing or curving. Several observed the object heading westward, in the opposite direction TWA 800 was flying. A few saw the 747 before the object collided with it. Yes, virtually every one of these acknowledged seeing the "trailing cascade of flames" highlighted in the CIA video, but all of them, save perhaps one, saw it as a fully separate event, and all of those saw the crippled plane heading only downwards.

Despite its consistency, this testimony moved Tauss not at all. In the face of all evidence to the contrary, he insisted, "The plane had exploded before [the witness] observations began." This was nuts. Delgado, Wire and more than fifty others saw the object as soon as it emerged above the horizon or the tree line or house line in front of them and tracked it for any number of seconds before the initial explosion. In his 2008 report, Tauss did even not try to explain away the testimony of Witness 73, the travel agent who called me years later at my office. He couldn't. She was looking at TWA 800 as the object approached it and "never took her eyes off the aircraft during this time." Her initial FBI report continued: "At the instant the smoke trail ended at the aircraft's right wing, she heard a loud sharp noise which sounded like a firecracker had just exploded at her feet. She then observed a fire at the aircraft followed by one or two secondary explosions which had a deeper sound. She then observed the front of the aircraft separate from the back. She then observed burning pieces of debris falling from the aircraft."

Given the specificity of her testimony, it was no wonder Tauss and/or his accomplices in the FBI turned her into a drunk. What they lacked in integrity, they compensated for in audacity. They blew off Witness 73 and every other witness as well. "What [the witnesses] were seeing," Tauss insisted, "was a trail of burning fuel coming from the aircraft." This was not, however, what the eyewitnesses were alleged to have seen in the 1997 CIA zoom climb video. The reader may recall the narrator's claim that "just after the aircraft exploded it pitched up abruptly and climbed several thousand feet from its last recorded altitude of about 13,800 feet to a maximum altitude of about 17,000 feet" and his subsequent assertion that "the eyewitnesses almost certainly saw only the burning aircraft without realizing it." In the 2008 CIA report, there was no mention whatsoever of this hypothesis. It vanished without explanation or apology.

By the time we were ready to launch *Silenced* in the summer of 2001, I knew most of this. I knew enough certainly to trust James Sanders more than the mainstream media. Although we chose not to discuss politics in *Silenced* or the source of the missiles fired, I had strong suspicions about both. I still had much to learn. That would come in time.

Chapter: SEVEN

THE GOOD BUREAUCRAT

T he editor of *Silenced*, Kelly Creech, hoped the project would be a learning experience for me. We had worked together on any number of videos before and shared thoughts on any number of subjects. One was the Kennedy assassination. A serious student of the event, Creech bought more or less into the Oliver Stone version of a government sanctioned turkey shoot. I dissented strongly enough that Creech offered to fly me to Dallas and walk me through Dealey Plaza. I argued then, and would argue now, that conspiracies of execution are not in our national character. The widely accepted rule of law among us and the generally cautious nature of the American civil servant weigh against that possibility.

Conspiracies of concealment are another matter altogether. It was not hard to imagine the FBI's J. Edgar Hoover or the CIA's John McCone shuffling the paperwork to avoid blame for Lee Harvey Oswald's unsupervised presence along JFK's parade route. In a similar vein, one did not have to be a conspiracy theorist to believe Richard Nixon would conspire with his subordinates to conceal a screwy, ill-advised break-in of the Democratic National Headquarters, especially in an election year. In these cases, the ambition of government employees made them all the more susceptible to pressure from above. "I was affected by how easily I said yes, sir," contrite Nixon aide Alex Butterfield told reporter Bob Woodward years later. "I had seen myself and heard myself get caught up in and be anxious and ready to facilitate an abusive government."[1] Access to power can be that seductive.

The CIA's role in the TWA 800 affair made sense to me. Its agents were in the business of deception. They got medals for it. I suspect that if they were asked to deceive the American people for reasons of the highest national security—to avoid war, say, or to protect a secret weapons system—they would have willingly obliged. Contrary to what its critics might think, the FBI is not in the business of lying. For those few in the know, the task could not have come easily. As shall be seen, at least one agent resisted.

Jim Kallstrom's assignment, I am convinced, scarred him for life, his bluster notwithstanding. Through some combination of carrots and sticks—and more on these later—the White House swayed him to its cause several weeks into the investigation. After all, the FBI did report to the Department of Justice, and, short of resigning, Kallstrom had little choice but to be a good soldier. As a young Marine platoon commander, he had served in Vietnam and fought in the grueling battle of Khe Sanh. He knew how to follow orders.

Much harder to understand was the complicity of the career professionals at the NTSB. Although founded in 1967, the agency was made fully independent in 1974. Its role was to investigate all major civilian transportation accidents in the United States and to do so without political pressure. For the first twenty-five years of its existence it did just that. The election of Bill Clinton in 1992 changed the equation. In his first appointment to the NTSB Board, the relentlessly political Clinton replaced a pilot/

aeronautical engineer/aviation lawyer with a good-old-boy Al Gore crony from Tennessee, Jim Hall. Unkindly but accurately, a *Washington Post* columnist described Hall as "a politically connected white male Democrat whose only transportation experience apparently is a driver's license."[2] Less than a year after his appointment, Clinton appointed the feckless Hall chairman. "I wouldn't trust Jim Hall as far as I could throw him," Reagan-era NTSB board member Vernon Grose told me. "He was locked up with Al Gore. I have no use for his integrity."[3]

As he often did—at the Department of Justice most relevantly—Clinton put his go-to guy in the less scrutinized second spot. That would be Robert Francis, a tall, balding patrician from Massachusetts. "Bob Francis," Pat Milton reported, "felt responsible only to the person who had appointed him: the president of the United States."[4] Francis had passed the previous nine years running the Paris office of the FAA. There, he had insinuated himself into the good graces of international courtesan and Democratic Party power broker, Pamela Churchill Harriman, Clinton's ambassador to France. In 1995, Harriman helped secure the NTSB gig for Francis.[5] Francis would prove to be the ideal *commissaire politique*. Clinton needed one. This was the most desperate stretch of his career. Virtually every move he and Hillary made in 1995 and 1996 was political, and few moves proved as salutary as the appointment of Francis. Although board members were expected to rotate through accident assignments, vice-chairman Francis somehow managed to catch two in a row: the May 1996 ValuJet crash in Florida, from which he had just returned, and now TWA Flight 800.

When the Department of Justice attorneys moved to take over the investigation, Francis was on the scene to let them. This move flirted with illegality. By law, the FBI could only seize control if DOJ attorneys declared the crash a crime scene, but this they did not do and never would. According to Title 49, section 1131(a)(2) of the U.S. Code, an NTSB investigation "has priority over any investigation by another department, agency or instrumentality of the United States Government." If the FBI were to run a parallel investigation, the NTSB was to authorize and oversee it. The opposite happened.

"There was something rotten in Denmark, just on the timing," said Grose. "The law is very clear," he told me. "The invitation is exclusively limited to when criminal action is suspected. And NTSB decides that distinction—not the FBI." In his experience, the NTSB enlisted the FBI's help if they thought there was a crime involved. He cited the October 1999 case of EgyptAir Flight 990, which crashed sixty miles south of Nantucket Island, Massachusetts, killing all 217 people on board. In that instance, the NTSB called in the FBI nearly two weeks after the crash when the recovered CVR pointed to a crime. The NTSB did not follow this protocol in the TWA 800 case. "The night of the crash," added Grose, who provided expert commentary for CNN into the early morning hours, "the FBI was already in charge."[6] From his perspective, to understand what happened to the investigation there is no more important problem to solve than who authorized the FBI takeover.

Hall and Francis yielded readily to the FBI takeover of the investigation. This was understandable. They were political people. They had their marching orders. If President Clinton lost in November, they would be out of work. A brief pep talk about national security would likely salve whatever conscience they brought to the job. Harder to understand were the motives of NTSB witness group head, Dr. David Mayer and his boss, Dr. Bernard Loeb, the head of the NTSB's Office of Aviation Safety. Nine years previously, Loeb had brought Mayer on board as a statistics and database specialist, and he had worked his way up to safety study manager by the time of the hearing.

Unlike the industry members of the NTSB witness group, Mayer was a federal employee. That said, he was not a political appointee. He had nothing obvious to gain from subverting the truth. And yet he participated in the sham 2000 NTSB hearing with overt enthusiasm. Fussy and officious, he seemed to me the good bureaucrat, one whose motives would have been clear to all good bureaucrats throughout history, if no one else.

Thanks to the video recording of the August 2000 hearings, we were able to give Mayer a featured on-camera role in *Silenced*. As the presenter for the witness section, Mayer came on in relief to save the game the CIA had run on the American people. If he succeeded, no witness account would ever be taken seriously. This was not an easy assignment, but Mayer was clearly the man for the job. He told the board that the FBI had begun interviewing witnesses on the evening of the accident and, within a week, had contacted more than five hundred of them.[7] This was true enough. "During this time," he continued, "safety board investigators reviewed the many witness accounts the FBI was documenting." This half-truth cloaked an insulting reality.

Two days after the crash, the NTSB's Bruce Magladry formed a witness group that included accident investigators from TWA, ALPA, and the FAA. On that same day, the FBI informed Magladry that no outside investigator could have any access to witness information. Two days later, Assistant United States Attorney Valerie Caproni told Magladry he could review FBI witness statements only if "no notes [be] taken and no copies made." A day later, he was told he could not even take notes during an interview and could only interview a witness in the presence of an FBI agent. Two days later, he gave up and slumped back to Washington.[8] It was hard to blame him. The restrictions rendered his task frivolous. That was not, however, how Kallstrom remembered it. "I cannot recall telling the NTSB not to interview anybody," he told Megyn Kelly of Fox News in June 2013. "They could interview whoever the hell they wanted to."[9] After years of fending off accusations, Kallstrom lied even when he did not have to.

Not until April 1998 did the NTSB receive the witness summaries from the FBI. The actual review began months later, now with Mayer as head of the witness group. Like the CIA's Tauss, Mayer made the case that reviewing these summaries was a "painstaking" task that took many months. In reality, a literate adult could read them all in an afternoon. Most are no more than a paragraph or two long.

Mayer endeavored to tell the board members what the witnesses, a quarter of whom were less than eleven miles away, actually observed. Some of what he said was true: only a few saw TWA 800 before it blew up; fewer still saw the nose section fall to the sea as it was not on fire; many saw what appeared to be a fireball breaking into pieces as it fell to the sea. Mayer claimed, however, that no one saw the initial explosion, which was not true. He insisted that the flaming fuselage, which looked like "a small light or streak," confused witnesses into thinking they saw a missile. This was egregiously false.

Mayer had some explaining to do, and he knew it. By the witness group's own count, 258 witnesses reported seeing a streak of light. There was, he conceded, "a remarkable consistency" among them. Of those 258 witnesses, fifty-six, by Mayer's count, put his casuistry to the test. These were the witnesses like Mike Wire and Joseph Delgado, who saw the object ascend straight up from the horizon. As to why these witness accounts "didn't seem to fit," Mayer offered two explanations, one more specious than the other. His best shot was to blame the FBI. Mayer admitted the agents did not record the interviews. They simply took notes, many of which were "incomplete" or "vaguely worded." As a result, "The documents may not always say what the witness said." This was true to a degree, especially in the second round of interviews in 1997. At that stage in the investigation, the agents were trying to dilute the strength of the testimony, even if it meant making a teetotaler a drinker.

Mayer's second rationale was more insulting than the first. This time the culprit was "memory error." Mayer cited the work of a hitherto obscure psychologist, Ira Hyman of Western Washington University, to the effect that people "combine knowledge from various sources with their own personal experience to create memory." Hyman's expertise was in recovered childhood memories. These fifty-six adult witnesses were telling authorities what they had seen a day or two earlier. Most gave their testimony unaware that others were giving comparable testimony. When re-interviewed, they stuck to their original stories, even after the media had ridiculed the missile theory and individuals such as Pierre Salinger who proposed it.

To make his point, Mayer walked the board through an utterly specious rendering of what Mike Wire saw from the bridge and Dwight Brumley saw from his US Air flight overhead. In each case, he either manufactured or contorted details to confirm his own "small light or streak" theory. Mayer then showed the results of a missile visibility test, one undertaken not to determine if a missile struck TWA 800—"We've known for a long time it wasn't"—but to show what witnesses at those distances might have seen. Not since the prosecutors dared O. J. Simpson to try on the gloves has a bit of show and tell gone so badly. Although positioned as far as sixteen miles from the launch site, "all of the observers," the NTSB acknowledged, "easily detected" the shoulder-fired missiles used in the test.[10]

The video of this test was priceless. We included it in *Silenced* and compared the missile in the test to what Wire and Delgado had seen. It was a near perfect match. "The rocket motor of the missile would be visible and it would look like a light ascending rapidly for about eight seconds," said Mayer. Wire used the word "zigzag" to describe the motion of the ascending object. Delgado used "squiggly." The missile in the video confirmed their observations. It squiggled and zigzagged. Both witnesses and many others noted that the missile seemed to disappear at the peak of its ascent. Unwittingly, Mayer explained why: "Then the motor would burn out and the light would disappear for as much as seven seconds." The missile used in the test was of the shoulder launch variety. A larger missile would have been more visible still.

In one of his less comprehendible moments, Mayer testified that in a "hypothetical missile attack" a witness would first have seen one streak of light, the hypothetical missile. Then he would have seen a second streak of light, the "airplane in crippled flight." This made no sense to anyone paying attention. Mayer was suggesting that a fuel tank explosion had already crippled the plane *before* the "hypothetical" missile struck. Mayer explained that since no witness saw both an ascending streak of light followed by Mayer's imagined "crippled flight" streak of light, they must have seen only the flaming fuselage of a crippled flight, never mind that several of the best eyewitnesses saw the missile heading in the opposite direction as TWA 800, and many more saw it ascend from the horizon. The NTSB produced its own video to show what a swooping, flaming, gently climbing plane might have looked like.

"They got smart when the CIA got laughed out of town by aviators," observed Commander Donaldson. "The NTSB figured they'd get away with half of it. So they said it climbed 1,700 feet. It didn't."[11] As with the CIA video, the NTSB plane streaked smoothly without the zigzags so many witnesses described. Mayer did not attempt to explain the discrepancy. There was a good deal more he chose not to explore, including the possibility that more than one missile hit the aircraft almost simultaneously and appeared, at least, to stop the 747 in its tracks.

Several witnesses testified to this perception. One fellow, Witness 551, who was sitting behind Dwight Brumley on US Air 217, said that TWA 800 came to a virtual halt "like a bus running into a stone wall."[12] Witness 233 "observed a large object seemingly stopping its forward momentum while igniting into a fireball."[13] Witness 150, Lisa Perry, who appeared in *Silenced*, gave very specific testimony along these lines.[14] As the FBI reported, Perry tracked a cylindrical object moving at a high speed when she then "noticed a large commercial airliner which appeared to be traveling at the same altitude. The object headed toward the side of the plane. She saw a puff of smoke, and then the plane simply seemed to 'just stop.'" Fissures developed throughout the plane, and it broke like a toy. "It was a 747, she knew, because it had a bump on the top." Her 302 continued, "The front was carried forward and arced down with its momentum. The right wing seemed to stay with the front of the plane.... A portion of the left wing began to fall separately down, yet forward with momentum. The tail section fell backward. There was 'blackness' in the rear. All of the pieces seemed to fall 'gracefully' down and widening, leaving a cloud in the sky." It would take weeks of investigation before the NTSB realized how accurate was the description Perry gave within days of the crash.

To be sure, Mayer made no reference to Perry's testimony or that of Witness 73, who described the destruction of the aircraft in similar terms. He did, however, make a passing reference to Captain Christian Baur, the Air National Guard helicopter co-pilot flying with Major Fritz Meyer. In his FBI interview on July 20, 1996, Baur reported seeing a flare-like object moving from left to right, towards JFK. He saw enough of it to ask the flight engineer, "Is that a pyro?"[15] Baur then saw a succession of explosions followed by a "huge fireball." As he told the FBI, he first "thought two things had flown into each other." Baur expanded on what he had seen during his interview with the NTSB in January 1997. "There was an object that came from the left," said Baur. "And it appeared to be like—like, a white-hot. Like a pyrotechnic."[16] Once it collided, or appeared to, with TWA Flight 800, said Baur, "It was almost as if the plane dropped in its tracks. It didn't keep going."

For Mayer, there were two major problems with this testimony. One was Baur's contention, shared by many of the better observers, that TWA 800 seemed to halt in the sky when struck. The second was that the object Baur saw was moving from east to west. TWA 800 was moving west to east. The streak Baur witnessed could not have been the flaming fusclage of Mayer's imagination. Mayer solved this problem by discounting Baur's testimony as something of a memory trick. Apparently, in his initial debriefing right after the incident, Baur did not talk of seeing a streak. Mayer seized on this. He spoke of Baur's later testimony to the FBI and NTSB as "an example of details being added over time." On night one, however, Baur had more pressing concerns, like dodging bodies as they fell from the sky and locating them for retrieval.

Had Mayer paid serious attention to what Baur and Meyer said he might have solved the mystery of the plane's demise. Interviewed by the NTSB witness group the same day as Baur, Meyer told his interrogators that he saw a streak moving in a gentle arc from right to left, the *same* direction as TWA 800.[17] He then saw a series of hard explosions "as opposed to soft explosion like gasoline or something." Only then did he see the fireball, which he described as "definitely petroleum." The two pilots were not confused. They saw two different objects, one heading in a westerly direction, one east, each exploding at or near TWA 800 and blowing it climactically out of the sky—no zoom climb, no gentle looping climb, no survivors.

When Mayer finished his presentation, the folksy board chairman Jim Hall asked Mayer a series of questions. Although Hall's probe seemed genuine, Mayer's answers were likely rehearsed in advance, and many of them were untrue. "Were your activities restricted in any way?" Hall asked. "No, sir," said Mayer. "There were no restrictions placed on us." This statement makes euphemism impossible: it was pure lie. No other word suffices. The DOJ shut the NTSB witness group out of the interview process on day two of the investigation. The FBI did not even allow its members to review the 302s until well after the CIA ruled out a missile strike. For Hall, these illegal actions were minor housekeeping details. "I want to acknowledge that normal board procedures were not followed in this investigation," he said, "and we are addressing that because that, unfortunately, has added to a lot of the misconception that has been generated around this."

Hall then asked other pertinent questions: "If you could show that the airplane did not climb after the nose departed, will that change your analysis?" Mayer replied, "Our analysis is not actually dependent on that." Lest he pull the curtain all the way back on the CIA's puppet show, Mayer claimed to "believe" the plane did ascend. Believe? That was not the only blow the NTSB quietly dealt to the CIA's theorizing. Mayer made no mention of the "sound propagation analysis" that inspired the CIA recreation. Hall addressed this as well. "Is sound a factor in this analysis you showed us?" he asked. "Again, we certainly gave sound a great deal of consideration," Mayer answered, "but our analysis is not based on sound so, no, sir, it's not."

Without calling attention to the fact, Mayer and Hall had fully subverted the FBI/CIA analysis. Sound was irrelevant. The zoom climb was a fantasy. The witness statements were impressively consistent and might have driven the investigation if the DOJ and FBI had not illegally prevented the NTSB witness group from seeing them. The observers in the missile test all saw pretty much what the witnesses had. "Is your analysis of the witness accounts dependent on the CIA work?" Hall asked lamely. It was not, said Mayer: "We were aware of their work but our work is not a derivative of theirs." Of course Mayer was aware. He had been working with the CIA. This I learned only recently, and it helps explain Mayer's performance. The access to power can turn a career bureaucrat's head all too easily.

Even if the other board members were serious about their responsibility, they would have been hard pressed to do the right thing. The NTSB witness group had been handed a rough hewn but well accepted fraud. Once appointed to head that group, Mayer smoothed out its rough spots, surely on orders from above, but let the fraud stand. To expose it might well have caused a constitutional crisis. The nation had just survived the impeachment of its president. Who, at this stage of the TWA 800 saga, would have investigated whom? Better to congratulate Mayer for what board member George Black called his "excellent literature review and report" and move on.

Before letting Mayer go, Hall had one more public relations problem to solve. Reed Irvine's Accuracy in Media helped organize the "TWA 800 Eyewitness Alliance." A week before the hearings, its members took out a full-page ad in the *Washington Times* boldly headlined, "We Saw TWA Flight 800 Shot Down by Missiles And We Won't Be Silenced Any Longer."[18] The ad featured the testimony of seven witnesses including Mike Wire, Dwight Brumley, Paul Angelides, Major Fritz Meyer, and Joseph Delgado. It was not easy to ignore.

"What do you think about those accounts?" Hall asked Mayer. At this juncture, Tom Stalcup could control himself no longer. The young physicist startled the audience in the Baltimore hearing room by yelling out, "Ask the eyewitnesses!" As Stalcup explained to us when interviewed for *Silenced*, there was no precedent for shutting the witnesses down like this. In place of their testimony, the NTSB satisfied itself with letting one its own officials sum up FBI reports he had already discounted as "incomplete" or "vaguely worded." Mayer himself had spoken to none of the witnesses. An outraged Stalcup would go on to fight this battle for the next fifteen years, but he would not prevail that afternoon. Hall very civilly threatened to have Stalcup removed if he said anything else.

Mayer had a copy of the *Washington Times* ad with him and breezed through the first five witness accounts with brief, specious counter claims not worth repeating. The sixth witness, William Gallagher, had earlier talked to the media about his frustration with the investigation. "I saw something hit the right side of the plane," the plainspoken New Jersey fisherman told the Riverside *Press-Enterprise* in October 1997. "My honest opinion, my gut feeling, is that we have the most brilliant people in the world and the best technology, [and] if they've been on scene for a year and they've not come up with something, as a critical thinker I have to ask, could they be covering up something?"[19] This was a question Mayer chose not to answer. He skipped Gallagher altogether.

Joseph Delgado, the seventh of the witnesses, gave Mayer the most trouble. As Mayer acknowledged, "Witness 649 described events that certainly do sound like a missile attacking the airplane." He noted too that Delgado was one of the eleven witnesses who were part of the Suffolk County Marine Bureau's line-of-sight study, chosen in no small part "because he provided some fixed reference points." The reader may recall that both in his phone interview and in his on-site interview at the running track, Delgado specified a "telephone pole next to the yellow fire hydrant."

To discredit Delgado, Mayer reached deep into his bag of propaganda tricks and pulled out a convincingly specific detail. "The yellow line that's been drawn shows his line of sight between those two flagpoles," said Mayer of Delgado while showing a supporting graphic. He argued that Delgado was looking in the wrong direction to see Flight 800 "when it would have been struck by a hypothetical missile." In making *Silenced*, we went to a location Mayer never visited, Delgado's school track. We showed why Delgado never mentioned a flagpole, let alone two. There was none. What Delgado showed the investigators were a fire hydrant and a telephone pole. Those were his reference points. Never did he imply that all the action was contained within them.

Given the work Mayer put into this presentation, it is hard to believe this reference was a mistake. If it were, he made exactly the same mistake that the CIA analysts did in discussing the apocryphal second FBI interview with Mike Wire. According to Analyst 1, Wire recanted his earlier statement that he first saw the object as it ascended from below the rooftop. In this second interview, Wire now claimed he first saw the object "high in the sky." How high? Analyst 1 had the answer: "[Wire] said it was as if—if you imagine a flag pole on top of the house. It would be as if it were on the top or the tip of the flag pole."[20] The flag pole gambit apparently worked. Both times. Who, after all, would disbelieve a detail that specific?

The media should have helped the citizenry see through the smoke. They didn't. As I heard from several reporters who covered this story, the *New York Times* owned this story. The FBI channeled virtually all new information through the *Times*, and the *Times* reported that information very close to uncritically. After the final FBI press conference in November 1997, for instance, the paper's opinion page editors congratulated the FBI for its "admirable thoroughness and openness" in an op-ed insultingly titled "Conspiracy Inoculation."[21] They were able to reach this hapless conclusion for one reason above all others: after the first day or two of the investigation, the *Times* did not interview a single one of the 258 "streak of light" witnesses.

If the media had paid attention to the investigation, they would have known by the time of the final NTSB hearing that they had been played. During the previous four years, government agencies had proposed at least four distinct scenarios to explain witness testimony. None of them made sense, but all went unchallenged.

The first was the bomb scenario sold successfully to the *Times* through August 1996. In fact, as early as July 19, the *Times* was reporting, "Some investigators think the most likely explanation was a terrorist or criminal bombing, a scenario apt to strike deep fear in the public."[22]

As to scenario two, the zoom climb, the CIA fixed upon this curiosity almost magically on December 30, 1996. Based on their fabled "sound propagation analysis," agency analysts concluded that after a spontaneous fuel tank explosion blew off the cockpit, the flaming, noseless fuselage streaked straight up more than three thousand feet. To reach this conclusion, of course, the CIA had to ignore the fact that no witness reported seeing the plane ascend, not a single one. Said Eastwind pilot David McClaine, TWA 800 "seemed to fall straight down."

An alternate possibility implicit in the CIA analysis was the cascading flame scenario. At the time of the November 1997 video premiere and FBI press conference, CNN paraphrased unnamed FBI officials to the effect that "what some witnesses thought was a missile hitting the plane was actually burning, leaking fuel from the jet after its front part had already broken off."[23] By 2008, the CIA had adopted this theory as well. "What [the witnesses] were seeing," analyst Tauss insisted, "was a trail of burning fuel coming from the aircraft."[24]

The fourth possibility is the one that Mayer proposed at the NTSB hearing. In this scenario, the center fuel tank exploded spontaneously but unseen. When the flames spread to the wings, the flaming fuselage, ascending gradually about 1500 feet, looked like "a small light or streak."

Then there is the fifth possibility, the one that Joseph Delgado, Mike Wire, William Gallagher, and scores of other savvy and responsible witnesses described in remarkably consistent detail. I refer here to the "events" that, in Mayer's words, "certainly do sound like a missile attacking the airplane." These events include the ascending flare-like objects, the smoke trail, the zigzag, the arc, the momentary disappearance, and multiple subsequent "bright white" explosions, followed by a fuel-fed fireball. Every one of the best witnesses saw a glowing object ascend and then saw the flaming plane descend. Their descriptions of the falling plane are as vivid and accurate as their descriptions of the ascending object. They did not confuse the two.

"It was important for us to determine if the witness accounts were generally consistent with the physical evidence," said Mayer at the final NTSB hearing. As should be clear, these accounts were not consistent at all with the physical evidence the NTSB presented. By the time we had completed *Silenced* in early summer 2001, I had every reason to trust the witnesses and none to trust the government. Officials who were willing to change witness testimony—or in some cases invent it—would have few qualms about editing tape, misreading data, misplacing parts, rearranging the debris field, or, if push came to shove, pulling out a hammer and bending the metal.

Chapter: EIGHT

RESPONSIBLE JOURNALISM

On June 6, 2001, we staged a pre-screening of *Silenced* for a tough audience, the Kansas City "hangar" of a semi-secret organization known as the "Quiet Birdmen." At the time the QBs were meeting at the Kansas City Club, a posh gentleman's retreat in downtown Kansas City. There were close to a hundred people in attendance, the great majority of them retired airline, military, and freight pilots with a heavy TWA representation. I was a little apprehensive. Every one in the audience knew more about aviation than I did. They sat in silence through the hour-long presentation. The video concluded with our own animation, as seen from the perspective of the man on the bridge, of a two-missile strike on the doomed aircraft. We did not speculate as to the type of missile fired or the perpetrator of the attack. We focused instead on the witnesses and the corruption of their testimony.

I did not know quite what to expect in the way of response, but when the lights came up, one gentleman rose angrily from his seat and shouted, "Follow the money!" He was a retired TWA pilot. Like many of his colleagues, he had been heavily invested in the company. He believed, as many of them did, that TWA management swallowed the government line to curry favor. At the time of this screening, the airline was in bankruptcy. It would cease to exist altogether within six months. If anyone in the room doubted that missiles had destroyed TWA 800, he kept his opinions to himself. Offered instead were corroborating details, particularly from angry TWA pilots, about the money trail and the inexplicable Pentagon visits of then TWA CEO Jeff Erickson. Said one TWA pilot: "90 percent of us believe there was a government cover-up." Many traced the airline's demise to that fateful night in July 1996.

Once we started distributing the video, the response we got from people within Boeing was equally encouraging. One engineer who had spent countless hours analyzing the aircraft's destruction on the company's Cray Supercomputers e-mailed me the following: "I brought [Silenced] to work today and showed it during lunch to eight of my fellow Boeing workers. The room was deathly quiet the entire time.... My impression then was a missile strike, and it is even more so today."[1]

Encouraged by the reception, I sent a copy to Claudia Anderson, the managing editor of the *Weekly Standard*, a publication I considered then and now to be the nation's smartest conservative journal. For the past few years I had been writing the occasional piece for the publication and had met Anderson during a recent visit. Not hearing back from her, I called to see if she had had a chance to watch *Silenced*. She claimed she tried but fell asleep while watching it. Taken aback, I suggested she watch it all the way through, this being the greatest untold story of our time, one with major political implications. She doubted she would.

I sensed correctly that my relationship with the *Weekly Standard* was over. Those who believe that the conservative media would jump at a story potentially damaging to the Clintons have no experience with conservative media. In Washington, at least, I had crossed the line from responsible journalist to conspiracy theorist. Peter Goelz certainly thought so. I knew Goelz from Kansas City, though not well. In a county without much in the way of Republican opposition, I did some political media for local Democrats, including future senator Claire McCaskill in her successful run for Jackson County prosecutor. Goelz worked as a Democratic consultant and lobbyist, and so our paths crossed once or twice.

Locally, Goelz was best known for his lobbying work with the "gaming" interests that were buying their way into Missouri. They nosed their way into the state with the pitch that the gambling would be limited to actual, floating, old-timey riverboats. In practice, the "boats" proved no more capable of floating than the Pentagon, but this was apparently "transportation" expertise enough to snag Goelz the spokesman's job on Jim Hall's staff at the NTSB. Being a political supporter of the ambitious Hall probably did not hurt either.

Spokesman for Jim Hall was not the job for which loyalist Goelz had been pining. His connections were strong enough that Clinton had tagged him in 1994 to head the National Indian Gaming Commission, a job rich with perks and possibilities. According to the *Washington Post*, however, nearly all the participating tribes were "furious" that the White House was ramming Goelz down their throats. So too was Democratic senator Daniel K. Inouye (D-Hawaii), chairman of the Senate Select Committee on Indian Affairs, who had been promised an open application process. Their collective disgust forced the White House to rethink its plans, and so Goelz ended up on Hall's NTSB staff.[2]

In May 2001, I wrote an article in support of *Silenced* for *Ingram's*, the business magazine that I served as executive editor. Goelz did not like it. In a dismissive letter to the editor in the next month's edition, he wrote, "In the end there were no missiles, no bombs, no mystery fleet, no fleeing ships, no terrorists, no U.S. Navy involvement. It was just a tired old 747 with an empty, explosive center wing tank."

In October 1998, Goelz singled out ABC News correspondent Lisa Stark and producer Tina Babarovic as being "very responsible about reporting the complexities" of the TWA 800 crash investigation. He likely made this point not so much to praise ABC News as to intimidate

ABC Entertainment. The network had recently commissioned filmmaker Oliver Stone to produce a one-hour prime-time special that would explore alternative TWA 800 scenarios. It never came to pass. According to the *New York Times*, the network dropped plans after "several ABC journalists" complained that viewers might confuse the Stone project with the news, and the news people knew for a fact that the missile theories were "groundless." In reporting on this conflict for the *Times*, Lawrie Mifflin elaborated that various theories about bombs and missiles had been "widely discredited."[3] Goelz emphatically agreed, calling all such theories "[a]bsolutely, completely groundless." At this time, the NTSB witness group had yet to read the eyewitness summaries, let alone come to any conclusions.

If nothing else, Goelz was skilled in turning one branch of the media against another. In August 1999, Kelly O'Meara, a reporter with *Insight* magazine, asked Goelz for an interview. She had quietly received some new radar data from an NTSB source and wanted Goelz's take on it. Fortunately, she recorded the interview. Within an hour of its conclusion, Goelz called the *Washington Post*'s Howard Kurtz to make a preemptive strike on O'Meara. Less than two days later, in an article thick with sarcasm, Kurtz quoted Goelz as saying, "She really believes that the United States Navy shot this thing down and there was a fleet of warships."[4] As her audiotape proved, O'Meara said or implied no such thing, but that is the way Goelz rolled, and the media rolled with him. Said former NTSB board member Vernon Grose of Goelz, "No other NTSB Managing Director has ever given interviews or delivered opinions about accidents."[5]

My turn was coming up. On July 16, 2001, I got a call from a producer at CNN asking if I would be willing to talk about TWA Flight 800 on air the following day, July 17, the fifth anniversary of the crash. Of course, I would. I would be beamed in remotely to the *The Point*, a show hosted then by Greta Van Susteren. There was nothing tentative about the arrangement. The producer might or might not select someone to go on with me as counterpoint, she told me, but barring a confession from wayward congressman Gary Condit, then too much in the news, the show would go on. That night I organized my thoughts as though I were to be the only guest.

The next morning the producer called back. Jim Hall had agreed to go on with me. Our dual appearance was billed on the CNN website and was promoted on conservative websites as well. The producer also directed me to the studio in Kansas City where the interview would be shot. It was KCPT, the local PBS station. I was pleased. The station had aired a half dozen of my documentaries.

After making the arrangements, I headed out to a local public swimming pool where I idled away my lunch hour. It seemed like just another summer day until that light bulb went off over my head. "Good God!" I thought. In six hours, I would have the chance to blow open the most successful cover-up in American peacetime history on CNN, the most respected of all cable news channels. I expected the deck to be stacked at least a little. A few years earlier the Truman Library in nearby Independence had asked me to debate the then retired Illinois Senator Paul Simon on Harry Truman's Fair Deal. The format went like this: Simon got twenty minutes. I got twenty minutes. Simon got twenty more minutes. Anticipating something similar, I concentrated on honing one killer question.

What I came up with was this: "By the NTSB's own count, fifty-six eyewitnesses saw an object rise up off the horizon, ascend, zigzag, arc over, and explode at or near the aircraft." I would continue, "The CIA—and what was the CIA doing on this case anyhow?—tried to tell us that the crippled plane rocketed upwards three thousand feet, confusing the witnesses. Aviators ridiculed this explanation. The NTSB disowned it. So my question to you, Mr. Hall, is what did the eyewitnesses see?" Hall, I imagined, would fumble out some kind of half-assed explanation. Then I would respond, "With all due respect, Mr. Hall, but the CIA had so little to go on that they manufactured—created out of whole cloth—an interview with their key witness, and I would be happy to show you the proof." At this point, the ref slaps the mat. Takedown! "Mr. Hall," I would say in conclusion, "I think you owe the American people an apology."

Of course, we would never get to this point. As soon as I formulated these questions, I knew the interview would never take place. Hall was much too slow, much too vulnerable. Unlike the president who appointed him chairman, Hall was not "an unusually good liar." Nor was he fast on his feet. Someone, I was certain, would get to him or to CNN and call this whole thing off. I just waited for the call to come. I did not have to wait long. Three hours before the show was to air, a chagrined young producer called to tell me my CNN debut was not to be. She did not hide her disgust. Jim Hall refused to appear on the show with me. And if I were to appear alone, as I had been scheduled to do just the previous day, then that would not be "responsible journalism."

An hour later, I e-mailed Kristina Borjesson, a former CBS producer who was canned for trying to break out the TWA 800 story four years earlier. "The producer and Greta Van Susteren are furious. Not their fault. This came from the top," I wrote. "The standards for responsible journalism seem to have changed overnight." A serious reporter, Borjesson called CNN to confirm the facts in my e-mail. After much searching, she found a source willing to speak anonymously.

"We had no idea we were going to run into this problem," the source told Borjesson. This CNN staffer went on to say that neither Hall nor Goelz would appear on this show with me so the decision was made to put Hall on alone. "If it is not responsible journalism for Cashill to go on alone, why is it responsible journalism for Hall to go on alone?" asked Borjesson. The answer was that Hall was a "legitimate news guest." Then the source said about me, "Lots of people warned us about this guy."[6]

That evening I watched *The Point* to see what responsible journalism looked like. Van Susteren began with a pointless canard. "At first," she said, "people suspected a bomb went off on the plane."[7] No, at first people suspected a missile and with good reason. She then talked about the "painstaking search" that led authorities to conclude that an electrical spark "probably" ignited vapors in the jet's empty fuel tank. Those vapors, she claimed, had been caused by the heat of the air conditioning units located under the tank. Much was made throughout the investigation about the plane sitting out on a hot tarmac, but these planes routinely sat out on tarmacs in places like Cairo and Phoenix. Plus, as one witness told the FBI, "It was a clear, chilly night." Van Susteren concluded her introduction musing about the "conspiracy theorists" that insisted the plane was shot down.

In her defense, Van Susteren almost assuredly did not write this opening. It would not surprise me if NTSB staffers had a hand in its creation. The "painstaking" trope smells of David Mayer, as does the all-purpose "conspiracy theorist." After the introduction, however, Van Susteren asked Hall a question that had the potential to derail him.

"Jim," she asked, "can you say with 100 percent certainty that the people who think that this flight was shot down, that they were wrong?" Hall tried to kill the clock with innocuous blather. "Well, Greta," he began, "I think the first thing that I need to say this evening is, we all need to remember first the 230 individuals who lost their lives in that tragedy." Throughout the investigation, Hall, Kallstrom and others held the grief of family members in ready reserve to ward off tough questions.

Hall prattled on for a minute or two before Van Susteren stopped him. "Does that mean, Jim," she asked, "that you are 100 percent certain that the conspiracists, who some say saw a white light traveling sky ward, zigzagging, disappearing, and then an orange ball of fire—can you say with 100 percent certainty that they're wrong?" Other than the irksome use of "conspiracists," this was a good question. An attorney, Hall knew enough to shade his answer. "Greta," he said, "in my mind, with 100 percent certainty, our investigators, based on the facts that we developed, they are wrong. They are incorrect." In his mind at least, Hall had dodged the bullet. It was not even hard.

CNN did not get off quite so easily. The Internet journal *WorldNet-Daily* ran a five-part series to support the release of *Silenced*. Its editors also heavily promoted my appearance on CNN. As Accuracy in Media reported, "The cancellation angered a lot of people."[8] Many of them communicated their disgust to the network. As a salve, CNN brass rescheduled me for August 2 but cancelled that one too. "We just didn't want to rush into something like we were rushing into it," said CNN executive producer Bruce Perlmutter in Yogi Berra–speak.[9] In my place,

CNN lined up Jim McKenna, a government-friendly aviation reporter but eventually dumped him for a news-less Gary Condit update. As would soon enough become clear, my lessons in responsible journalism were just beginning.

Chapter: NINE

SEPTEMBER 11

"**Y**ou've got to hear what I was just told," said the caller. The time was late summer 2001. The fellow on the other end of the line was Steve Rosenbaum, the founder and then executive producer of an innovative, New York–based production company, Broadcast News Networks (BNN). Rosenbaum was working to help us find a cable network home for *Silenced*, but up to this point he was agnostic on its thesis.

"You got my attention," I said.

As Rosenbaum explained, he was sitting on the rooftop deck of his New York City offices, interviewing a potential new hire for a job as BNN technical director, when a plane passed overhead. The plane got Rosenbaum talking about *Silenced* and TWA Flight 800.

"You know," said the job candidate, "I saw the video."

"You saw *Silenced*?" asked a surprised Rosenbaum.

"No," said the candidate, "I saw the actual video, the video of the missile." The fellow had been working late at MSNBC the evening of July 17, 1996. The network was airing an amateur video of the missile strike in regular rotation until "three men in suits" came to the fellow's editing suite. They demanded every copy of the video that the network had and cautioned that there could be serious consequences for this fellow and his colleagues should they choose to talk about the video, let alone air it again.

Although I had not seen the video, I had heard a good deal about it, including a rumored bidding war for its purchase. Over time, at least a hundred people have sworn to me they saw it. No one was quite sure which station aired it, but MSNBC seemed a likely suspect. The network debuted on July 15, 1996, two days before the crash. That its execs would go all in to obtain the video made good marketing sense.

In early 2009, I received my most precise confirmation as to its contents, this from a 747 pilot named Thomas Young. In early August 1996, Young explained, he was laid up in a Seventh Day Adventist hospital in Hong Kong for ten days with a back injury. His employer, Polar Air Cargo, flew his wife Barbara out to join him. They had little else to do but watch TV. Here, according to Young, is what they saw on the local news, both on an English language channel and a Chinese channel, over and over again:

> The videotape began with people milling about on a deck facing a body of water. In the background, a streak of light can be seen leaving a point below the edge of the deck, accelerating as it climbed; it passed behind what appeared to me to be a thin cloud layer and continued upward out of the frame, from right to left. As the streak of light disappeared beyond the edge of the frame, after a slight pause, there is a generalized, dim flash on the upper left side of the screen, followed by a brighter and more pronounced flash.[1]

Young had a distinct perspective on what he was seeing. For six years in the 1980s he had worked at Boeing, much of that time in its Space and

Strategic Missile Systems Division. There he had reviewed scores of videotapes of missile launches, covering a wide range of missile types. Given the TV reception in his Hong Kong hospital, Young could not identify the type of missile that took out TWA 800, but he was confident he was looking at a missile. "If this was a Navy missile," Barbara recalled her husband saying at the time, "there goes Clinton's re-election." Apparently, the FBI had not yet made its way to Hong Kong. This description, of course, tracks precisely what the best eyewitnesses saw. When Young returned to the United States, he was "absolutely shocked not to see the video on the air."[2] He asked his fellow pilots if they had seen it and was shocked again that they had not. Young's testimony has added value in that he had little to gain by telling me this, and even less in lending his name to the account.

In the summer of 2001, Rosenbaum had asked us to extend our sixty-minute documentary to ninety minutes to make it more marketable. We all agreed that an interview with Rosenbaum's job candidate would be a useful and newsworthy addition. The fact that Rosenbaum decided to hire the fellow made him all the more accessible, but it did not make him any less fearful. He flat out refused to speak on the record or even off it, at least to me. I have only Rosenbaum's word for what the fellow experienced, but Rosenbaum had no reason to exaggerate.

If nothing else, this refusal gave us more time to devote to the family members of those who died in the crash. For *Silenced*, we interviewed Marge Krukar, a former TWA flight attendant whose brother Andrew Krukar was among the victims. In Paris, Andrew had planned to meet up with his sweetheart who was to come on a later flight. There he would surprise her with an engagement ring—one shattered dream out of many. Marge's testimony was as powerful as Andrew's story. She had vowed to find out who was responsible for her brother's death and, to this point, the authorities only stood in the way.

Don Nibert was no more satisfied with the investigation than Marge Krukar. Like too many other residents of Montoursville, a pleasant little town in central Pennsylvania, he lost a child on that flight. Alone among the townspeople, he would openly challenge the official explanation. I agreed to meet Nibert at 2 p.m. on August 30, 2001, at the Montoursville Cemetery where his daughter Cheryl, her fifteen fellow French Club members, and their five chaperones were buried. I contracted with a video crew out of Scranton to meet us there as well. I was staying in western New York at the time and drove down. The day was dreary, the sky close and ominous, the worst kind of light for shooting a video. As I found my way to Montoursville and approached the cemetery, however, the clouds parted just a little, and the sun struggled through. There was something mystical about the light—something mystical about the whole experience, for that matter.

Tall and taciturn, Nibert did not seem like a fellow given to fabulation. He had a story to tell, and was not afraid to tell it. After showing me the grave of Cheryl and her schoolmates, he told me the story of that tragic evening. In its early hours, he was picking berries in his small commercial orchard, completing a job Cheryl had been intent on finishing before he shooed her away. Just as the sun was setting, he heard a voice behind him in the Ohio valley accent he had grown up hearing and heeding. The voice was his mother's. He did not doubt its source for a moment. "Don, Cheryl is okay," said the voice. "She is with me. You even sent her with raspberry stains on her hands." His mother had been dead for years.

A professor of agriculture at a nearby college, Nibert has the mind of a scientist. Still, he did not discount what he had heard. He and his wife Donna finished their work in the orchard and went back to the house. There the phone rang. It was the mother of one Cheryl's classmates. She was frightened. A plane had crashed off Long Island. Did Don know the flight number of the kids' plane? Nibert did not have to know the number. He knew the plane was theirs. At that awful moment, the long, nightmarish saga began—the desperate phone calls, the trip to JFK, the meeting with authorities, the identification of the body, the grief, the numbness, the despair, and, for Nibert, the mendacity. "I trusted the government before we went through this," he said. "I do not trust them now." The lies would make him an activist.

After the meeting at the cemetery, Nibert and I drove by the high school Cheryl attended. He had something he wanted to show me. In a small park next to the school stood a statue of a tall bronze angel, its head bowed, encircled by twenty-one young maple trees, one for each victim. Nibert explained that three days after the crash, during a memorial service, a cloud in the shape of an angel hovered over the town. Almost to a person, the parents took it as a sign their children were in good hands. Today, an angel in front of a public high school might be considered something of a provocation. I asked Nibert whether he was concerned that the ACLU might sue to have it removed. "Let 'em try," he said drily. Clint Eastwood could not have said it more convincingly. When we returned to his home, Nibert showed me a photo of that cloud, and my own skepticism melted. The resemblance was uncanny.

Twelve days later, before we had a chance to edit the footage from Montoursville, the world turned upside down: it was September 11, 2001. Despite the horrifying events of the day, the Kansas City parish to which I belonged chose to go ahead with its annual dinner. Our young French priest reasoned that people would all the more feel the need to connect with those they knew and cared for, and no one disagreed. Not until I arrived, however, did I learn that the scheduled speaker's plane had been forced down in Indianapolis. The priest asked me to speak in his stead. "You know something about airplanes," he said. "Father," I replied, "I'm not sure this should be about airplanes." In fact, I was pretty sure it shouldn't be, but until about five minutes before my time to speak, I wasn't sure what to speak about. Then it hit me. I would talk about the Angel of Montoursville. It was a natural topic.

Given the national mood, we decided to shelve *Silenced* for a while. BNN agreed. We did, however, glean some useful insights on the day of September 11 itself. One came from George Stephanopolous, the Clinton advisor turned ABC News correspondent. On the afternoon of that endless day, Stephanopolous was speaking to ABC News anchor Peter Jennings about President George Bush's relocation to the situation room at Offutt Air Force Base in Nebraska. Likely to show he deserved his generous salary, Stephanopolous served up some inside info about a second, more secure White House Situation Room about which few people knew. There, he told Jennings, the various military chiefs could teleconference with the president and other officials. "In my time at the White House," confided Stephanopolous, "it was used in the aftermath of the Oklahoma City bombing, in the aftermath of the TWA Flight 800 bombing, and that would be the way they would stay in contact through the afternoon."[3] To the degree this remark garnered attention, it was for Stephanopolous's use of the word "bombing." If "bombing" was a slip of the tongue, his assertion about the Situation Room was surely not. This was newsworthy. The Pentagon does not involve itself in civilian plane crashes, certainly not in the United States. Nor, for that matter, does the White House. This had never happened before.

Jim Kallstrom had his own moment of revelation as well. While speaking with Dan Rather on CBS News about the events of the day, he blurted out in no particular context, "We need to stop the hypocrisy." He then quickly added, "not that hypocrisy got us to this day."[4] Kallstrom knew more than he was prepared to say. Hypocrisy did help get America to that day. By convincing America that a mechanical failure destroyed TWA 800, Kallstrom and his superiors relegated talk about aviation terror to the overnight radio shows, if there. The failure to take the problem seriously left America more vulnerable than it needed to be. Kallstrom was the public face of this deception, and for just that one honest moment on September 11, he rebelled against the role he had felt compelled to play.

In the days following September 11, several commentators alluded to the destruction of TWA 800, but only one did so twice, and that was John Kerry, then a senator from Massachusetts. Senator Kerry first mentioned TWA 800 on September 11 itself. "We have always known this could happen," Kerry told Larry King. By "we" he meant the Senate Select Committee on Intelligence. By "this" he meant the use of planes as flying bombs. "I can remember after the bombings of the embassies, after TWA 800, we went through this flurry of activity, talking about it, but not really doing hard work of responding."[5]

I knew of at least one person who called Kerry's office for clarification about his inclusion of TWA 800. A Kerry staffer told her she must have misunderstood. There was no misunderstanding Kerry's second mention. I saw it as it happened. Kerry was a guest on *Hardball with Chris Matthews*, then on CNBC.[6] "We've had the *Achille Lauro*, the Munich Olympics, the pipe bomb at the Olympics in Atlanta, the TWA 800, the bombing of embassies, and it's not going to disappear overnight," Kerry told Matthews, again adding "TWA 800" to a list of terrorist actions.

In between Kerry's first mention of TWA 800 and the second, one major newspaper broke the story of how former vice president Al Gore undermined an air safety commission he himself chaired. According to Kerry's hometown newspaper *Boston Globe*, Gore sold out the commission, formed after the TWA 800 disaster, for campaign cash. Reporters Walter Robinson and Glen Johnson knew an Achilles heel when they saw one. The collapse of Gore's commission struck them as "the clearest recent public example of the success that airlines have long had in defeating calls for more oversight."[7] I speculated at the time that Kerry's followup on Chris Matthews's show was fortuitous. He was playing *hardball*. Gore stood in the way of his run for the White House, and he wanted him out. I may have been right. After Gore's surprise announcement he would not be a candidate in 2004, he endorsed Howard Dean over Kerry.

I was not the only one who caught the many references to TWA Flight 800 by the various commentators. So too did retired TWA Captain Albert Mundo. Mundo knew something about TWA 800. He served as flight engineer on the plane's trip in from Athens earlier on the day of its demise and inspected it before its final flight. On September 25, 2001, he sent a letter to Greta Van Susteren.[8] He pointed out the various terrorist references by Kerry and others and lamented the cancellation of my scheduled appearance on CNN two months prior. "Had the real cause of the destruction of TWA 800 been made public," he wrote, "then there surely would have been a heightened awareness of the terrorist threat to this nation."

Bestselling novelist Nelson DeMille noticed as well. He was on Long Island the night of July 17, 1996. News reports of the plane's destruction spooked him. He had put his college-age daughter on that same plane three nights earlier. Two years later, his research on a new novel dealing with Mideast terrorism, *The Lion's Game*, put him in touch with several FBI agents and members of the Joint Terrorism Task Force (JTTF). During one interview he casually mentioned TWA 800, and the agent answered brusquely, "What does that have to do with Mideast terrorism?" When DeMille mentioned the possibility of a missile strike, the agent shot back that it was a center fuel tank explosion and concluded, "That's all I'm going to say about that."

The agent's tone intrigued DeMille. He kept asking the question of other involved parties and kept getting the same cryptic answers. One New York cop he interviewed worked the case through the JTTF. Not being a federal agent, he felt freer to talk. He had interviewed two dozen witnesses and convinced DeMille those witnesses had seen *something*. After September 11, at the suggestion of the NYPD/JTTF officer, DeMille got hold of the FBI witness summaries, the 302s, and he came to much the same conclusion that I did upon reading them at the Sanderses' home in Florida.

Before beginning a novel on TWA 800, DeMille conferred with retired TWA international captain, Jack Clary. "I don't know what it was," said Clary as to the cause of the crash, "but I know what it wasn't. It wasn't a short-circuit spark in the center fuel tank." As Clary asked rhetorically, and this more than five years after the crash, "Do you see the FAA requiring any remedial action on the center fuel tank of the 747s?" The answer was no, not even on Air Force One. There had never been a comparable explosion before and has not been one since. Thomas Young, in fact, had told me that his Boeing colleagues thought the spark in the fuel tank theory "laughable."[9]

Soon after, DeMille ran into a neighbor at a Long Island restaurant. In passing, the man asked what he was working on.[10] DeMille said he was thinking about writing a novel based on TWA 800. "We saw that," said the fellow. "We were on our boat that night." DeMille arranged to interview the couple and their children. On the night in question, this family and another were out boating. "Look, a skyrocket," said one of the kids. And then everyone on the boat, four adults and five children, "watched as a streak of light rose off the water and headed into the sky." DeMille knew these people and trusted them. They had nothing to gain by embellishing. They convinced him there was a story to be told. The subsequent novel, *Night Fall*, opens on July 17, 1996, and culminates on September 11, 2001. Not to give too much away, but the story begins with a steamy encounter on the beach that the couple decides to videotape. DeMille knew a real video was out there, and the plot of his novel revolves around it. Although the real video was confiscated, the hunt for it would continue. More on this later.

Chapter: TEN

FIT TO PRINT

"**C**ashill, you are either stupid, delusional or complicit," wrote one correspondent. "Hey bozo," wrote another, "what are you going to do with that little bit of money you are being paid to spew that elementary, zombie riddled, falsity?" No, the NTSB's Peter Goelz was not calling me out for being a conspiracy theorist. Just the opposite. The readers of a piece I had written about September 11 were calling me out for *not* being enough of a conspiracy theorist. One summed up my failings nicely. "You are no better than the rest of the hacks out there with something to sell," he wrote. "Only you are willing to excuse the murder of thousands of citizens by our own government to do it."

In the offending piece, I suggested a media version of Gresham's law: bad conspiracies drive out the good. In the wake of September 11, a variety of wildly speculative inside job theories threatened to trivialize the most consequential real conspiracy of our time. This was the environment in which James Sanders and I were writing in 2002, having signed a book contract early that year. A former accident investigator, Sanders was the nuts and bolts guy. I was more interested in the logic, the why. None of the 9/11 conspiracy theories passed the "why" test. For a theory to make sense, all the pieces must fall in place, not just some, and there has to be a compelling logic as to why they would. The challenge in discerning the logic of the TWA 800 misdirection was that the logic kept shifting. A walk through the first two months of the *New York Times*' reporting on the investigation sheds useful, if imperfect, light on that shift.

After the downing of TWA 800, the *Times* reporters swarmed Long Island, producing as many as a half dozen articles a day. Little of that reporting went beyond what they were told by the FBI. If nothing else, the *Times*' dependence on the FBI provided clearer focus on the pressures Kallstrom and his colleagues faced and some insight into why they responded the way they did. The pressure was coming from several different sources: the White House, largely through the Justice Department; Clinton's go-to guy at the NTSB, Robert Francis; and, most curiously, the CIA.

The *Times*' first full article on July 18 leads with the fact that the FBI had taken over jurisdiction of the investigation. The reason for the takeover was that "witnesses reported an explosion, raising the possibility that a bomb went off on the jetliner."[1] On day one, "federal law enforcement authorities" were leading the *Times* away from a missile. In fact, the word "missile" does not appear in the article, and each of the eyewitnesses interviewed saw the plane only after it exploded. That the *Times* failed to mention the widely bruited speculation about a missile suggests that its reporters were asked not to. The article concluded, however, with a federal official saying, "It doesn't look good," meaning, the reporter conceded, "a terrorist act." A day later, July 19, the *Times* published the president's remarks on the crash. "We do not know what caused this tragedy," said Clinton. "I want to say that again: We do not know as of this moment what caused this tragedy."[2] To drive home a lie,

Clinton had the habit of repeating an assertion as if repetition signaled sincerity. He did this most memorably in January 1998. "I want you to listen to me. I'm going to say this again," the president told the nation. "I did not have sexual relations with that woman, Miss Lewinsky."[3] We know he was lying in January 1998. The evidence strongly suggests he was lying in July 1996 as well.

In a separate article on July 19, the *Times*' David Johnston introduced the possibility of a missile strike. "In public," Johnston wrote, investigators were talking about an "accident," but "in private" they hinted at a "terrorist's missile." The *Times*' account was straightforward. Eyewitnesses "had described a bright light, like a flash, moving toward the plane just before the initial explosion, and that the flash had been followed by a huge blast—a chain of events consistent with a missile impact and the blast produced by an aircraft heavily laden with fuel."[4] There it was. This was the most honest description of the plane's demise that the *Times* would publish. Of note, this same article reported that air traffic controllers "had picked up a mysterious radar blip that appeared to move rapidly toward the plane just before the explosion."

Based on his language, Johnston's sources seemed to be local. Later that same day, a separate article by Matthew Purdy showed "federal" law enforcement officials struggling to regain control of the narrative.[5] They claimed to have looked at radar records and were "giving less credence" to the missile theory in no small part because TWA 800 was flying too high for most shoulder-fired missiles to reach. This was true, but there was no mention of the kind of missiles that did have range enough to destroy a 747 at more than 13,000 feet. Curiously, the *Times* quoted both Major Fritz Meyer and Paul Angelides, the last two witnesses to a likely missile strike the *Times* would cite. Both would press their case in the years to come, but the *Times* had no interest in hearing what they or other eyewitnesses had to say. On July 20, the *Times* ran a notice asking people who saw "events in the sky" to call an FBI hotline. The FBI, however, would not share the results of these calls with the NTSB for nearly three years and never with the *New York Times*.

Recently published CIA documents show that the White House had recruited the agency within a day of the crash, not to hunt for international terrorists but to suppress missile speculation. In a July 20 internal memo obtained by a Ray Lahr FOIA request, a CIA analyst reported "no evidence of a missile" in the radar data.[6] That same memo argued that the aircraft was beyond the range of virtually all shoulder-fired missiles. In no memo was there any mention of a possible naval misfire even though one memo acknowledged the Navy was "reportedly conducting an exercise in the area." The analyst mentioned the exercise only because he was interested in seeing if any of the ships had raw radar video recordings to share.

Sure enough, by July 21, "experts" were telling the *Times* that the radar blip was actually "an electronic phantom image." They insisted too that TWA 800 was flying beyond the range of even the "most sophisticated shoulder-launched missiles."[7] It was not hard for the authorities to make the radar mean whatever they wanted. A CIA analyst would admit in an internal memo that the FAA did not "store or record" the original radar video data. The only imagery available was "post-detection," meaning copies or representations.[8] Jim Holtsclaw had the advantage of talking to controllers who witnessed the event in real time. These experts also told David Johnston that no one either saw or heard a missile launch, a claim they could not begin to substantiate.

On July 24, the *Times'* Matthew Purdy reported that investigators had yet to find proof of an explosion.[9] Speaking to reporters, President Clinton claimed to have learned nothing new about "the cause of the *accident*" (italics added). On July 26, the paper of record published the president's remarks on his and Hillary's meeting with the families of the victims. "We do not yet know what caused Flight 800 to crash, whether it was mechanical failure or sabotage," he insisted. "But we will find out."[10]

By July 26, investigators had established the false dialectic that would hold for the next two months. The cockpit voice recorder captured only a brief sound before it stopped recording. This, reported Matthew Wald, "added strong support to the theory that a bomb destroyed the plane."[11]

That much conceded, "aviation experts," surely the NTSB, could "not exclude mechanical failure." There was no mention of a missile. This same dialectic played out a day later. The NTSB's Francis insisted that mechanical malfunction still could not be ruled out but his comments shriveled under a headline that read, "Backing a Bomb Theory: Devices Stopped in Unison."[12]

The bomb scenario enabled Clinton to appear presidential. On July 26, *Times* editors praised his decision to install bomb detection systems in advance of any NTSB findings.[13] On July 28, *Times* readers learned that "within days" the weight of the evidence would "prompt the Government to announce that the cause was sabotage, and that the case is being taken over by the F.B.I."[14] The word "sabotage" implied "bomb," but investigators had every reason to believe the culprit was a missile. In a July 30 internal memo, headlined "Hold the Press," a CIA analyst warned of an impending FBI report on a likely missile strike. After interviewing 144 witnesses, the FBI was convinced there was a "high probability that the incident was caused by a MANPAD," meaning a shoulder-launched surface-to-air missile. According to the reporting agents, all three of whom had aviation experience, the evidence was "overwhelming." The witnesses were "excellent" and their testimony "too consistent" for the cause to be anything other than a missile.

The unnamed CIA analyst boasted of how he discouraged the FBI from pursuing this angle. "I reported to [the FBI agent] the majority if not all our concerns, issues and problems with the determination that the incident was most-likely caused by a MANPAD." Said the analyst of his FBI counterpart, "He had little to refute our concerns." At this point, even internally, all missile talk revolved around terrorism. The FBI agents appeared to be sincere in their beliefs; the CIA analysts not so much. In any case, the FBI never did go public with this report even though it had "only minor corrections left to make," and the future performance of the CIA suggests it played a role in assuring the same.[15]

On August 2, 1996, two weeks after the crash, President Clinton shared his thoughts on TWA 800 with Taylor Branch. About once a month over the course of his presidency, Clinton allowed the Pulitzer

Prize–winning historian to interview him. The understanding between the two was that these conversations could not be published before 2010, time enough, one presumes, to give Hillary her shot at the presidency. When published, *The Clinton Tapes* offered little in the way of the new or useful. Even in private, Clinton could not stop spinning, but on August 2, 1996, Taylor caught up with Clinton before the spin had become dogma. At the time, it appears that the Clinton White House was still finessing the TWA 800 narrative. "Unless some telltale chemical survived the brine," Clinton told Branch, "[the investigators] must try to reassemble the plane to determine the cause."[16] Clinton also told Branch that the FBI was "rechecking" its interviews with "some fifteen ground witnesses who saw a bright streak in the sky near the plane." If corroborated, Branch added, this "could suggest a missile rather than a bomb." By August 2, of course, the FBI had interviewed more than 500 witnesses, at least 144 of whom were considered "excellent." Clinton had to know this. He knew enough certainly to tell Branch that a Stinger fired from land was out of the question, but not a surface-to-air missile fired from the sea.[17]

Perhaps as a form of dress rehearsal, Clinton floated the Eisenhower option by Tower. "They want war," Branch quoted Clinton as saying of Iran. Never one to take his eye off the prize, Clinton was convinced that, given his investment in the Mideast peace process, fundamentalists in Iran and elsewhere wanted war to "undermine [his] chances for reelection."[18] After the Khobar Towers bombing in June 1996, the president's first instinct was to have advisor Dick Morris run a quick poll. Morris found that Americans approved of his handling of the terrorist attack 73 to 20 percent. "SAUDI BOMBING—recovered from Friday and looking great," Morris wrote in his notes. Only 18 percent held Clinton responsible.[19] If Morris polled about Clinton's handling of TWA 800, he has never discussed it publicly.

Given how little information was available to the public or even to Clinton's cabinet, the Iran angle seemed to make sense. In their 1998 book *TWA 800: Accident or Incident*, Kevin Ready and Cap Parlier made a plausible, if speculative, case that a surface-to-air missile fired from an Iranian ship destroyed the airliner.[20] They traced the Iranian motivation to the U.S. Navy's accidental shoot down of Iranian Airbus 655 in July 1988. Both Ready and Parlier have serious credentials, Ready having served as a military intelligence officer and Arabic linguist and Parlier as a U.S. Marine Corps lieutenant colonel. *No Survivors*, a 2013 CNN special report, made the case that the White House did indeed think terrorists attacked TWA 800, with Iran the leading suspect. "I think our first thought," said national security advisor Anthony Lake, "was that, when we got this news, that if it was terrorism, we wanted to especially look for an Iranian connection."[21]

Subsequent events suggest, however, that Clinton was hedging his bets with history. He knew more than he was telling Branch or even his aides, but on August 2, 1996, he had yet to fix on an end game. If the FBI found Clinton's "telltale" chemicals, its agents could argue for a bomb and declare the crash a crime. In the interim, the FBI and CIA would continue to marginalize the witnesses. Both agencies had been doing that from day one. With the witness testimony suppressed, the investigators could "reassemble the plane" as Clinton suggested to Branch,[22] and the tedious reconstruction of the massive 747 would take the investigation past the November election. The missile talk would remain strictly private. Greg Norman. Greg Norman.

The White House could live with a bomb scenario. For the first two weeks of August, the bomb theory dominated the *Times* reporting. Relentlessly political, Clinton attempted to exploit public anxiety about terrorism. In an article with the none too subtle headline, "Seizing the Crime Issue, Clinton Blurs Party Lines," the *Times* told its readers that the tough talking president "scrapped his party's traditional approach to crime and criminal justice." In its stead, he recommended a series of punitive measures that "threatened the Republicans' lock on law and order."[23]

On August 14, four weeks to the day after the crash, the *Times* offered the first detailed account of the plane's break-up sequence. The most salient revelation was that the center fuel tank caught fire as many as twenty-four seconds after the initial blast. This meant that the "only good explanations remaining" were either a bomb or missile.[24] Reporter Don Van Natta described the destruction of the plane in much the same way the best eyewitnesses had weeks earlier. "The blast's force decapitated the plane, severing the cockpit and first-class cabin, which then fell into the Atlantic Ocean," he wrote. Witness 73, for instance, "observed the front of the aircraft separate from the back." Witness 150, Lisa Perry, told of how the plane broke apart like a toy: "The front was carried forward and arced down with its momentum." In no subsequent report by the FBI, NTSB, or CIA did any witness get credit for such an observation. To admit the witnesses reported the break-up sequence accurately would be to concede they knew what caused the plane to break up.

In their later embrace of the CIA zoom climb scenario, *Times* editors ignored Van Natta's accurate description of a plane going nowhere but down. "The rest of the plane flew on, descending rapidly," he wrote, "and as it did thousands of gallons of jet fuel spilled out of the wings and the center fuel tank between them. At 8,000 feet, about 24 seconds after the initial blast, the fuel caught fire, engulfing the remainder of the jetliner into a giant fireball."

On August 17, in an article prophetically titled "To T.W.A. Crash Investigators, Not All Witnesses Are Equal," Andrew Revkin introduced *Times* readers to Witness 136, Michael Russell. On July 19, Russell told the FBI he was working on a survey vessel a mile off shore when "a white flash in the sky caught his eye."[25] Within seconds of that flash, Russell "observed a burst of fire forming a huge fireball." According to Revkin, who identified Russell by name, "His sober, understated story was one of only a few that investigators have judged credible." As reported, there were "fewer than a dozen" accounts believable enough to aid the investigation. Of course, the FBI knew there were many, many more.

The FBI judged Russell's story credible because it fit with the Bureau's already skewed plot line. This was not Russell's fault. His observations were honest and accurate. He caught the "white flash" out of the corner of his eye. He did not happen to see the ascending object that caused it. That said, the white flash suggested a high explosive, meaning one that detonates at a high rate of speed, as in a bomb or a missile. The subsequent fireball, more yellow in color, he correctly identified as "a substance of extreme flammability being suddenly ignited." An engineer, Russell knew the difference. Russell's account, Revkin reported, "bolstered the idea that a bomb, and not an exploding fuel tank, triggered the disintegration of the airplane." More to the point, his account "substantially weakened support for the idea that a missile downed the plane." That was the article's money quote, and the reason readers were allowed to hear from Michael Russell.

The investigators who introduced Russell to the *Times* imagined a level of happy collaboration among the agencies that had defied reality. As they assured the *Times*, "teams of Federal agents and safety board officials" were carefully interviewing witnesses, reading their body language, and culling out "the pleasers." This was nonsense. In reality, the FBI agents were imprecise and inconsistent. They had shut out safety board officials altogether and prevented witnesses from reading and correcting the 302s.

Amateurism was only part of the problem. The Clinton White House was improvising a strategy to make missile talk go away and exploiting FBI weaknesses to make it happen. In this highly compartmentalized investigation, the great majority of those working it had no suspicion there was a strategy in place other than seeking the truth. Kallstrom knew, but he could not have known what conclusion he would be allowed to reach. As late as six weeks after the crash, I seriously doubt if Clinton knew what would be the final explanation for the crash. What the insiders did know, however, was that there could be no missile strike—a bomb maybe, but no missile—at least until November.

On Thursday, August 22, the investigation took an unexpected turn. Reporter Dan Barry noted that Kallstrom was "conspicuously absent" from the podium he shared with the NTSB's Robert Francis during the routine press briefings.[26] Francis told reporters not to read too much into Kallstrom's absence as Kallstrom had other responsibilities to attend to. Taking Francis's cue, Barry failed to follow up. He should have. For the first time, Kallstrom had been called to meet with government officials in Washington.

From a political perspective, the meeting came a day or two too late. "Three senior officials" had already provided the *Times* enough information to generate an above the fold, front-page headline on Friday, August 23, reading, "Prime Evidence Found That Device Exploded in Cabin of TWA 800."[27] If Van Natta, the author of the article, called one of the president's people for confirmation, that call may have triggered the August 22 meeting. According to Pierre Salinger, August 22 was also the specific date Dick Russell composed his nervy e-mail, and that may have factored in as well.[28] Kallstrom blamed the DOJ attorneys for informing the *Times* about the residue finds, but this accusation was not credible on any level.[29] DOJ officials did not have the knowledge to generate a story of this magnitude. More to the point, just days before the Democratic National Convention, the attorneys at the deeply politicized DOJ did not have the motive.

The Van Natta article could scarcely have been more definitive. Investigators had found "scientific evidence" of an explosive device, specifically traces of PETN, or pentaerythritol tetranitrate, a component found in bombs and missiles. As Van Natta reported, the FBI had announced as early as July 29 that "one positive result" was enough to declare the plane's destruction a criminal act, a condition repeated often over the next few weeks. This was not the first article in which the *Times* reported evidence of explosives. On August 9, Van Natta noted that ATF agents had detected traces of explosives on some pieces of wreckage, but "later tests at the F.B.I. turned out negative."[30] On August 14, Van Natta reported that in ten field tests on the scene in Long Island, chemists had detected "residue consistent with an explosive," but in each case further tests at the FBI lab in Washington were "not conclusive." On August 24, Dan Barry reported that five days after the crash, investigators on Long Island had found a trace of PETN on a piece of the right wing, but "more sophisticated" tests at the FBI lab failed to replicate the result.[31]

At first glance, this may seem as if the FBI was just being thorough, but in fact the EGIS Explosives Detection System at the Calverton investigation site was as at least as sophisticated as any device the FBI had in its lab. In his book on criminal forensics, Dr. Harold Trimm called EGIS "the ultimate in speed, accuracy, and sensitivity—without compromise."[32] EGIS developer David Fine described the technology as "extremely sensitive" and noted that false positives were "very rare if ever."[33]

A further complication was that the FBI lab was then subject to what the *Times* described as a "long-running internal inquiry" by the Inspector General of the DOJ. This inquiry cautioned FBI brass "to wait for incontrovertible evidence before saying publicly what most of them acknowledge privately: that Flight 800 was deliberately downed by an explosive device."[34] When Kallstrom finally did go public with his evidence—he sat on it for two weeks—he likely felt safe because the explosive residue had been found in the plane's interior. This revelation kept the investigation on the "bomb" track. Still, the White House could not have been pleased with the timing.

Despite Clinton's lead over Republican Bob Dole in the polls, presidential advisor Dick Morris reminded the president that he had "a soft underbelly." Too many voters did not trust this former draft-dodger in his role as commander in chief.[35] As Morris well knew, a missile attack against America, by friend or foe, would have exposed that vulnerability. A bomb scenario was more manageable but still problematic.

For whatever reason, the *Times* reporters and editors failed to comment on the political backdrop against which this drama was playing out. The other above-the-fold headline on August 23 read as follows, "Clinton Signs Bill Cutting Welfare; States in New Roll."[36] The president was dramatically tacking to the center, as he had been doing on the terrorism issue. The signing of this bill three days before the start of the Democratic National Convention in Chicago was hardly a coincidence. There, Clinton hoped to sell the party's peace and prosperity message. Front page headlines about explosive devices destroying an American airliner, by a bomb or especially by a missile, would remind America of what Clinton was not—namely, a trustworthy wartime leader.

Back from Washington on the day the article appeared, Friday, August 23, an apparently chastened Kallstrom reversed direction. According to *Times* reporter Jim Barry, Kallstrom staged a "hastily announced" news conference. Investigators, said Kallstrom, lacked "the critical mass of information" necessary to declare the crash a criminal act.[37] "The three theories are on the board," he added. "When we confirm one of them, we'll take the other two off." When asked the provenance of the PETN if not a bomb or a missile, Kallstrom alluded vaguely to "some other means." Barry followed this comment with an unusually critical observation, "But on Thursday night, a senior law enforcement official laughed out loud at the suggestion of this possibility."

Although there is no published record of any Washington meeting, Kallstrom returned to Calverton a changed man. Based on his subsequent performance, he seemed to have no more urgent task than to negate the *Times* reporting on explosive residues. Front-page headlines like "Prime Evidence Found That Device Exploded in Cabin of TWA 800" were not easily explained away, and it fell to Kallstrom to do the explaining.

Without noting the significance of the date, Christine Negroni traced the effort to find an alternate explanation to the very day the "Prime Evidence" headline appeared, August 23.[38] For the FAA, this meant a worldwide search to determine whether local police had ever used explosives in dog-training exercises on the plane that would come to be designated TWA 800.[39] This would be no simple task. The FAA had never systematized these records. For its part, the FBI ceased to look for eyewitnesses. Agents would do no more interviews for the next two months, and only a handful after that, almost inevitably for the wrong reasons. The investigators working through the NTSB continued to do their work in good faith, but in a highly compartmentalized investigation most knew little more about the mischief afoot than did the public. That too would soon change, and people who noted the mischief would suffer for it.

Chapter: ELEVEN

BLACK HOLE

O n August 22, 1996, the day Jim Kallstrom was called back to Washington, the White House blunted the forward momentum of the investigation (just as surely as missiles had TWA 800's five weeks earlier). Those five weeks had to have been a tumultuous stretch in the life of President Clinton. A U.S. airliner had been blown out of the sky two days before the start of the Atlanta Olympics, and the White House was making plans to retaliate. Richard Clarke called this crisis "the almost war," and he was not exaggerating. As late as two weeks after the incident, Clinton was telling historian Taylor Branch that we were on the verge of attacking Iran.

Given the gravity of the situation, one would have expected Clinton and his advisors to feature this saga in their respective memoirs, especially since all this chaos and uncertainty unfolded in the heat of a presidential campaign. Yet save for Clarke, they did not, not at all. So suffocating was the shroud of silence that cloaked the TWA 800 investigation that the individuals most deeply involved all but refused to talk about it. As a case in point, in his 957-page 2004 memoir, *My Life*, Bill Clinton spent one paragraph on TWA 800 and that a thoroughly dishonest one. "At the time everyone assumed—wrongly as it turned out—that this was a terrorist act," Clinton wrote. "There was even speculation that the plane had been downed by a rocket fired from a boat in Long Island Sound."[1]

No, the fifty-six certified NTSB witnesses who claimed to see an object ascend from the horizon all traced its provenance to the Atlantic Ocean, south of Long Island. The Sound is north of Long Island. "While I cautioned against jumping to conclusions," continued the former president, "it was clear that we had to do more to strengthen aviation safety." He then added a second paragraph bragging about the intrusive and irrelevant measures he and Vice President Al Gore took—or promised to take—to avoid future bombings. That was it.

A week after the crash, Bill and Hillary spent three heart-wrenching hours meeting with the victims' families. Clarke described the president "praying with them, hugging them, taking pictures with them." He spoke of how "Mrs. Clinton" retreated alone to a makeshift chapel, there to pray "on her knees."[2] For someone who liked to boast of her empathy with ordinary people, Hillary could have made literary hay with a scene this poignant. She did not. In her 528-page memoir, *Living History*, Hillary spent just one-third of a sentence on TWA 800, which, for her, was merely one out of several "tragic events" that summer.[3]

In his memoir, *My FBI: Bringing Down The Mafia, Investigating Bill Clinton, and Fighting the War on Terror*, former FBI director Louis Freeh mentioned the crash in passing as a footnote to the Khobar Towers bombing in Saudia Arabia: "Three weeks later, on July 17, TWA flight 800 exploded off Long Island minutes after taking off from John F. Kennedy International Airport. No one knew what brought it down: mechanical failure, a bomb, a ground-to-air missile all seemed possible in the early stages."[4] No investigation during Freeh's tenure generated more news coverage or demanded as much FBI attention, and yet Freeh begrudged it only two sentences, neither of which answered the question as to what did bring the plane down.

In his memoir *Off With Their Heads*, presidential advisor Dick Morris teased his audience but did not deliver. He cited TWA 800 as one of "three attacks" in the "terror summer of 1996." Wrote Morris, "Americans demanded action. But all they got from Clinton were speeches."[5] He did not shy from speaking in detail of the other two "attacks"—Khobar Towers and the Olympic Park bombing—but about TWA 800 he had nothing to say beyond its listing with the other two. On July 15, 2003, I got the Morris treatment firsthand when he and I were phone-in guests on Paul Schiffer's Cleveland radio show. Three times I asked Morris to elaborate on his TWA 800 remarks. Three times he responded as though he had not even heard my question.

Although he was inadvertently open about TWA 800 with ABC's Peter Jennings on 9/11, George Stephanopolous did not spare the incident a single word in his 1999 memoir *All Too Human*. In June 2013, Stephanopolous sat mutely during a three-minute discussion of TWA 800 by two of his ABC colleagues on his own show, *Good Morning America*. Again, he said not a word.[6]

In the aftermath of the plane's destruction, George Tenet served as acting director of Central Intelligence. The new CIA documents show him to have been involved in the investigation from very nearly the beginning. Indeed, he signed off on the CIA's ultimate explanation months before the FBI shared that explanation with the public. Yet he too failed to even mention the disaster in his 2007 memoir *At the Center of the Storm*. Clinton's chief-of-staff Leon Panetta called the president with the news of the plane's downing. "The concern at that moment was that this might very well be a terrorist act," Panetta would tell CNN.[7] The concern was apparently not memorable enough to earn even the slightest mention in Panetta's 2014 memoir, *Worthy Fights*.

TWA 800 and the ensuing investigation would seem perfect fodder for the Senate Select Committee on Intelligence. The committee's "Special Report" for that period of time explored the terrorist bombing of

Khobar Towers in Saudi Arabia three weeks before the TWA 800 disaster and a variety of other intelligence-related stories in the news. The report, however, was fully silent on the subject of TWA 800.[8] This was all the more troubling given the CIA's own acknowledgement that "the DI [Directorate of Intelligence] became involved in the 'missile theory' the day after the crash occurred."[9] Equally curious is that on the same day the report was issued—February 28, 1997— CIA analysts presented a comprehensive PowerPoint titled, "A Witness by Witness Account: A Review of the TWA 800 Witness Reports," to an unspecified internal audience.[10]

Tim Weiner covered TWA 800 for the *New York Times*. In his 2008 bestseller, *Legacy of Ashes: The History of the CIA*, he had the opportunity to make amends for the paper's failure to smoke out CIA mischief during the course of the investigation. To no one's great surprise, he chose not to even mention TWA 800. Sicilian mobsters could learn a thing or two about *omerta* from the *Times* newsroom.

As the lone White House chronicler of the TWA 800 aftermath, Richard Clarke buttressed the administration case just when the 9/11 Commission might have been tempted to scrutinize it. Unfortunately, little of what he wrote was true. "The FAA," he reported, "was at a total loss for an explanation. The flight path and the cockpit communications were normal. The aircraft had climbed to 17,000 feet, then there was no aircraft."[11] In fact, if the FAA had no explanation, its people would have likely contacted the NTSB. Clarke was summoned precisely because the FAA did have an explanation: the radar data showing an unknown object approaching TWA 800 just before it blew up. It was the radar data, not the eyewitness reports, that prompted Clarke's meeting. As to the "17,000 feet" reference, Clarke incorporated the CIA's zoom climb altitude into this 1996 story long before the CIA imagined it and repeated the altitude in his 2004 book long after the NTSB disowned it.

Roughly four weeks after the crash, the late FBI terrorist expert John O'Neill reportedly told Clarke that the witness interviews "were pointing to a missile attack, a Stinger."[12] Since O'Neill died at the World Trade

Center on September 11, Clarke could put whatever words in O'Neill's mouth he chose to. For the record, no witness ever mentioned a "Stinger." As early as July 22, CIA analysts and FBI agents had concluded that a missile "would have to come from a boat under the flight path" and would most likely have been "an IR SAM," meaning an Iranian surface-to-air missile.[13] O'Neill was correct, however, in telling Clarke the FBI was convinced a missile had taken down the plane. This bears repeating. Within two weeks of the disaster, FBI agents had interviewed 144 "excellent" eyewitnesses and found the evidence for a missile strike "overwhelming." Clarke used his book to help scrub this information from the record. In the days following the crash, he wrote, "No intelligence surfaced that helped advance the investigation."[14]

Clarke cited the small, shoulder-fired Stinger missile as a way of discrediting all terrorist or missile-related theories. The CIA memos showed its analysts taking the same tack with the FBI. "[TWA 800] was at 15,000 feet," Clarke reportedly told O'Neill. "No Stinger or any other missile like it can go that high." Confident no one in the media would challenge his numbers, Clarke did not bother to get the altitude of TWA 800 right or even consistently wrong. The actual altitude at the time of TWA's destruction was 13,760 feet.

Although Clarke would pass himself off as a man above politics, the Clintons had seduced him if by no other means than granting him an access to power that George W. Bush never did. Clarke openly relished his role as a Clinton insider. A week after the crash, the president was telling Clarke and others that he was convinced terrorists had downed the plane and at that point, Clarke may not have known enough to disbelieve him. Soon, however, Clarke would become an active agent of disinformation. Based on his own timeline, he assumed this role a "few weeks later," or roughly a month after the crash. As Clarke related in his book, he visited the investigation site at a "giant hangar in Beth Page, Long Island" where the plane was being "rebuilt."[15] Although he did not reveal why he was at the hangar or who sent him, Clarke did see fit to report on a remarkably convenient exchange he had with a random, unnamed technician:[16]

"So this is where the bomb exploded?" I asked. "Where on the plane was it?"

"The explosion was just forward of the middle, below the floor of the passenger compartment, below row 23. But it wasn't a bomb," he added. "See the pitting pattern and the tear. It was a slow, gaseous eruption, from inside."

"What's below row 23?" I asked, slowly sensing that this was not what I thought it was.

"The center line fuel tank. It was only half full, might have heated up on the runway and caused a gas cloud inside. Then if a spark, a short circuit..." He indicated an explosion with his hands.

The technician went on to tell Clarke that those "old 747s" had an "electrical pump inside the center line fuel tank," and he cited the pump as the likely source of ignition. In truth, the whole story rings false. The giant hangar was in Calverton, forty-five miles east of Beth Page, and the decision to rebuild the plane was not made until the second week of November, at least two months after this serendipitous meeting.[17] These "old" 747s could idle for hours on runways in Phoenix or Cairo without overheating, let alone on a cool summer evening in New York. The plane's fuel pumps were suspect until finally recovered and found blameless. The NTSB admittedly never did find an ignition source.

Why Clarke chose to tell so strange a story is bewildering. Something of a glory hound, he may have wanted to claim credit for showing the White House the way out of this monstrous political mess. He elaborated, in fact, that he returned to Washington that same day and shared his fuel tank theory with Panetta and National Security Advisor Tony Lake, even to the point of diagramming the interior of the 747. Neither Panetta nor Lake has confirmed this account, but then again they, like everyone but Clarke, have kept their accounts to the bare minimum. "Does the NTSB agree with you?" Lake reportedly asked Clarke. "Not yet." He added the telling comment, "We were all cautiously encouraged."[18] The word "encouraged" gives away more than Clarke intended.

A fuel tank explosion brings no one back to life, but it would spare the president a Greg Norman moment.

"Unfortunately," Clarke concluded, "the public debate over the incident was clouded by conspiracy theory." Speaking of conspiracies, Clarke failed to sort through the conflicting details of the one the CIA had orchestrated. Although he accepted TWA's 800 apocryphal ascent to 17,000 feet, he claimed that what the witnesses saw was not the zoom climb but "a column of jet fuel from the initial explosion and rupture, falling and then catching fire."[19] If he never quite got his story straight, it was because he did not have to. The media held the Clinton White House to a different standard than they did that of his successor, George W. Bush. When Clarke's book came out in March 2004, he got a ton of exposure, including sixty minutes on *60 Minutes*. No one asked him about his preposterous take on TWA 800. This was an election year after all. He was telling the media that Bush had done "a terrible job on the war against terrorism,"[20] and that was all they needed to hear.

Chapter: TWELVE

DOG DAYS

As the Long Island summer slogged into its dog days, the news from the investigation slowed as well. The immediate problem for Jim Kallstrom was that he sold the bomb theory too well. The victims' families believed it. So did the media. In the days after his return from Washington in late August, he seemed to be playing for time—to what end was not quite clear. Despite earlier promises, he refused to declare the crash a criminal act.

On August 31, the *Times'* Don Van Natta complicated matters for the White House. He reported that investigators had found "additional traces of explosive residue" on the interior of the aircraft near where the right wing met the fuselage.[1] Earlier, investigators had found explosive traces on the exterior where the right wing met the fuselage. "This is the spot believed to be the focal point of the explosion that destroyed the

plane," Van Natta reported. For the record, Witness 73 had also identified "the aircraft's right wing" as the initial point of contact. So too had
fisherman William Gallagher. This residue was RDX. RDX and PETN
are the prime ingredients of Semtex, a plastic explosive that can be
molded into any shape and slipped easily past an X-ray machine. For this
reason, Semtex had become, wrote Van Natta, a "favorite of terrorist
bombers." Publicly at least, the FBI and the NTSB continued to insist
that until they found telltale "physical evidence" they could not designate
the explosion a criminal act. Still, noted Van Natta, they offered no
alternative explanation as to how these chemicals got on the plane.

It was about this time that the dynamics of the investigation appeared
to change. Few people noticed the difference, but one who did was senior
NTSB accident investigator Hank Hughes. Hughes had been on the go-
team that arrived immediately after the crash and worked on-site for
months thereafter. At Calverton, Hughes led the team that reconstructed
the interior of the aircraft. It was not until May 1999 that he and other
NTSB and ATF officials were able to take their concerns public. The
setting was a Senate Judiciary Subcommittee hearing chaired by Republican Senator Charles Grassley.[2] Those testifying complained that the
FBI, although allegedly running a "parallel investigation," bullied its
working partners from day one. FBI agents let the others see only what
they wanted them to see, and sometimes they restricted them from seeing
anything at all. Kallstrom was nonplussed. In his typically brusque fashion, he dismissed the hearing as a "kangaroo court of malcontents."[3]

As the hearing revealed, the NTSB was predisposed to deconstruct
accidents. Its officials resented the FBI and failed to understand why its
agents leaned towards a crime. "It was not whether someone was going
to find evidence of a bomb," said NTSB metallurgist Frank Zakar, "it's
a matter of when." To Zakar and others, if a bomb at least seemed plausible, a missile did not. "Possibly the FBI had knowledge of something
we were not aware of that could possibly have led them to believe it was
a missile damage," said Zakar naively. This was nearly three years after
the incident. That Zakar still did not know about the radar data or the
witness testimony is striking. This lack of knowledge, when coupled with

a resentment of the FBI, led the NTSB rank-and-file to push for a mechanical explanation without much in the way of prompting.

Hughes, however, was seeing something more sinister. The FBI's failure to respect the evidence and honor the chain of custody frustrated him, but it was the "disappearance of parts from the hangar" that truly alarmed him. Whole seats were missing, and other evidence was disturbed. At one point, he set up an overnight video surveillance that recorded two FBI agents in the hangar without authorization at 3 a.m. On another occasion, he saw an FBI agent trying to flatten out a piece of metal with a hammer. Indeed, if one visual image captured the spirit of the investigation, this was it.

"You don't alter evidence," Hughes told Grassley. He had no idea what the agent's intentions were, and he had no authority to stop him. When Hughes reported problems, he was ignored. As he would come to recognize, an FBI with this much control could literally hammer the metal to make an external explosion look like an internal one. Metaphorically, it could hammer the evidence to fit almost any outcome it desired.

Hughes started noticing this phenomenon about two months into the investigation. He was not alone. Jim Speer, representing ALPA, the Airline Pilot's Association, watched the FBI skew the investigation and shared his misgivings in *Silenced*. With twenty-five years of experience as an Air Force fighter pilot and additional experience with TWA, Speer brought a rich experiential knowledge into his work. None of this impressed the FBI. Speer had to be inventive to learn much of anything. On one occasion, he identified a suspicious-looking part from the right wing and brought it to the FBI's field lab at Calverton. He was convinced a high explosive had damaged it but dared not say as much. Instead, he told the FBI testers that he had done some chemical testing in college and was curious to see how the EGIS technology worked. When they agreed to show him, he grabbed the suspect part and passed it off as one of the million parts—literally—retrieved from the ocean floor.

"I asked them to swab it and test that in their demonstration, which they did, and the part tested positive for nitrates," said Speer. This threw the testers into a panic. One of them picked up the phone, made a call, and in "nanoseconds" three agents in suits came running in. The agents huddled with the testers before informing Speer the machine had frequent false positives. They ran the tests several times without letting Speer watch. When finished, the lead agent turned to Speer and said, "All the rest of the tests were negative; we will declare the overall test negative and the first one you saw, we'll call it a false positive."[4]

TWA's Bob Young, who worked with the NTSB on the investigation, witnessed this incident. As he noted, and Speer confirmed, the FBI sent this part to Washington for further testing. It never came back.[5] This was a common phenomenon. In his otherwise innocuous testimony before Grassley's subcommittee, Donald Kerr, the FBI Lab director, casually boasted that FBI Lab examiners sent "116 pieces of debris" to the FBI lab in Washington for further testing.[6] This was 116 more pieces than Kallstrom would admit to sending.

FBI Director Louis Freeh had appointed Kerr, an outsider, to clean up the lab in the wake of a major scandal that rocked the FBI while the TWA 800 investigation was in full swing. Dr. Frederic Whitehurst, who blew the whistle on that scandal, failed to understand why any part from Calverton should have been sent to the D.C. lab. For one, he believed that the EGIS technology was "very specific and very sensitive." For another, he argued that in delivery the part ran the risk of contamination.[7] That these parts tested positive for explosive residue after weeks of immersion suggests that a high explosive blast outside the aircraft was more than the proverbial figment of a conspiracy theorist's imagination.

The boldest among the malcontents was Terry Stacey, the TWA senior manager who worked on the investigation through the NTSB. Stacey knew the aircraft well. He had flown the 747 in from Paris the day before its tragic end. Originally assigned to the NTSB witness group, he did not protest when the FBI neutered it. He was a team player by nature. Elizabeth Sanders described him as "a straight arrow, go-by-the-rules kind of guy."[8] A couple months into the investigation, he too noticed a subtle shift in FBI behavior. Always secretive, the agents now seemed intent on concealing potential evidence of a missile attack. In October

1996, James Sanders flew up from Virginia to meet with Stacey at Newark Airport. "What he told me over those first hours," said Sanders, "was one thing—'I know there's a cover-up in progress.'"[9]

Sanders pored over the data Stacey provided in subsequent meetings. What the two concluded was that an initial blast outside the right wing appeared to leave a reddish-orange residue trail across two rows of nearby seats. In late August 1996, the FBI had the residue tested but refused to share the results with Stacey and others working with the NTSB. In September 1996, the residue trail was much discussed at Calverton. Stacey had planned on scraping off some of the residue, but when it refused to yield, he cut out a few square inches of material and FedExed it to Sanders. Sanders had the material tested at an independent lab on the West Coast, and its elements were found to be consistent with elements present in the exhaust residue of a solid-fuel missile.

After Sanders went public with his findings in March 1997, the FBI counter-claimed that the material was simply glue. If this were so, the FBI brass would not have needed to classify the results under national security, but they did. If this were so, they could have simply informed Stacey it was glue before he sacrificed his career to get at the truth, but they did not. If this were so, they would not have felt compelled to arrest Stacey and the Sanderses, but apparently they did.

One did not have to be a conspiracy theorist to distrust the FBI. Gene York, an experienced 747 pilot who worked the investigation through the NTSB on behalf of the ALPA, does not believe a missile brought down the plane. He concedes he is among the minority of pilots who feels that way, but having helped reconstruct the plane, he is firm in his beliefs. A former Marine like Kallstrom, York had little use for the FBI honcho's bullyboy style. "He couldn't put a sentence together without a four-letter word," York told me. He described Kallstrom at work as "a bull in a china shop."[10] York had real problems with the way the FBI agents ran the show. "They would pick up things that looked like a crime and go hide it," he said. When he protested, they retaliated by trying to get him thrown off the investigation. They even threatened to bring him up on charges of mishandling government equipment. He believes they tapped his phone as well. The whole experience left York disillusioned. "Don't ever ask me to trust the government," he said. "These guys do what they want to do and we are just hanging on for the ride."

On September 19, 1996, the government went public with its change in direction. The news this time came out of NTSB headquarters in Washington, not out of Calverton. Putting it in play was Gore family retainer and NTSB chair, Jim Hall. "Convinced that none of the physical evidence recovered from T.W.A. Flight 800 proves that a bomb brought down the plane," Matthew Wald led in his *Times* article, the NTSB was now planning tests "to show that the explosion could have been caused by a mechanical failure alone."[11]

Wald cautioned that not everyone had signed on to this shift. Boeing did not think a fuel tank explosion capable of doing that kind of damage. Without passion, Kallstrom insisted the FBI would continue its parallel investigation. And Wald reminded his audience why many thought a mechanical failure unlikely, including the explosive residue, the lack of any emergency transmissions, and the dramatic fracturing of the plane. Unmentioned in the article was any reference whatsoever to eyewitnesses, at least a few of whom described the break-up sequence in detail before the NTSB confirmed the same. Forgotten too were the two military helicopter pilots who watched objects strike TWA 800 from opposite directions. As for the "mysterious radar blip that appeared to move rapidly toward the plane," the authorities had been incrementally erasing that from the record for more than a month. In sum, Wald made eight references to a bomb in the article and only one to a missile and that briefly in the negative.

In her account from this same period, Pat Milton likewise deleted talk of missiles from the record. Given her access to Kallstrom, she was able to recreate a conversation between him and trusted deputy Tom Pickard. The two were apparently confused because a trace of RDX was found on a curtain in the rear of the plane as well as in the area near the right wing. "How about multiple bombs?" Kallstrom reportedly mused. "Multiple bombs?" said Pickard. "But how do you detonate multiple bombs on a single plane?"[12] If Milton is to be believed, both seem to have forgotten that three of their more capable agents had interviewed 144 "excellent" witnesses less than two months prior and found the evidence for a missile strike "overwhelming."

The balance between bomb and mechanical failure lasted exactly one day before the weight swung fully the way of "mechanical." On Friday, September 20, the FBI released a statement claiming the TWA 800 aircraft had "previously been used in a law enforcement training exercise for bomb-detection dogs."[13] On September 21, the *Times'* Matthew Purdy filled in the details. Reportedly, on June 10, 1996, the St. Louis police used the TWA 800 plane to train a bomb-sniffing dog. The trainer placed explosives throughout the plane and encouraged the dog to find them. One law enforcement official told Purdy the explosives were kept in tightly wrapped packages but conceded that "testing can leave traces behind."[14]

The following day, September 22, the *Times* published what would prove to be the investigation's obituary. "Can you imagine what a defense lawyer would do to us?" one investigator told Van Natta. "This pretty much knocks out the traces, unless we get something much more concrete."[15] By "concrete" he meant physical evidence of a blast, like the explosive residue that had been blasted into the corner of a baggage container in the bombing of Pan-Am 103 in 1998. But that piece was only ten inches long.

From the beginning Kallstrom argued that the critical piece of evidence was most likely "a small piece of metal." With the weather worsening, and that evidence likely deep under water, the search had become what Van Natta called "a race against the calendar." Van Natta was right, but not in the way he intended. For the White House, the search had always been a race against the calendar—a race, that is, to November. If the officials under its sway could keep the public pacified and the airways open until then, they would win the race. The investigation was proving less stressful than the Clintons might have imagined. If the media believed the outcome hinged on a small piece of metal, how hard could it be to lose that piece or never find it?

In looking back at the case, I am struck by the sincerity of so many hundreds of hard-working investigators, and I am forced to wonder whether I have read too much into the inconsistencies. Then I come face to face with some appalling act of deception, and I file my doubts away. The CIA zoom climb animation comes to mind. So too does David Mayer's creepy, CIA-influenced performance at the 2000 NTSB hearing. And the fabrication of witness statements would unsettle the media in the better class of banana republics. The dog-training story, however, came first and hit the serious investigators, said one, like "a punch in the gut."[16] All the work he and others had done finding explosive residue was undone—in this case by a training exercise that never took place.

To sell the dog story took any number of lies. It also required victims. One for sure was the St. Louis police officer that did the training, Herman Burnett. A second may well have been Ohio Congressman James Traficant who exposed the training for the fraud it was. So willing were reporters to believe Kallstrom—or to protect the Clintons pre-election— that they failed to confirm a story that could not withstand the least bit of scrutiny. Taking its lead from the FAA, the FBI had agent Jim Van Rhein interview Burnett on September 21, 1996.[17] The alert reader may recall that the FBI put out its press release on this exercise the day before that interview, September 20. The *Times* published a comprehensive dog-training article on September 21. Incredibly, the FBI and the *Times* broke this story nationwide before a reporter or even an agent spoke to Burnett.

Six years after the incident I asked a police officer friend to persuade Burnett to talk to me, and Burnett obliged. As Burnett told me, I was the first person in the media to call him. Burnett had a story to tell. In fact, the FBI had no proof he had ever done a training exercise on the plane that would become TWA 800. In a September 1997 letter to Rep. Traficant, Kallstrom asserted, "The [airport] manager on duty, whose name the patrolman could not recall, told him that a wide body was available at gate 50." The FBI did observe that Burnett "made no notations regarding the tail number of the aircraft, as it was not his policy to do so." Nor was it Burnett's policy to note the gate number, but that detail was left out of the record.[18] What Burnett did list on the form were specific start and stop times and the notation "wide body." That was all the information anyone had to go on.

The lack of documentation should have nipped the story in the bud. To repeat, no known record put Burnett and his dog at gate 50 or on the Flight 800 plane. The FBI claim that Burnett remembered the gate number after three months was unbelievable on its face. Yes, a 747 bearing TWA #17119, the number for the Flight 800 plane, was parked at gate 50 that day. According to the FBI, the plane was there "from shortly before 700 hours [7 AM] until approximately 1230 hours [12:30 PM] on that date." No one disputes this. The FBI also acknowledged that Burnett "began the placement of the explosives at 10:45 AM." No one disputes this either, but these time details undercut the whole FBI construct.

On that June day, as usual, Burnett placed the training aids throughout the passenger cabin in a "zigzag" pattern. He let the explosives sit for a while, as FAA regulations dictate, and then returned to his car to retrieve Carlo, his dog. "At 11:45 AM," again according to the FBI, "the patrolman began the exercise by bringing the dog into the aircraft. The exercise lasted 15 minutes, and the dog located all the explosives." Carlo's mission accomplished, Burnett led him out of the plane and back to the car. Burnett then returned to the plane to retrieve the scattered training aids. He placed each aid on the galley counter and carted them all back out. Burnett estimated this activity to have taken fifteen minutes. Based on the FBI's own timetable, Burnett could not have left the plane earlier than 12:15 p.m. Yes, the Flight 800 plane was at gate 50 until 12:30 as the FBI indicated.[19]

There was a reason the plane left the gate. As clearly documented in several places including Captain Vance Weir's "Pilot Activity Sheet," Weir and his passengers took off for Honolulu in that very same 747 at 12:35 p.m.[20] Burnett did not leave the plane until 12:15 p.m. at the earliest and saw no one. To clean the plane, stock it, check out the mechanics, and board several hundred passengers would have taken more than the fifteen-minute window of opportunity offered in the FBI's own timetable. Much more.

Even if the FBI had been unaware of TWA regulations that mandated an hour on-board preparation time for the crew, its agents would have known just from experience that a Hawaii-bound 747 would have been busily stocking up and loading passengers long before the plane took off. Burnett, however, was alleged to be exercising his dog in a "sterile" environment and seeing no one. As it happened, another 747, a veritable clone, was parked at gate 51. This second plane—bound for JFK International as TWA Flight 844—would not leave the gate until 2:00 p.m.[21] This later departure would have allowed Burnett and Carlo plenty of time to execute the training undisturbed. In its response to Traficant, the FBI failed to acknowledge this second plane. "You know for sure the dog was on the plane?" Rep. Traficant asked Kallstrom at a congressional hearing in July of 1997. "We have a report that documents the training," dodged Kallstrom.[22]

How, one must ask, could so flagrant a deception unfold with so many people looking on? The answer seems fairly obvious. Immediately after Kallstrom was called to Washington on August 22, federal officials began searching the nation, and probably the world, to find an airport at which a dog exercise had taken place on a day when the Flight 800 plane was parked there. Almost all of those involved in this search performed it in good faith, but not everyone. At the end of the search, some few people—Kallstrom was surely one—made an executive decision not to scruple over the details. The pressure to justify the investigation's shift in direction forced their hand. They may have been reluctant collaborators, but their collaboration killed the investigation.

As was obvious from the beginning, too, Burnett did not put his training aids anywhere near where the explosive residue had been found. He told the FBI he made five separate placements of explosive devices within the plane in a zigzag pattern. These included smokeless powder, water gel, detonator cord, and ammonia dynamite. All of these were placed outside the area of damage on the right side of the plane, rows 17–27, in which the explosive residue had been found. And none of these aids combined PETN and RDX, the elements of Semtex that the FBI had reported finding in late August.

Van Natta reported this discrepancy in his September 22 article on the subject. "Records show the packages were not placed in the same place where the traces were located," Van Natta wrote, citing "several" unnamed investigators as his source. These investigators also pointed out that an explosive trace had been found on the right wing, a location clearly beyond Carlo's skill set. CNN's Negroni used named sources to make the same point. "Where the bureau got hits on the wreckage," said FAA bomb technician, Calvin Walbert, "there was no explosive training aids anywhere near that."[23] Said Irish Flynn, FAA associate administrator, "It's a question of where those traces came from. The dog doesn't answer the questions."[24]

To defend the FBI's conclusions, Kallstrom would dishonor his good name and damage Burnett's. At the July 1997 hearing, Rep. Traficant prodded Kallstrom, "Isn't it a fact that where the dog was to have visited, that it is not the part of the plane where the precursors of Semtex were found?" Said Kallstrom, growing defensive and defiant, "That's not true." He added in agonizingly dishonest detail, "It is very important where the packages were put, Congressman. And the test packages that we looked at, that were in very bad condition, that were unfortunately dripping those chemicals, were placed exactly above the location of the airplane where we found chemicals on the floor." In fact, Kallstrom elaborated, "An incredible amount of this chemical leaking out of these packages fell into that spot."[25] The "tightly wrapped packages" of September 1996 were dripping chemicals less than a year later exactly where Kallstrom needed them to be dripped. This was a multi-tiered *lie*. No euphemism can paper over what Kallstrom said and did.

In her 1999 book, Milton changed any number of details to make the story work. She had Burnett loading the plane with "enough plastic explosives to blow the airport sky-high." She referred here specifically to "five pounds of SEMTEX, or C-4."[26] In his 1997 letter to Traficant, however, Kallstrom specified a "1.4 block of C-4." With all due respect to Ms. Milton, SEMTEX and C-4 are not the same. Unlike SEMTEX, C-4 does *not* contain PETN, and it was the discovery of PETN traces that first prompted the "bomb" stories in the *Times*. Besides, Kallstrom admitted in 1997 that Burnett placed the C-4 in a seatback pouch outside the suspected area.

In cleaning up Kallstrom's account after the fact, Milton put the finishing touches on Burnett's reputation. "Yeah, I could have spilled more than a little," Burnett reportedly told the FBI. "The packages were old and cracked and we hadn't used them in a while, so more than usual might have come out." Milton referred to the incident as the "dog fiasco" and concluded her account with Kallstrom and his colleagues laughing at "Carlo" jokes. Officer Burnett, an African American, did not find the incident funny. "I am pissed off to this day," he told me. "I never lost any. I never spilled any. There was never any powder laying loose." As to his alleged confession of the same, he said, "I just hate that they twisted my words. I know what I did, and how I did it."[27] As should be clear by now, his were not the only words that were twisted in this investigation.

Three weeks after the dog-training story broke, and four weeks before the election, President Clinton signed an aviation bill into law that included a range of cumbersome programs designed to prevent passengers from bringing bombs onto commercial airplanes. "It will improve the security of air travel," said Clinton. "It will carry forward our fight against terrorism."[28] In attendance at the White House signing were several people who lost loved ones on TWA Flight 800, unwitting props in Clinton's effort to "showcase himself as a can-do steward tackling the nation's problems." Nowhere in the *Times* article just cited was the word "missile" even mentioned. That possibility had largely been relegated to the realm of the grassy-knollers. With more than a little help from the media, Clinton managed to turn a national security disaster of major proportions into a pre-election photo-op. Sixteen years later, Hillary Clinton would attempt to do much the same with Benghazi.

The Navy P-3 was hovering a mile or so above TWA 800 when the plane exploded. That was the command position the P-3 routinely assumed during a Cooperative Engagement Capability (CEC) missile test, illustrations of which were publicly available in 1996.

Chapter: THIRTEEN

LOST AT SEA

Although fully confident that TWA 800 was shot down—I would not have embarked on this adventure were I not—I was not certain about who pulled the trigger. In *Silenced*, Sanders and I remained agnostic on the subject. For *First Strike*, which was published in 2003, we knew we would have to offer specifics, even if speculatively. From the beginning, Sanders believed the U.S. Navy had tragically misfired and said so in his 1997 book, *The Downing of TWA Flight 800*. For my part—and here is where what scientists call "confirmation bias" sneaks into the process—I did not want to believe that was true.

In *First Strike*, as the name of the book suggests, we arrived at a plausible speculation, namely that the Navy took out TWA 800 in the process of destroying a small terrorist plane filled with explosives. This theory is not at all fanciful, and Sanders still believes it possible. Several eyewitnesses talked about a small plane. Witness 550, for instance, reported seeing "a plane coming from west to east and then what looked like a 'smaller' plane coming from the northeast on a dead course heading towards the nose of the larger plane." He heard a "crackling sound" when the two planes "crunched up." In addition to witness testimony, we heard from at least two military sources that the flying bomb scenario was indeed the case. Even the CIA speculated early on that a "small airplane" might have intercepted TWA 800.[1]

A few months after the book was published, I was a guest on Barbara Simpson's San Francisco radio show. One call from a local banker intrigued me enough that I had the producer take the caller's name and number off-air. I followed up later that day. A Navy veteran, the fellow struck me as entirely credible. As he told the story, one of his banking customers was a TWA executive. Having served as a radar man during several missile-firing exercises on the Pacific missile firing range, the banker was curious about TWA 800 and asked the exec what he knew. Citing the TWA CEO as his source, the exec told him the U.S. Navy shot down the 747 by accident. This the banker had heard before, and he remained unconvinced. One added detail, however, caused the banker to reevaluate the possibility of a shoot down, specifically the exec's suggestion that the U.S. Navy was not running a test but was actually trying to take out a small terrorist plane when its missiles inadvertently destroyed TWA 800.

In his 2003 book, *Dereliction of Duty*, retired Air Force Lieutenant Colonel Robert "Buzz" Patterson related an incident that makes this theory sound at least plausible. As mentioned previously, Patterson carried the "nuclear football" for the president. One morning in "late-summer" 1996, Patterson was returning a daily intelligence update to the National Security Council when he "keyed on a reference to a plot to use commercial airliners as weapons."[2] The plot went under the rubric "Operation Bojinka," Bojinka being the Serbo-Croatian word for "loud bang."

The mastermind of the plot was Islamic terrorist Ramzi Yousef. Yousef was on trial in New York for his role in Bojinka on the day TWA

800 went down. Although the plot's best-known feature was a scheme to blow up eleven American airliners over the Pacific, a secondary feature had Yousef and/or his cohorts chartering a plane, loading it with explosives, and crashing it into an American target.[3] In moving these documents between offices, Patterson saw the president's hand-annotated response to Bojinka. "I can state for a fact that this information was circulated within the U.S. intelligence community," Patterson wrote, "and that in late 1996 the president was aware of it."[4] Knowledge about the use of planes as bombs would emerge as a contentious issue during the 9/11 Commission hearings in 2004. As early as the summer of 1996 Clinton and his staff were aware of the threat. It is altogether likely that Clinton's review of these documents was related to TWA 800's destruction, if only to establish an alibi.

All this being said, I do not believe that Yousef had anything concrete to do with the demise of TWA 800. Nor have I seen sufficient evidence in the thirteen years since *First Strike* was published to believe a terrorist plane threatened TWA 800. If Yousef played any role it was to heighten anxiety, already keen three weeks after the terror bombing of the USAF's Khobar Towers facility in Saudi Arabia. Two days before the start of the Atlanta Olympics, the Clinton administration reportedly had the U.S. Navy on the highest state of alert since the Cuban Missile crisis.[5] In this hair-trigger environment, accidents could happen.

Accidents had happened before in such an environment. On Sunday morning, July 3, 1988, at the tail end of the Iran-Iraq War, an Aegis cruiser, the USS *Vincennes*, fired two Standard Missiles at a commercial Iranian Airbus, IR 655. IR 655 had reached 13,500 feet, a final altitude almost identical to TWA 800's, when Captain Will Rogers III gave the order to fire. Rogers and his crew had mistaken the ascending passenger jet with 290 people on board for a descending Iranian F-14, a fighter plane.

Four years after the incident, in July 1992, *Newsweek* teamed up with ABC News's *Nightline* to produce an exhaustive exposé on the incident and its subsequent cover-up.[6] *Newsweek*'s John Barry and Roger Charles reported that the $400 million Aegis system was capable of tracking every aircraft within three hundred miles and shooting them down. The weakness of the system was its complexity, especially when managed by people with little experience in high-pressure situations. "Some experts," observed the reporters, "question whether even the best-trained crew could handle, under stress, the torrent of data that Aegis would pour on them."

In retrospect, Rogers and his crew could have used more training. Working under a time crunch in the ship's windowless combat information center (CIC), they made a series of oversights and misinterpretations that quickly turned tragic. With IR 655 just eleven miles away, Rogers switched the firing key to "free" the ship's SM-2 antiaircraft missiles. Given the green light to fire, a nervous young lieutenant pressed the wrong keys on his console twenty-three times before a veteran petty officer leaned over and pressed the right ones. Thirty seconds later, the first missile blew a chunk of the left wing off the airliner with an engine pod still attached, and the rest of the plane quickly plunged into the sea. The job done, Rogers gave the order to steam south out of Iranian waters.

Within twelve hours, Admiral William Crowe, chairman of the Joint Chiefs of Staff, called a press conference at the Pentagon to announce that, yes, the Navy had accidentally shot down a commercial airliner. That was about all the truth Crowe was inclined to offer. Relying on the information Rogers provided, Crowe stuck to the story that the Iranian plane was descending, picking up speed, flying outside the commercial air corridor, and refusing to identify itself. As their colleagues would do after the TWA 800 disaster, the naval officers closed ranks and kept other investigating bodies at bay. By July 14, 1988, when Vice President George H. W. Bush reported on the incident to the United Nations, Crowe knew that Rogers's initial report was false in almost every detail but chose not to share that information with Bush. "The U.S. Navy did what all navies do after terrible blunders at sea," *Newsweek* reported. "It told lies and handed out medals."

Newsweek ran this lengthy cover story while Bush was running for reelection. It did his campaign no good. Following the article's publication,

Les Aspin, Democratic chairman of the House Armed Services Committee, held public hearings on the *Vincennes* incident in July 1992 and grilled a defiant Crowe. "The accusations of a cover-up are preposterous and unfounded," Crowe told the House committee.[7] After the hearing, Aspin vowed that there would be further hearings on the subject. There were not. On September 19, 1992, two months after testifying before Aspin, the politically savvy Crowe made an unlikely pilgrimage to Little Rock, Arkansas.

This was a crucial visit. The great majority of military officers, active and retired, loathed the draft-dodging Clinton. With the candidate beaming by his side, Crowe dismissed Clinton's draft record as "a divisive and peripheral issue" and threw his considerable weight behind Clinton's bid for the presidency.[8] A month later, Crowe wrote a *New York Times* op-ed defending his position. He conceded that Ronald Reagan, who first appointed Crowe chairman, did an excellent job handling the Soviet Union. He admitted too that George H. W. Bush, who extended Crowe's chairmanship, did great work in defeating Saddam Hussein. That said, Crowe argued unconvincingly, "America needs new leadership, which will imaginatively and boldly address the problems facing our citizens and threatening our prosperity."[9] Upon being elected, Clinton appointed Aspin secretary of defense, and the probe into the *Vincennes* quietly died. Helping it stay dead was the newly appointed chairman of the president's Foreign Intelligence Advisory Board, none other than Crowe. When TWA 800 blew up, the retired admiral was serving as the ambassador to the United Kingdom.

Barring a deathbed confession, the exact details of what the U.S. Navy did on the night of July 17, 1996, may never be known. What the media learned from the *Vincennes* incident, however, was that the mismanagement of the U.S. Navy's prized Aegis system could and did result in the accidental destruction of a commercial airliner. They learned too that the Navy was capable of deceiving the citizenry about a misfire of this magnitude. What they chose not to learn, however, was that Bill Clinton was capable of exploiting vulnerable naval officers to improve his political chances.

In the election year of 1996, the media chose to forget the little they did learn from the *Vincennes* incident. Most conspicuously, the *New York Times* failed to voice the least suspicion about the role of the U.S. Navy in TWA 800's demise. On September 17, two months to the day after the crash, Andrew Revkin wrote an article on Internet-based conspiracy theories, one of which suggested that a Navy Aegis guided missile cruiser "let loose a practice shot that went awry."[10] The Pentagon denied any involvement, and Kallstrom assured the *Times*' readers that the probability of a Navy misfire was "as close to zero as you can get." This was the most probing penetration of the naval involvement the *Times* would deliver. It was as if the *Vincennes* incident and its subsequent cover-up had never taken place. Had the *Times* reporters persisted, they would likely have encountered what *Newsweek* did in pursuing the *Vincennes* story—"months of stonewalling by senior naval officers"— but there was no indication they bothered.

Although Revkin did not name a source for the Internet-based theory, he was likely referring to the Holtsclaw-Russell communication. Russell recalls sending his provocative e-mail about a month after the crash. Interestingly, Pierre Salinger cited August 22 as the specific date of the e-mail.[11] This was the same day Kallstrom was summoned to Washington for that game-changing session with the DOJ. According to the Russell e-mail, on the night of July 17 a Navy P-3 participated in a missile firing practice in W-105, a warning area off the southeast coast of Long Island. For the record, the P-3 is a long-range, antisubmarine warfare patrol aircraft with advanced submarine detection and avionics equipment. It can help provide a fleet commander oversight of an engagement at sea and relay information among the various ships in a battle group. As it happens, the presence of an Iranian P-3 near IR 655 heightened the suspicions of Rogers and his crew on the *Vincennes*.

The AP's Pat Milton provided the only serious window into Kallstrom's knowledge base at this time, especially in regards to the U.S. Navy. Writing two years after the incident, Milton explored the P-3 issue in some detail. In her retelling, FBI agents interviewed the crewmembers the day after the crash and satisfied themselves with the crew's explanation that

the P-3's proximity to the exploding TWA 800—less than a mile away—
was a "harmless coincidence."[12] Wanting more assurance, Kallstrom sent
agents back to interview the crew again on the following day. This time
Captain Ray Ott resisted the interrogation. "Are you saying I'm lying?"
he told the agents. "Are you questioning my patriotism here?" Ott refused
to share details of his flight and told the agents the mission was classified.

An irritated Kallstrom contacted the chief of the Atlantic fleet,
Admiral Bud Flanagan, and asked him to intervene. "They've given you
all the information relevant to your search, sir," Flanagan reportedly told
Kallstrom. "Anything else is outside what you need to know." According
to Milton, Kallstrom then leaned on his old Marine Corps colleague,
General Charles Krulak, to get at the truth, and Krulak shared Kallstrom's concern with his fellow Joint Chiefs. The verdict: "Friendly fire
did not play a role in the downing."[13] Still, Kallstrom persisted, and the
Navy obliged by allowing his agents to interview the P-3 crew a third
time. To this point in the investigation, there is no reason to doubt Kallstrom's sincerity.

Some time before the third interview, the FBI learned that the P-3's
transponder, the homing device that enables air traffic control to track
the plane, was off during the flight. Holtsclaw knew this before Kallstrom did. He told Russell the P-3 was "a non-beacon target (transponder OFF) flying southwest in the controlled airspace almost over TWA
800." In his third interview with the FBI, Ott explained that the plane's
transponder was "faulty" and only worked "intermittently." In their
interview with the NTSB in March 1997, P-3 crew members insisted the
transponder "failed after takeoff" and was soon replaced through the
normal Navy supply channels.[14]

According to Milton, after the explosion the P-3 circled back to the
crash site with the crew offering to help. The plane then returned to its
original practice mission, dropping sonobuoys to track the USS *Trepang*,
a submarine.[15] At a November 1996 press conference, Rear Admiral
Edward K. Kristensen, who managed the Navy's end of the investigation,
claimed the P-3 was conducting the training exercise with the *Trepang*
eighty miles south of the crash site,[16] a figure Milton would repeat. In

March 1997, however, the P-3 crew told the NTSB much the same story about the training exercise but added that the sonobuoys were all dropped "a minimum of 200 miles south" of the crash site.[17]

The authorities staged the aforementioned November 1996 press conference to refute Pierre Salinger's claim of an accidental shoot-down. In no previous article had the *Times* so much as mentioned the P-3. Its readers still did not know what Russell's colleagues knew, namely, that the P-3 was flying almost immediately above TWA 800 with its transponder off. This, as shall be seen, was a critical detail. Kristensen chose not to mention it at the press conference. A savvy reporter might have asked one devastating question: if Washington were on veritable war footing immediately after TWA 800's destruction, and a terrorist missile attack was suspected, why did the P-3 continue on a routine sub-hunting exercise 80 miles (or 200 miles) to the south? After all, no naval asset was more capable of finding the culprit. Two answers suggest themselves. One is that the P-3 crew, knowing the Navy's culpability, heeded orders to vacate the area. The second, and much less likely, is that the crew remained ignorant of a potential terrorist threat.

Reporters had good cause not to ask tough questions. Kristina Borjesson, then a CBS producer, attended this press conference. She watched in shock as Kallstrom exploded at a fellow who asked how the U.S. Navy could be involved in the investigation when it was a possible suspect. "Remove him," Kallstrom shouted. Two men promptly grabbed the reporter by the arms and dragged him out of the room. Wrote Borjesson, "Right then and there, the rest of us had been put on notice to be on our best behavior."[18]

A veteran freelance cameraman who worked the TWA 800 case every day for months confirmed Borjesson's account. "I watched some astounding things I never saw before, nor saw since," said the fellow who asked that I not reveal his name. "It all unfolded before me—firsthand: official stories changing, Pat Milton cozying up with the FBI, tapes confiscated, threats to boycott TV networks if those shows persisted with the missile theory, press thrown out of press conferences for simply asking a question."[19]

When Russell's e-mail surfaced, the authorities sensed they had a problem on their hands. Russell knew about the naval training exercise. He knew about the P-3. He knew that the P-3's transponder was off. And he knew about the radar data. The readers of the *New York Times* knew none of this. That the e-mail apparently surfaced on August 22 might have been a coincidence, but the investigation overflowed with coincidences, like the one that put the P-3 with its allegedly broken transponder right above TWA 800 as it exploded. Another coincidence, of course, was that the radar data just happened to mimic a missile arcing over and intersecting TWA 800 in the second before its identifier vanished from the screen.

Kallstrom was in way over his head. He and his agents knew nothing about radar data or P-3s or submarines or guided missile cruisers. Although the FBI's November 1997 summary listed all the Navy assets its agents reportedly checked out, those agents depended fully on the Navy for that information. If the crew of the P-3 felt free to blow them off, the skippers of the cruisers and subs surely felt the same. Navy higher-ups had to know the president had their back, and Kallstrom had to have figured that out. In November 1996, with all options still in play, he insisted there was no Navy involvement in TWA 800's destruction. "We have looked at this thoroughly," he blustered, "and we have absolutely not one shred of evidence that it happened or it could have happened."[20] In truth, he did not have a clue.

In addition to the P-3, three submarines and at least one cruiser were in the mix that night. Kallstrom claimed early on that no naval asset was "in a position to be involved," but the FBI was never sure where those assets were. The information Milton got from the FBI put one of those subs, the USS *Trepang*, 80 miles south of Long Island. (The P-3 crew, as mentioned, said the *Trepang* was 200 miles away.) Milton put a second sub, the USS *Wyoming*, 150 miles south. A tugboat captain spotted a third sub about fifty miles away off the Long Island coast about midnight on July 17. Milton identified that sub as the *Albuquerque*.[21]

As to the cruiser, Rear Admiral Edward K. Kristensen claimed at the November 1996 conference held to discredit Salinger that the USS

Normandy was the "nearest ship" to the crash site about 185 miles southwest.[22] By this time, however, Kallstrom had to know Kristensen was being deceptive. According to Milton, shortly after the crash Kallstrom learned of a "gray warship" that two flight attendants spotted off the Long Island coast an hour before the crash steaming south. FBI witness Lisa Perry and her friend Alice Rowe likely saw the same ship about two hours before the crash near the coast of Fire Island and heading east. "The ship was so big and close," said the women, "that you couldn't capture the entire profile in one glance." They described it as battleship gray with a large globe and impressive gunnery. "It was quite obviously a military fighting ship."[23] Other witnesses had seen this ship as well. Kallstrom was not at all pleased to learn how badly he had been played. He reportedly called Admiral Flanagan's office in a huff. Only then was he told there had, in fact, been a Navy ship in the area—a Ticonderoga-class cruiser, the USS *Normandy*.

If Kallstrom ever did learn the location of the *Normandy* at the moment of TWA 800's destruction, he did not share that information with Pat Milton. According to Milton, the FBI verified "the precise location" of the ship as "181 miles southwest of the crash site, at latitude 37 degrees, 32.8 minutes north, longitude 74 degrees, 0.92 minutes west, off the Manasquan inlet in New Jersey." Milton passed these numbers along without doing her homework. The coordinates do place the USS *Normandy* at a site roughly 181 miles from TWA 800's debris field but nowhere near the Manasquan inlet. If the coordinates were accurate, the *Normandy* was off the coast of Delaware-Maryland-Virginia, at least 150 miles south of Manasquan. The ship that witnesses had seen just hours before the crash might have made it to Manasquan by 8:31 p.m., but given the timeline, the ship could not have made it to Virginia. Whatever ship the witnesses did see the FBI apparently failed to inspect. No surface vessel other than the *Normandy* was listed in the FBI's final summary.[24]

Chances are the *Normandy* was where Kristensen said—180 or so miles southwest of the crash site. The coordinates given to Milton put the ship off the coast of Wallops Island, home of NASA's Wallops Flight

Facility and site of a rocket testing range. That is where the ship was positioned when retired U.S. Air Force Lieutenant Colonel and then active TWA 747 captain Allen Strasser had the opportunity to witness a missile test in March 1995, sixteen months before the fatal shoot down. As Strasser told me, he was a guest aboard the ship.

About five to ten miles away from the *Normandy* that day was a second ship. On the night in question, slightly after midnight, a target missile was launched from Wallops Island. The second ship then launched an intercept missile. Strasser stood on the starboard wing bridge of the *Normandy* and watched the missile ascend. After the launch, Strasser returned to the ship's combat information center where fewer than ten people monitored its computer systems, reprogrammed to put all of their computing power into the intercept shot. The purpose of the test, said Strasser, was to help upgrade the U.S. Navy standard arm missile from a ship-to-air, antiaircraft missile to a ship-to-air, anti-missile missile. The test that night proved fruitful, the first success after two previous failures. Prophetically perhaps, the successful intercept took place high over the ocean just south of Long Island.

According to Strasser, on the night TWA 800 went down, an American Airline captain reported seeing a missile ascend from Wallops Island. Strasser argues that if a Navy ship fired the fatal shot, the crew may not have known the missile had a booster rocket capable of propelling it farther and higher than a typical standard arm missile. The missile would have been loaded in a vertical launch system, which was not visible to the crew. This may help answer the question of why no sailor has come forward, publicly at least, to report the incident.[25]

Channeling the FBI, Milton wrote of the *Normandy*, "The agents told [Kallstrom] that the ship had been 181 miles south of the crash site when Flight 800 exploded, and not in the position to hit the plane with any of its armaments."[26] This information is misleading. In the test that Strasser observed, the *Normandy* programmed and monitored the missile. It did not fire any missiles itself. "I believe the loss of TWA 800 was by a missile," Strasser told me, "and there is a 75–85 percent chance it was our own missile." Strasser and I had this communication in 2008.

Over the years I have heard from any number of people in and around the incident. Most do not want their names repeated. Strasser was an exception. "Feel free to use the information as is," he said. "It is all true. The initial three people who let this out of the bag were arrested by the FBI to scare them into submission." A one-time top gun, Strasser was not easily intimidated.

In its final press release, the FBI boasted that its agents had done an "accounting of all armaments capable of reaching Flight 800." Despite their efforts, they had little idea of what those armaments were. Few people did. One of my correspondents suggested why. He cautioned that his information was limited, but his insights have merit nonetheless. "Mack" (not his real name) was a crewmember on the USS *Albuquerque*. Several days before TWA 800 was destroyed, Mack was involved in loading what he was told were "experimental missiles" aboard the sub.[27] "This was not your normal load out," he said. The sub was heading for the testing area off the coast of New Jersey and south of Long Island. Mack did not go on that cruise. When the TWA 800 news first broke and talk of missiles was still in the air, his wife asked, "Do you think it was a terrorist?" Said Mack, "God, I hope so. My boat was out there." If a terrorist did not down the plane, he feared the Navy might have.

This fear was widespread. It accounted, at least in part, for media reluctance to pursue this angle and the insider reluctance to share information. Still, some facts were too obvious to ignore. In its final report[28] the NTSB conceded that FAA radar picked up four unidentified vessels within six miles of the TWA 800 explosion. Three of the six were leaving the scene at between twelve and twenty knots "consistent with the speed of a boat." A submarine goes under the rubric "boat." The fact that all three of these radar tracks disappeared right after TWA 800 crashed raised the question of whether these boats were submarines.

Kallstrom never said otherwise. The final FBI summary located the three subs in question—the USS *Wyoming*, the USS *Albuquerque*, and the USS *Trepang*—in the "immediate vicinity of the crash site." In a recorded September 1998 phone interview AIM's Reed Irvine asked Kallstrom about the unidentified vessels within six miles of that site. Said

Kallstrom, "I spoke about those publicly. They were Navy vessels that were on classified maneuvers."[29] No, Kallstrom had never spoken publicly about classified maneuvers. He was having a hard time keeping his story straight.

Radar picked up a fourth vessel radar within six miles of the crash site, and this one the authorities never managed to explain away. The ship was spotted twenty minutes before the explosion heading southwest. At the time TWA blew up, it was less than three miles away. Instead of heading back to the site to look for survivors, its captain committed a nautical sin of the highest order. He fled the scene at a speed the FBI estimated at between twenty-five and thirty-five knots. That captain has never been held to account. "Despite extensive efforts," the FBI's Lewis Schiliro told a House subcommittee, "the FBI has been unable to identify this vessel." Schiliro added the meaningless disclaimer, "Based on our investigative efforts, we are confident it was not a military vessel."[30] The FBI identified the other vessels in the area and conducted interviews as appropriate, claimed Schiliro, but he declined to name the other vessels for fear of compromising the investigation.

According to Schiliro, the fleeing ship was "believed to be at least 25–30 feet in length." This was pure guesswork, if not outright disinformation. A Navy cruiser measures in the hundreds of feet. A routine radar scan cannot gauge length, but it is much more likely to pick up a Navy cruiser than an ordinary pleasure boat. Whatever the nature of the ship, whether Navy or pleasure or terrorist, the people on board would have had a better perspective on the incident than just about any witness. Admittedly, FBI agents never talked to them. Nor did the FBI explain how it was able to identify every other vessel in the area except the most conspicuous one.

On subjects nautical, the FBI had little choice but to take the Navy's word. From day one, however, naval officers were sparing with the truth. The directive to be evasive had to come from on high. How high one can only conjecture, but the White House would be a reasonable guess. Were the shoot-down the result of a secret test gone awry, a president could easily have invoked "national security" as the rationale for concealing the truth from the American people. Only a few high ranking officers would have needed to know the details, but it is hard to believe they would or could have misdirected the investigation of their own accord.

For the first week after the crash the documentation of its cause lay buried, presumably on the ocean bottom. Investigators believed, with good cause, that when they retrieved the so-called "black boxes" they would discover the truth. These durable fluorescent orange containers protected the cockpit voice recorder (CVR) and the flight data recorder (FDR) respectively. Between them, the CVR and FDR had the potential to spell out precisely what had gone wrong.

Investigators knew how skilled the U.S. Navy was in retrieving these boxes and expected quick results. In February 1996, the Navy used a remote-control submersible vehicle to recover the CVR and FDR from Birgenair Flight 301, a Turkish charter plane that crashed off the coast of the Dominican Republic. The devices had sunk with the wreckage to a depth of 7200 feet. The FDR revealed in explicit detail the mechanical flaws that caused Birgenair 301 to crash, and the CVR recorded the pilots' desperate attempt to cope with the impending disaster. As in most crashes caused by mechanical failure, the cockpit drama lasted for several excruciating minutes. In this case, it began with one pilot saying, "There is something wrong, there are some problems," and it ended three minutes later with the other pilot crying out, "Oh, what's happening?"[31] The FDR data proved just as revealing. Between them, the two devices told in inarguable detail the story of Birgenair 301's undoing.

On the night of the TWA 800 crash, would-be rescue boats had picked up the distinctive "ping" from the black boxes' underwater locator beacon. The next morning, July 18, two NTSB investigators set out to find the boxes. This should not have been hard. The sea was smooth. The sky was crystal clear. The searchers used the latest in sounding devices. And the aircraft wreckage lay only 120 feet beneath the surface. Birgenair 301 had settled *sixty* times deeper. Wrote CNN's Negroni, "The men left the inlet that afternoon optimistic they'd soon have what they were after."[32] They found nothing, heard nothing.

The *New York Times* expressed little curiosity about the delay, but the Long Island–based *Newsday* sensed something amiss. On July 22, the paper ran an article titled, "Divers Wait as Devices Scan Ocean." According to *Newsday*, Navy divers still had not gone into the water. They had been relying instead on various remote devices that had yet to find the elusive boxes. "They should be down there diving," a captain of a nearby diving boat operation told *Newsday*. "[Federal officials] said it was too rough out there, but my boat had 27 divers in the water on Saturday [July 20]."[33]

Navy Captain Chip McCord told *Newsday* that those remote devices were a "quicker and better" way to locate the boxes, but in the first four days the Navy found nothing. *Newsday* paraphrased McCord as explaining, "Signals from the black boxes have not been heard because the devices are broken, destroyed or covered with sand or other material." Whether intentionally or not, McCord was misleading the reporters. On July 24, two Navy divers finally went in. I have seen the underwater video of the Eureka moment, a moment Negroni described accurately enough. No sooner was the first diver lowered to the ocean floor, she wrote, than he saw "an orange box with FLIGHT RECORDER stenciled on its side." Seconds later, the other diver "came into view. In his arms he carried another orange box." Said diver Kevin Gelhafen, "Recovering the boxes was merely picking them up, setting them in the basket, and tying them down."[34] Like Milton, Negroni expressed no wonder at the ease with which the divers found the boxes.

With the boxes successfully recovered, President Clinton's "on again/ off again"[35] trip to New York was on again. Arriving at JFK the morning after their retrieval, Clinton spun their recovery to his best political advantage. "Just last night the divers who were braving the waters of the Atlantic to search for answers recovered both flight data recorders," boasted the president at a press conference afterwards. "Our experts are analyzing their contents at this very moment. This is major step toward unraveling the mystery of Flight 800."[36] As to what that mystery might be, Clinton laid out two possibilities, "mechanical failure or sabotage." The word "sabotage" implied a bomb, not a missile.

A major part of that "mystery" was the length of time it took to find the boxes. No sand or other material covered the CVR and FDR—not that any such covering would have muffled their distinctive ping. Nor were the beacons broken. In its first formal report from November 1997, the NTSB addressed the condition of the two boxes. Although banged up and even ripped open, the boxes protected the recording devices, both of which were in good working order. The NTSB also examined the underwater locator beacon on the CVR, the "pinger," and it "operated normally when tested."[37] This report failed to mention the condition of the FDR beacon, but there is every reason to believe that it worked as well.

Stranger still, when the NTSB agents examined the recordings, they found no useful information at all. The last words out of the cockpit were "power set," a casual acknowledgement of an air traffic control order to continue ascending. This was said nearly a minute before the tape ended.[38] The FDR ended at the exact same time as the CVR, also revealing nothing of consequence. According to former NTSB Board member Vernon Grose, this complete lack of information was unusual to the point of extraordinary. As Sanders and I discussed in some detail in *First Strike*, there is every reason to believe the boxes were recovered immediately after the crash, edited, and put back in place. I will not go into detail here because the evidence remains inconclusive.

Some facts, however, speak for themselves. Most notable is the inexplicable failure of the CVR and FDR to reveal any crash-related information whatsoever. Another is a CIA intra-agency memo from early in the investigation in which an analyst expressed surprise that the recorders would go silent. "To get the electrical power to shut down," wrote the anonymous analyst, "[a missile] would need to 'miss' the engines, and instead hit the electrical compartment by mistake."[39] There was no evidence this happened. Finally, there is Executive Order 13039. Although the president preferred to work through his fixers, on March 11, 1997, Clinton quietly signed this order effectively removing all federal whistleblower protection from anyone, civilian or military, associated with U.S.

Navy "special warfare" operations.[40] This would include any Navy divers charged with moving the black boxes.

The date of the executive order is worth considering. On the following day, March 12, the *New York Times* reported that government officials had "unleashed a pre-emptive strike" to neutralize an upcoming 57-page article in the *Paris Match*. That article explored in depth the Navy's role in the destruction of TWA 800.[41] The *Times* also noted that on the day before, March 11, the same day as Clinton's executive order, the Riverside *Press-Enterprise* broke the story of James Sanders's residue test. Having cause to fear the collapse of the cover-up, Clinton for the first time left his fingerprints on the investigation. The media failed to notice.

Much more alert than the media, Montoursville's Don Nibert had deep suspicions about the black boxes. The technically inclined Nibert used his status as a bereaved family member to get information. As he would tell CNN, he asked for a copy of the flight data recorder tape to have it analyzed independently, and the NTSB obliged him. Nibert delivered the tape to audio expert Glenn Schulze. For the thirty years prior Schulze had worked as an independent consultant with high profile clients like the U.S. Navy and the Applied Research labs at the University of Texas. Schulze concluded there were at least two seconds purposely deleted from that tape. Nibert believed they were removed to conceal "an outside explosion next to the airplane." When CNN asked NTSB Board member John Goglia for clarification, he responded unhelpfully, "We talked about there being an event of something that the data was missing and it's unexplainable, it's just missing."[42]

Nibert's proposed scenario, if accurate, would not have shocked Jim Speer. Representing the representing the Airline Pilot's Association, Speer recalled watching a video of the ocean floor early in the investigation and noticing that the tape had been jacked with. "Look at the gaps in the time clock here," Speer told his FBI chaperone. "There is no reason for gaps to occur unless the tape has been edited. I want to see the unedited version."[43] Said the agent, "No." End of conversation.

With the black boxes saying nothing, and the media saying not much more, the Navy was off the hook. More importantly, so was the president. Missiles, friend or foe, had been edited out of the equation as surely as the troubling shots of the ocean floor in Speer's video and the revealing last few seconds of data from the black boxes. For the White House, things were looking up.

Chapter: FOURTEEN

MR. SMITH GOES TO WASHINGTON

In late November 2002, I was strolling the concrete banks of Brush Creek, a channelized waterway that runs through the heart of Kansas City. As usual, I walked Huck Finn–style along the edge. With *First Strike* about to be released, scads of people had told me to "watch my back." What they should have told me was to "watch my step." Lost in thought, I stepped off into space and immediately knew I was going in the water. As in the cartoons, it took about a half hour to get there. On the way, I had time to contemplate the absurdity of what could happen were I to drown in the smelly, semi-toxic Brush Creek. Who would ever believe I just fell in? A whole conspiracy industry could grow up around my literal liquidation. I hit the water almost laughing.

The laughing stopped, however, when I realized I could not get out. I was wearing sweats, now about as heavy as I was, and boots. The walkway was about a foot and a half above the water. I could not quite pull myself out or throw my foot up over the edge. The harder I tried, the wearier I got. Few people in our overly antiseptic metropolis walk the creek even in the best of weather. In late November, no one does. But then—*mirabile dictu!*—a hefty, heaven-sent fellow came ambling down the walkway. "Hey, Mac," I said to my new guardian angel, "could you lend me a hand?" Again as in the cartoons, he did a comic double take. My guess is that he had not seen too many swimmers in this waterway, especially in November. He cheerfully obliged and spared the conspiracy mills a story even the *New York Times* might have felt compelled to investigate.

Upon the book's publication three months later, our young publicist Bob Keyser and I descended on the nation's capital. Our goal was to find someone higher up the media chain to take an interest in the information Sanders and I had gathered. Thanks to the Internet, we had much more information at our disposal than the *Times* newsroom had a year after the crash, but we lacked the institutional clout to prod authorities to return our phone calls. That is not to say we didn't try. We simply did not succeed. I had no illusion that we could break open this story ourselves.

As I had yet to acquire a reputation as a "loose cannon"—that would come in time—a few media people of note proved willing to talk with us. We began with AIM's Reed Irvine, who had been helpful throughout. He knew what doors to knock on and what numbers to call and graciously shared those numbers with us. One door led to Don Phillips, an aviation reporter who covered the TWA 800 affair for the *Washington Post*. We met with him in the *Post*'s lobby. Although he told us little that was new or useful, Phillips did not disguise his contempt for a process that relegated him and every other reporter not with the *New York Times* to a lower media caste. By funneling its inside information to the *Times*, the FBI made the Grey Lady a co-dependent, and she obliged, wittingly or not, by enabling the White House's disinformation campaign.

I never did meet the one person I thought could move the TWA 800 saga into the mainstream, but in deference to Irvine, that fellow did take my calls. In addition to being the most effective reporter of his generation,

Bob Woodward was a U.S. Navy vet. He served for five years as a lieutenant after graduating from Yale in 1965. During those years, by his own account, he sometimes acted as a courier between the White House and Admiral Thomas H. Moorer, then the chief of naval operations.[1] Moorer, long since retired, publicly supported the work Irvine was doing to reopen the TWA 800 investigation. In January 1998, at an AIM-sponsored press conference, he and Commander Donaldson made the case that a surface-to-air missile brought down the aircraft.[2] Despite Moorer's credentials and Donaldson's expertise, the media blew them off. During Clinton's second term, reporters showed little interest in knowing any more than they had to about the workings of the administration.

Woodward was not nearly as dismissive. He let me make my case almost without comment. Not above a little flattery, I assured him he was the only reporter capable of breaking this open, which was very close to the truth. I added, a bit presumptuously, that TWA 800 would make a nicely symmetrical capstone thirty years after Watergate. Woodward reminded me that the war in Iraq was just about ready to kick off. He suspected it would grab the media's attention in a way a seven-year-old story could not. That I could not deny. In any case, Woodward remained polite throughout our two or three phone conversations and asked me to send a book to his home address, which he provided. I have not heard from him since. If he left anything unspoken, it was a general sense of apprehension, the kind that, if voiced, might have translated, "Don't you know what you are getting yourself into?"

I did get to meet one mainstream reporter in Washington with a reputation for uncovering things presidential: Michael Isikoff, then with *Newsweek*. Isikoff became very nearly a household word early in 1998 when Matt Drudge broke an Isikoff story that *Newsweek* had spiked, namely that President Clinton had been dallying with intern Monica Lewinsky in the Oval Office. Sex was the one scandalous slice of Clinton's life that defied the media's best efforts to suppress it.

With Isikoff in *Newsweek*'s cramped Washington office was a colleague who covered the TWA 800 story for the magazine, Mark Hosenball. In fact, no reporter endorsed the CIA zoom climb hoax more enthusiastically than did Hosenball. His article on the subject began with a *pro forma* dig at "conspiracy theories" and went nowhere positive from there.[3] Indeed, without intending to, Hosenball revealed how painfully little America's major newsrooms knew about TWA 800 even in November 1997, sixteen months after the crash. Worse, what he did know he got from the CIA. Its analysts had convinced him that "infrared images captured by spy satellites" showed what really happened during the plane's last forty-nine seconds.

This revelation may have come as news to Kallstrom. The FBI's comprehensive summary issued just a week before Hosenball's article did not once mention the word "satellite." The NTSB's final report made only vague mention of "infrared sensor information from a U.S. satellite" and that in reference to the CIA video. In his 2008 report, the CIA's Randolph Tauss claimed a satellite detected a "heat plume associated with the crash" but said it was not "crucial" to the analysis. In her book, CNN's Christine Negroni made no mention of satellites, and AP's Pat Milton made only fleeting references. The *New York Times* avoided the subject altogether. Yet here was Hosenball saying that the CIA had "spy satellites designed to monitor unfriendly foreign countries pointed at the Eastern Seaboard." This at least sounded plausible. Two days before the start of the Atlanta Olympics, and three weeks after the terror bombing of the Khobar Towers in Saudi Arabia, the military was on an extremely high state of alert.

Family member Don Nibert heard about the satellites as well and wanted to know more. "I learned that they had three satellites that would have coverage of the site near the 8:30 time period," Nibert observed wryly. "All failed."[4] Nibert asked John Clark, an aviation safety deputy with the NTSB, what were the odds all three would cease working at the same time. Clark responded that this information was considered classified.

This was bunk. If the satellites showed what Hosenball claimed, federal officials would not have needed the CIA's trumped up zoom climb video. Surely too the FBI and NTSB would have used the data to buttress their shaky, inconclusive summaries. In a letter to then congressman John

Kasich two months after the press conference, the CIA quietly buried the subject: "No satellite imagery of the disaster exists."[5] This translates, "No satellite imagery exists that would help us make our case."

Hosenball fell hard for the CIA video. Under his byline, *Newsweek* ran a fully affirmative, nine-frame, full-color recreation captioned with the unlikely boast, "CIA Photos." For Hosenball, the video provided a necessary rebuttal to "speculation about a mystery missile." As he told the story, "some" of the "244" FBI witnesses claimed to have seen a streak of light arcing across the sky. In reality, that "some" was 258, and the "244" was 736. But who was counting? Not Hosenball. He had information enough to assure his readers that what the witnesses really saw was the fuselage of the burning, climbing plane rocketing upwards some three-thousand-plus feet.

Indeed, had Hosenball been on the CIA payroll he could not have done more to legitimize the agency's crude rewrite of history. Among the major media only Robert Hager of NBC rivaled Hosenball in the uncritical affirmation of government talking points. In fact, the CIA cited Hager in an in-house newsletter as an example of how well the media received the zoom climb animation. "The work was riveting," the newsletter quoted Hager as saying. Hager too marveled at the satellite data and congratulated the CIA on its "fascinating, highly informed" presentation.[6] In the years to come, authorities could rely on Hager to pass off TWA 800 agitprop as news.

Our goal in meeting with Isikoff and Hosenball was not to make enemies but to make converts. Unfortunately, we had no success. Hosenball resisted fiercely. He countered my objections to the CIA animation with the claim that Boeing executives had assured him the 747 fuel tank was a veritable time bomb. I had a hard time believing any executive anywhere would say something that incriminating, but Boeing did have reason not to make enemies at the White House. When the crash occurred, Boeing was in the middle of negotiations to buy McDonnell Douglas, its only real competitor in the American commercial airliner market. The airlines closed the deal in December 1996 with a $13 billion price tag, pending government approval.[7]

Among others, consumer advocate Ralph Nader denounced the proposed merger, arguing that it would give Boeing a near monopoly on the industry as well as "dramatic political power."[8] Despite Nader's impassioned plea, the Federal Trade Commission (FTC) approved the merger on July 1, 1997. This was a mighty subjective decision. Just the day before, the head of the FTC was reportedly "delighted" when a federal judge blocked a proposed merger between Office Depot and Staples. The *New York Times* dryly noted that the decision was "controversial" in antitrust circles given that the merged entity would "would control only 6 percent to 8 percent of the overall office products market."[9]

In November 1997, with the merger concluded, Boeing execs seemed confident enough to distance the company from the CIA zoom climb animation. "Boeing was not involved in the production of the video shown today, nor have we had the opportunity to obtain a copy or fully understand the data used to create it," said a company press release posted immediately after the video's airing. "The video's explanation of the eyewitness observations can be best assessed by the eyewitnesses themselves."[10] The release concluded with an odd disclaimer, "Since the beginning of the investigation, Boeing has never subscribed to any one theory."

Isikoff did not patronize us the way Hosenball had. He just did not express much interest. He asked me which three pages of the book he should read. "Given that this is the great untold story of our time," I responded, "how about a chapter?" I suggested chapter fourteen, our summary chapter. As I explained, there is a binary quality to any such investigation: gate open or shut, explosive device or mechanical failure, internal explosion or external explosion. To transform an external explosion into a mechanical failure someone had to alter or suppress every known variable.

As I explained to Isikoff, in chapter fourteen of our book we reviewed all the relevant variables—the physical evidence, the eyewitness testimony, the debris field, the medical forensics, the explosive residue, the residue trail, the Navy information, the radar data, the FDR, the CVR, the satellite data, and more—and showed how the authorities lost, stole, concealed, erased, deleted, denied, or simply ignored every variable that did not fit the preferred outcome. Where need be, I continued, they even manufactured new evidence—the zoom climb, the imaginary flagpoles, bogus interviews, counterfeit dog training. Losing patience, Isikoff looked at me skeptically and repeated, "Which three pages?"

Mr. Smith, welcome to Washington.

Chapter: FIFTEEN

THE FIXERS

"They were careless people," wrote F. Scott Fitzgerald, "they smashed up things and creatures and then retreated back into their money or their vast carelessness, or whatever it was that kept them together and let other people clean up the mess they had made." Fitzgerald, of course, was writing here about his fictional characters Tom and Daisy Buchanan in *The Great Gatsby*. The Buchanans, however, had nothing on the Clintons. Throughout their political careers, Bill and Hillary made one unseemly mess after another and in every case let other people clean up.

The clean-up people rarely got the top jobs. Those required Senate confirmation. They got the number two spots or, in Webster Hubbell's case at the Department of Justice, the number three spot. Unfortunately, Hubbell had messes of his own and no one to clean up after him. A year into his tenure as associate attorney general, the Clintons' old Arkansas pal was forced out for sundry corruptions back at his and Hillary's law firm in Little Rock. For the Clintons this was just as well. The ungainly Hubbell would not have been up to the TWA 800 mess—the Clinton's most complex and consequential, Monica included. This clean up had to be managed through at least three agencies: the NTSB, the CIA, and the FBI, as well the Departments of Defense and Justice.

In that it controlled the FBI, the DOJ had the most demanding job. Making it tougher still was the disarray within the department. From the moment Hillary Clinton staked out Justice as her personal fiefdom, the department had been in chaos. Nanny issues sidelined the first two attorney general candidates as well as the first would-be deputy AG. Insisting that a woman—any woman—head the department, Hillary finally settled on the feckless Miami prosecutor Janet Reno. For the next eight years the Clintons would have to work around her. Needing someone to work through, they finally found a fixer worthy of the number two position, a little known DC litigator named Jamie Gorelick. With Gorelick's appointment as deputy attorney general in February 1994, Hillary had three women occupying the most powerful posts in federal law enforcement, criminal division head Jo Ann Harris being the third.

Gorelick proved to be a much more capable and subtle problem solver than the blundering Hubbell. In June 1996, a little more than a month before the TWA 800 crash, *Newsweek*'s Mark Hosenball—yes, that Mark Hosenball—took note of Gorelick's insider role. In a rare glimpse at the political workings of the feminized DOJ, Hosenball observed that Gorelick had set up "a campaign-like 'war room'" to combat alleged smears from the Bob Dole campaign. Wrote Hosenball without a hint of disapproval, "In a campaign year, Justice can't afford to be totally blind."[1]

In that stormy campaign year, Justice was very nearly omniscient. A month after the Hosenball revelation, still in war room mode, Gorelick directed the FBI to take over the TWA 800 investigation. Heading up Justice's operation on the ground in Long Island was United States Attorney Valerie Caproni. As attorneys and officers of the court, Gorelick and

Caproni knew the FBI was the subordinate agency. They knew too the NTSB could not legally be restricted in its pursuit of information. They simply ignored the law. The FBI reported to Justice. The NTSB did not.

While Reno contented herself with "policy issues," Gorelick ran the department. The media acknowledged as much, but they missed Gorelick's crucial role in the TWA 800 investigation. In her book *Deadly Departure*, CNN's Christine Negroni never once mentioned her. The *New York Times* made only one reference to Gorelick in regards to TWA 800. That came on July 20, three days post-crash. Identified as a member of an "interagency task force," Gorelick told the *Times* that investigators were still entertaining "multiple possibilities" as to the cause of the crash. That was it. Of note, at the time of the interview, she was traveling to the Atlanta Olympic games "with the presidential party." In a lapse of taste given the mess in Long Island, the *Times* headlined this article, "Clinton Tells U.S. Athletes, 'I Want You to Mop Up'."[2]

Only with the release of Pat Milton's book three years after the crash did Gorelick's name surface in any meaningful way. Milton identified Gorelick as the most serious player at the August 22, 1996, meeting in the attorney general's office, the meeting that reversed the momentum of the investigation.[3] Presuming Kallstrom told Milton about Gorelick's presence at that meeting, he did not share her apparent message, namely that investigators had to find some explanation other than a bomb, let alone a missile. Although undocumented, the rough outlines of the strategy shift would not be hard to interpret.

What followed in the next several weeks was the most ambitious and successful cover-up in American peacetime history. At its quiet center was Gorelick. With the help of a complicit media, she and her cronies transformed a transparent missile strike into a mechanical failure of unknown origin. Given her role, the months after the crash had to have been emotionally harrowing. She did not know whether she would wake up one morning to find *Washington Post* reporters at her door eager to make her their John Mitchell or H. R. Haldeman. Perhaps such anxiety may have inspired her to leave the DOJ in January 1997. If so, the media missed the story. In an article on her departure, the *New York Times* failed to explain why the "hard-driving, efficient" deputy was stepping down or what she intended to do next. Nor did the paper mention her role in the TWA 800 investigation.[4]

There was nothing routine about Gorelick's next career move. In May 1997, the Clintons found a way to reward their trusted deputy for her steely performance. To the best of my knowledge, not one reporter even questioned why a middling bureaucrat with no financial or housing experience would be handed the vice-chairmanship of Fannie Mae, a sinecure the *Washington Monthly* aptly called "the equivalent of winning the lottery." Had the reporters inquired, they might have learned that Clinton had appointed five reliable hacks total to the Fannie Mae Board, including the chief of staff and deputy campaign manager from his 1992 campaign, a former White House aide, a major DNC fundraiser and Lincoln bedroom guest, and a GOP real estate mogul who endorsed Clinton in 1992. The *Washington Monthly* summarized a board appointment as "a nice way for a president to say 'thank you' to a political ally." One does not have to be a conspiracy theorist to suspect that Clinton had something to do with Gorelick's appointment. Gorelick would make $877,573 in that first half-year alone.[5]

Another understated player in the TWA 800 drama was George Tenet. A party loyalist, Tenet hopscotched from one congressional staff position to another before wending his way to the deputy directorship at Central Intelligence. On July 17, 1996, he was serving in that position under John Deutch. A respected intellectual, Deutch brought much to the office, but, unlike Tenet, he did not bring the one quality the Clintons most valued: blind fealty. In September 1996 Deutch confirmed White House suspicions by testifying to Congress that Saddam Hussein was stronger than he had been after the 1991 Gulf War. Reported the *Times'* Tim Weiner, "The White House was furious at Deutch for speaking the truth in public."[6] Clinton dismissed him two months later.

The memos the CIA released in response to various FOIA requests reveal the CIA's complete engagement in the investigation by the day after the crash. In that all names are redacted, I cannot tell whether Tenet sent or received any of these memos. He was sufficiently involved, however, to lend his imprimatur to agency disinformation by March 1997. That month Tenet sent FBI director Louis Freeh a letter assuring him that "what these eyewitnesses saw was the crippled aircraft after the first explosion had already taken place."[7] This was eight months before the FBI shared the counterfeit CIA thesis with the public. For all the FBI's bluster and the NTSB's statutory authority, the CIA gave the impression of being the agency in charge.

To secure a meeting with the analysts responsible for the zoom climb video, for instance, the NTSB's Jim Hall had to send a humble pie letter to Tenet explaining how NTSB group members would "appreciate learning more about the CIA's evaluation of witness statements."[8] Hall sent this letter two years after Tenet informed Freeh as to what the witnesses were alleged to have seen. In March 1997 the White House rewarded Tenet for his faithful service by naming him director of central intelligence. Opined the *New York Times,* more accurately than its editors knew, "The rise of Mr. Tenet is proof of the rewards of being a loyal and obedient servant to one's boss, be he a senator, a spymaster or the President of the United States."[9]

For all their power within the administration, neither Tenet nor Gorelick could have undone the TWA 800 investigation without Kallstrom's support. In the way of compensation, Gorelick had one precious carrot to dangle: the freedom of Kallstrom's good friend and FBI colleague, R. Lindley DeVecchio. For thirty years, until his arrest in 1992, a Brooklyn hit man named Greg Scarpa worked as a "top echelon confidential informant" for the FBI. DeVecchio managed that relationship for many of those years. In return for the intelligence Scarpa provided on New York's La Cosa Nostra families, the FBI protected Scarpa, a capo in the Colombo family, and kept him out of prison.

During the years he was under FBI protection, however, Scarpa murdered as many as fifty people. Ultimately, three of DeVecchio's fellow agents accused him of losing his moral balance and, at the very least, providing Scarpa with the kind of FBI intelligence that allowed him to target his enemies.[10] This was a serious charge and not without parallels elsewhere. A similar relationship with mobster Whitey Bulger in Boston would earn FBI agent John Connolly a forty-year sentence for murder.

According to the *New York Times*, the Clinton Justice Department began its investigation of DeVecchio in 1994 based on the testimony of his FBI colleagues. In April of 1996, with DeVecchio still in FBI limbo, Kallstrom had his attorney send a memo to FBI director Louis Freeh warning that the DOJ investigation of DeVecchio threatened future prosecutions and "casts a cloud" over the New York Office.[11] In July 1996, the DeVecchio case was still active when Freeh assigned Kallstrom to head up the TWA Flight 800 investigation.

On August 22 of that year Gorelick summoned Kallstrom to Washington. In early September 1996, the Justice Department abruptly closed its thirty-one month long investigation and informed DeVecchio that a prosecution was not warranted.[12] By mid-September 1996, Kallstrom had ended all serious talk of a missile and pushed through the administration's "mechanical failure" narrative. In October, DeVecchio resigned with full pension. Of course, the DOJ's abrupt clearance of DeVecchio in 1996, like Gorelick's Fannie Mae bonanza and Tenet's directorship, may all have been happy coincidences, but the coincidences in the TWA 800 investigation make hash out of the laws of probability.

In any case, the State of New York was not as forgiving as the Department of Justice. In 2006, its prosecutors indicted DeVecchio for his alleged role in abetting the Scarpa murders. At the time of his indictment, Kallstrom came defiantly to his friend's defense. "Lin DeVecchio is not guilty and did not partake in what he's being charged with. It's as simple as that," said Kallstrom, still speaking in absolutes. Then serving as senior counterterrorism advisor to New York governor George Pataki, Kallstrom apparently saw no conflict in publicly raising money for a man whom New York State had indicted for murder.[13] Although the case against DeVecchio eventually fell apart, the evidence was strong enough for the State of New York to risk alienating the FBI by bringing it to trial.

Kallstrom left the FBI in December 1997 immediately after the close of the TWA 800 case. Like many of his peers, Louis Freeh included, he took an executive position with the MBNA Bank before assuming New

York State's top security post in response to 9/11. Today, he serves as a regular contributor to Fox News on the subject of terror. The NTSB's Peter Goelz did pretty well too. He proved to be a good enough soldier during the early rough going of the TWA 800 investigation that Jim Hall named him managing director of the NTSB on December 4, 1997, a week before Kallstrom resigned.[14] On the next day, December 5, the FBI arrested James and Elizabeth Sanders. The NTSB's David Mayer would have to wait a little longer for his ship to sail in, but in July 2009, he was named managing director of the NTSB. The CIA's Randolph Tauss meanwhile got his medal. Washington takes care of its own.

If Gorelick's sweet Fannie Mae deal passed under the media radar, Webster Hubbell's did not. In the same spring Gorelick was plotting her career options, Hubbell was fending off any number of government interrogators. They were hoping to learn why Hubbell's "clients" paid him more than $400,000 in the months after he stepped down from Justice to face criminal charges. The most generous of those clients, the Riady family of Indonesia, had been bailing Clinton out since his White-water days in Arkansas. According to the *Times*, the Riadys had their hand in a $2 billion American-Chinese project whose White House endorsement international bagman Commerce Secretary Ron Brown had the dishonor of trumpeting. He did so, said the *Times*, while "on a groundbreaking trade mission to Beijing."[15]

This groundbreaking mission to China took place two months after the Riadys put Mr. Hubbell on their payroll. Without saying so explicitly, the *Times* strongly implied that the disgraced White House fixer was paid to keep quiet during his eighteen months in prison. The headline said as much, "Payment to an Ex-Clinton Aide Is Linked to Big Chinese Project."[16] The Whitewater independent counsel, the Justice Department, and Congress were all investigating Clinton fundraising but were getting nothing out of Hubbell.

"I'm not going to talk about my clients," he told the *Times*, as if he could have provided any useful service to anyone other than his contin-ued silence. The president claimed to have learned about the payoff only by reading about it in the newspapers. "The charge is serious; we need to get to the bottom of it,"[17] said Clinton with enough of a straight face to keep the *Times* from branding this scandal a "scandal" and running with it the way its editors would have had Clinton been a Republican.

As Hubbell's case suggested, a fixer's obligation to the Clintons did not end when he or she left their employ. In January 2004, the *Times* reported matter-of-factly that Jamie Gorelick was resigning from Fannie Mae "to spend more time on the national commission investigating the Sept. 11 terrorist attacks and to pursue other interests."[18] What the *Times* did not report is that during her five-plus years with that self-serving enterprise, Gorelick self-served herself to the queenly sum of $26,466,834 in salary, bonuses, performance pay, and stock options.[19]

Gorelick was either the most self-sacrificing of American patriots or an anxious fixer with a mess to clean up. As one of only five Democrats on that commission and the only one to give up a $5-million-a-year gig to secure a seat, the latter option seems most likely. Gorelick hinted at what that mess might be when she told the *Times* that the commission's work focused "on the period of 1998 forward."[20] She said this to deflect criticism that she would be investigating her own responsibility for the 9/11 attacks, but her timing suggested a deeper truth.

If the Clintons asked Gorelick to give up her extravagant Fannie Mae salary, they asked even more of their ultimate fixer, Sandy Berger. Like *Pulp Fiction*'s Winston Wolf, Berger's job was to "solve problems." Berger and the president went way back. They worked together on the McGovern campaign in 1972, and twenty years later Berger urged Clinton to run for president when others friends shied away. In his first term, Clinton rewarded this trade lawyer and lobbyist with the deputy national security advisor job, not because of Berger's foreign policy experience, which was slight, but because of his political instincts, which were keen.

In his second term, Clinton appointed Berger national security advisor. Unlike virtually all of his predecessors—General Colin Powell, Rear Admiral John Poindexter, Zbigniew Brzezinski, Henry Kissinger—Berger had no serious foreign policy expertise. What he did have was the president's confidence. Clinton had entrusted the then deputy with some highly sensitive assignments, and Berger delivered. That Berger reportedly remained in the family quarters with the Clintons during the first night of the TWA 800 saga testified to the trust between the two men. So too did his designation as Clinton's point man on China. On the controversial trade missions abroad, it was Berger who pulled the strings that made Ron Brown dance.

In April 2002, the former president called in his chits. He designated Berger as his representative to review intelligence documents in advance of the various hearings on 9/11. As a 2007 report by the House Committee on Government Oversight and Reform specified, Berger did not ask for this assignment, not at all.[21] According to the archivists, Berger "indicated some disgust with the burden and responsibility of conducting the document review." The Clintons, however, had a hold on Berger. To appease them, he risked everything—his reputation, his livelihood, his very freedom. According to the House report, Berger made four trips to the National Archives. His stated reason for the visits was to prepare for his upcoming testimony before the Graham-Goss congressional committee and the 9/11 Commission. The first of his visits was in May 2002, the last in October 2003. He clearly left his mark. "The full extent of Berger's document removal," said the House report, "is not known and never can be known."

In the absence of substantive reporting by the major media, please allow me an informed speculation as to why Berger risked his all. On his first visit, according to Archives staff, "Berger was especially interested in White House terrorism advisor Richard Clarke's personal office files."[22] According to the Committee, "Had Berger seen 'a smoking gun' or other documents he did not want brought to an investigatory panel's attention, he could have removed it on this visit." If there were a "smoking gun," it might well have involved the idea of using planes as bombs.

Understandably, the 9/11 Commission was concerned about who knew what when in regards to the use of planes as bombs. Before the Atlanta Olympics, in fact, Clarke had warned security planners about the possibility of someone like Ramzi Yousef hijacking a 747 and flying it into Olympic Stadium.[23] Two days before the start of those Olympics, on July 17, Saddam's National Liberation Day, with the U.S. Navy on an extremely high state of alert, TWA Flight 800 blew up inexplicably off the coast of Long Island. The fact that the president was reviewing Bojinka plans soon after the destruction of TWA Flight 800 made the versions of those plans with his hand written notes on them all the more critical. If found and revealed, those plans, at the very least, would have shown the president's interest in the possible use of planes as bombs five years before September 11.

Berger's task, I believe, was to make sure all references to Bojinka, planes-as-bombs, and/or TWA Flight 800 were rooted from the Archives, especially any documents with hand-written notes that led back to co-conspirators Berger, Clarke, Tenet, Gorelick, or Clinton. For what other reason would Berger have risked so much?

Paul Brachfeld, the inspector general of the National Archives, threw a major wrench into the Clintons' scheme. Unlike so many career bureaucrats, Brachfeld spoke out forcefully about the criminal activity he was witnessing, namely Berger's theft and destruction of sensitive government documents. Unfortunately, he met resistance from other career bureaucrats less committed to the national interest than he was. On January 14, 2004, the day Berger first testified privately before the 9/11 Commission, Brachfeld met with DOJ attorney Howard Sklamberg. Concerned that Berger had obstructed the 9/11 Commission's work, Brachfeld wanted assurance that the commission knew of Berger's crime and the potential ramifications of it. He did not get it. On March 22, 2004, two days before Berger's public testimony, senior attorneys John Dion and Bruce Swartz informed Brachfeld the DOJ was *not* going to notify the commission of the Berger investigation before his appearance.

DOJ's failure to notify the commission set up one of the most bizarre days in the annals of American history—Wednesday, March 24, 2004. Testifying together before the commission were George Tenet, Richard Clarke, and Sandy Berger.[24] Evaluating their testimony was Jamie Gorelick, one of only ten commissioners. Berger had already been apprehended stealing and destroying documents that the commission was expected to review. The commission members, at least the Republicans, did not know this. This much was evident in Chairman Thomas Kean's initial exchange with Berger.

"We are pleased to welcome before the commission a witness who can offer us considerable insight into questions of national policy coordination, Mr. Samuel Berger, who served as President Clinton's national security advisor," said Kean. To those in the know what Kean asked next must have sounded like a punch line: "Mr. Berger, we would like to ask you to raise your right hand. Do you swear or affirm to tell the truth, the whole truth and nothing but the truth?" Even more perversely amusing were Gorelick's final words to Berger, "Thank you very much for your testimony and your service to the country."

The Republicans on the commission questioned Berger and Clarke about President Clinton's inaction after the bombing of the USS *Cole* and other terrorist attacks. In a dazzling display of political moxie, both men cited the false TWA 800 narrative to make their inaction seem virtuous. "We thought TWA 800 was terrorism," said Berger. "It was not terrorism. People actually—dozens of people saw the missile strike TWA 800 as it went up over Long Island." At this point, Commissioner John Lehman interjected, "Yes, but you just told us...." Berger snapped back, "Preliminary judgments, I have come to learn, are not the same as judgments."

Clarke elaborated on this theme in his defense of Berger. "He pointed out that in the days and weeks after the TWA 800 crash, we assumed it was a terrorist attack," said Clarke confidently. "There were eyewitnesses of what appeared to be a missile attack. But after exhaustive investigations that went on for years, in the case of the NTSB and the FBI, a determination was made that it was not a terrorist attack." With Berger having purged the files and with Gorelick monitoring the commission, Clarke had every reason to feel confident.

Clarke came to the hearing well prepped. In this critical election year, several major media partisans had collaborated to turn this hitherto obscure bureaucrat into a celebrity swift boater. His soon-to-be-bestseller *Against All Enemies* had been published two days prior. He appeared on *60 Minutes* the Sunday before the hearing and on *Meet the Press* the following Sunday. At every turn, he played the selfless public servant who, unlike President Bush, was man enough to apologize for failing to prevent 9/11. In testifying before Gorelick and her fellow commissioners, Clarke asked that intelligence analysts "be forgiven for not thinking about [aviation terror] given the fact that they hadn't seen a lot in the five or six years intervening about it."

Of course, to think about aviation terror would have kept TWA 800 in the conversation. As the memoirs of the various participants suggest, no one wanted it there. Although Clarke talked about the crash in 2004, he helped kill the investigation in 1996. Berger and Gorelick signed on to make sure it stayed dead. Unfortunately, the Clintons and their cronies did so good a job burying the truth that no one passed information about potential aviation terror on to the next administration. This became apparent with the very first question posed to Bush national security advisor Condoleezza Rice in her appearance before the commission on April 8, 2004.[25] Asked Kean, "Did you ever see or hear from the FBI, from the CIA, from any other intelligence agency, any memos or discussions or anything else between the time you got into office and 9-11 that talked about using planes as bombs?" Rice had not.

Tenet avoided the subject of TWA 800 at the hearing, but he caused problems for Gorelick on another front. In explaining intelligence failures before 9/11, he first addressed the "wall that was in place between the criminal side and the intelligence side." Tenet made that barrier sound impenetrable. "What's in a criminal case doesn't cross over that line. Ironclad regulations," he insisted. "So that even people in the Criminal Division and the Intelligence Divisions of the FBI couldn't talk to each other, let alone talk to us or us talk to them."

This testimony flummoxed those of us researching TWA 800. Kallstrom and his colleagues certainly used the "wall" to protect the FBI's criminal investigation from the NTSB, but they welcomed, or at least accepted, the involvement of the CIA from day one on. In the ensuing months, they fed the CIA analysts a steady stream of information about a presumed crime against American citizens on American territory. This cooperation, in which Tenet himself was involved, showed the wall to be more vulnerable to presidential politics than to any pressing issue of national security.

In her response to Tenet, Gorelick acknowledged the wall and claimed to have used "brute force" in her attempt to penetrate it, but she took no responsibility for its creation. The task of assigning credit was left to Attorney General John Ashcroft. In fact, he was the first witness to call attention to the inherent conflict in Gorelick's double agency. "The single greatest structural cause for Sept. 11 was the wall," Ashcroft testified before the commission on April 13, 2004.[26] He was referring here to the same memo that Tenet had, one issued in 1995, which provided instructions on the "separation of certain foreign counterintelligence and criminal investigations."[27] These instructions, as Tenet noted, disallowed FBI agents from communicating with intelligence gatherers at the CIA and elsewhere. "Full disclosure," Ashcroft continued, "compels me to inform you that its author is a member of the commission."

That author, of course, was Gorelick. "We predicted Democrats would use the 9/11 Commission for partisan purposes, and that much of the press would oblige," thundered a *Wall Street Journal* editorial. "But color us astonished that barely anyone appreciates the significance of the bombshell Attorney General John Ashcroft dropped on the hearings Tuesday."[28] For all their passion, the *Journal* editors themselves failed to see the significance of the Ashcroft revelation. The Clintons and their allies had handed an inexperienced functionary a $5 million a year job. She then gave that job up to join the 9/11 Commission despite a work history that, when exposed, would embarrass the Democrats. Having kicked TWA 800 down Clinton's ample memory hole, the *Journal* and all other media overlooked one outstanding fact: under Gorelick's watchful gaze the CIA and FBI collaborated splendidly on the zoom climb video. In so doing, they proved there was nothing "ironclad" about those regulations. By 2004, this collaboration was a matter of record.

While the commission hearing moved on, its best story lines suppressed or ignored, the National Archives' Brachfeld kept prodding Justice. On April 6, 2004, two weeks after Berger's appearance before the 9/11 Commission, he called DOJ's Inspector General Glenn Fine and again expressed his concern that the commissioners remained unaware of Berger's theft. Fine organized a meeting for April 9. Brachfeld reported to those gathered, "Berger knowingly removed documents and therefore, may have purposely impeded the 9/11 investigation." Some of those documents, Brachfeld added, might have been "original."

For all of his efforts, Brachfeld was unable to persuade Justice to inform the 9/11 Commission of Berger's actions. The commissioners remained in the dark until July 19, 2004, three days before the 9/11 Commission released its final report, too late for any significant amendment. They might not have known even then had there not been a leak from somewhere in the Bush administration. At the time this story broke in July 2004, Berger was serving as a campaign advisor to Senator John Kerry. "Last year, when I was in the archives reviewing documents, I made an honest mistake," he told reporters.[29] His attorney Lanny Breuer called the removal of these documents an "accident" and shifted the blame to the Bush White House for using the revelation as a campaign ploy. A year later, when Berger pled guilty, the *Times* wrote off the theft and the surrounding hoopla as "a brief stir" in the campaign season.[30]

In truth, there was nothing honest or accidental about what Berger had done. Among his more flagrantly criminal acts, Berger swiped some highly classified documents, and then, during a break, stashed them under a trailer at a construction site. He retrieved them at the end of the day and admittedly used scissors to cut the documents into little pieces before throwing them away. These repeated thefts should have caused a whole lot more than a brief stir. "His motives in taking the documents remain something of a mystery," reported the *Times* after Berger pled guilty.[31] How different history would have been had the *Washington Post* contented itself with writing, "The motives of the Watergate burglars remain something of a mystery."

Finally, on Friday, April 1, 2005, the Bush Department of Justice announced its plea deal with Berger, an embarrassingly lenient one at that—a $10,000 fine and the loss of his top-level security clearance for three years.[32] That was it. Berger repeatedly stole and destroyed classified documents, lied about it to authorities, and received a much lighter punishment than James Sanders had for receiving and testing a purloined pinch of foam rubber. In September 2005, a federal judge upped the ante on Berger's treachery but not by enough to hurt. Judge Deborah Robinson raised the fine to $50,000—chump change for the wealthy attorney—added two years of probation, and threw in one hundred hours of community service. Robinson said she took into account Berger's "otherwise exemplary record" and "sincere expression of remorse" in her sentence. Berger was remorseful only about getting caught. "I let considerations of personal convenience override clear rules of handling classified material," he lied on the very day of his sentencing. There was nothing convenient about shredding documents and nothing exemplary about the reasons he had to do so.[33]

As I watched these events unfold, I presumed the Bush DOJ went soft on Berger to honor some unwritten pact among presidents to protect their predecessors' national security secrets. On closer inspection, however, it seems that the Bush White House lacked control of its own Justice Department. For the record, Dion, Swartz, Sklamberg, and Fine were all holdovers from the Clinton administration. As far as I could tell, Fine, Swartz, and Sklamberg have only contributed to Democratic candidates in federal races and Dion has no record of federal contributions.[34] During the course of the investigation, Alberto Gonzales, a Republican Janet Reno, replaced the much shrewder John Ashcroft as attorney general. For whatever reason, Gonzales consented to the absurdly lenient plea agreement offered to Berger. In the final analysis, the decision to protect Berger may have had more to do with saving the Clinton legacy than with protecting national interests.

Less than a year later, Berger was back in the news. The global strategy firm over which he presided, Stonebridge International, added a new member to its advisory board. That member just happened to be the vice-chair of the 9/11 Commission, Lee Hamilton, a former congressman. The *chutzpah* of this appointment still astonishes. Berger had thoroughly sabotaged the work of the 9/11 Commission and then had the nerve to appoint the highest-ranking Democrat on that commission to the five-member advisory board of his private firm. Again, the media chose not to notice. The media failed to notice as well when Berger helped plot the political assassination of the one man in Washington most willing to expose his and the Clintons' criminal mischief, Rep. Curt Weldon, a ten-term Republican from Pennsylvania. In the process, the unrepentant Berger would help turn Congress over to the Democrats.

In March 2006, Berger held a fundraiser for the designated hit man, Joe Sestak, a former vice admiral forced into retirement for what the U.S. Navy charitably called "poor command climate." This would-be congressman had not lived in Weldon's suburban Philadelphia district for thirty years before being tabbed to run against Weldon.[35] Berger lent more than his money and support. He volunteered Stonebridge's Director of Communications to serve as Sestak's campaign spokesperson.[36] Before the campaign was through, Berger and his allies would bring in the big guns, none bigger than Bill Clinton and none more lethal than the FBI.

Unaware of the plot against Weldon, I stumbled into the middle of it. Mike Wire, the TWA 800 witness on the bridge, had wrangled an appointment with Weldon and asked if I wanted to come along. Wire lived in suburban Philadelphia, and I happened to be down the New Jersey shore that week. So he and I and his wife Joan drove down together. We did not expect much. If Weldon were like other authorities we had tried to contact, he would have listened politely for a few minutes and promised to have some staffer look into it.

Given Weldon's interests, I had expected to meet a much harder guy. The year before our visit Regnery Publishing had published Weldon's *Countdown to Terror: The Top-Secret Information that Could Prevent the Next Terrorist Attack on America—and How the CIA Has Ignored It*, a book whose very title made serious enemies in the intelligence establishment. Weldon had also shed light on Able Danger, the Army intelligence unit that had targeted 9/11 conspirators months before the attack only to be thwarted by various bureaucracies.

The Weldon we met, however, was a congenial, grandfatherly fellow who took more pride in his service as a volunteer fireman than he did in fighting the CIA. He had served a couple of terms as a small town mayor and seemed no more regal than that. Nor did the session go as we had anticipated. Not at all. Weldon ushered us into his office at 11 a.m., and he and Russ Caso, his chief intelligence aide, kept us there for more than two hours. In fact, I was the one who broke up the meeting as I had to be back in New Jersey for an extended family gathering.

Wire told a compelling story. His straightforward, no-nonsense account has made a believer out of many a skeptic. I supported his account by showing other witness testimony from *Silenced* and explaining the motivation and the logic of the conspirators. Weldon did not need much convincing. He had been investigating the dark side of the Clinton security apparatus for years, including Berger's woefully under-punished destruction of government documents.

Weldon was well aware of the forces massing against him. And he thought he knew why. He had made it his business to find out what Berger had been seeking in the National Archives and how he had gotten off so lightly. In fact, when we left Weldon, he was on his way to review the Berger evidence. He was the one man in Washington willing and able to put all the pieces together of a scandal that, if pursued, could shake the DC firmament. The very fact that Berger was overseeing a campaign against the man most likely to expose him had the potential to move the political Richter at least a few notches.

The Clintons and their cronies invested a good deal of energy in neutralizing Weldon. During an unusually testy Chris Wallace interview with President Clinton on Fox News in late September 2006, the nation saw just how much energy. "A three-star admiral," Clinton announced out of nowhere, "who was on my National Security Council staff, who also fought terror, by the way, is running for the seat of Curt Weldon in Pennsylvania."[37] He did not even mention Sestak. In fact, he mentioned only two Republicans in the interview: Curt Weldon and President George Bush. A week or so later, Clinton visited Weldon's district to stir up the base.

Popular ten-term congressmen don't go down easily. With three weeks remaining before the election, despite the outsized efforts of the Sestak campaign, Weldon retained a seven-point lead in the polls.

Weldon's enemies, however, had a nasty little ace up their sleeves. Dealing it was Greg Gordon of the Democrat-friendly McClatchy Newspapers' Washington Bureau. Two anonymous sources had allegedly told Gordon that Weldon had "traded his political influence for lucrative lobbying and consulting contracts for his daughter."[38] Two days later, on October 15, the *New York Times*, in a surprisingly lengthy article on the race, confirmed that law enforcement officials "were investigating [Weldon's] role in securing lobbying contracts for his daughter's international public relations firm."[39]

Alleging a need to act quickly because of the leak, the FBI raided the homes of Weldon's daughter and a friend on Monday morning, October 16. Within hours, Democrat protesters were waving "Caught Red-Handed" signs outside Weldon's district office in Upper Darby.[40] The story received a great deal of unreflective attention from a media desperate for a Democrat win. My attempt to educate reporters at the McClatchy papers and the local *Delco Times* fell on willfully deaf ears. The narrative had already been established, and the media saw no need to rework it. On election night, Sestak and his pals had cause to celebrate. He won his district with 56 percent of the vote, and the Democrats retook Congress.

It took a good long while for the local media to wise up. "It was assumed by some at the time that the Justice Department wouldn't have taken the extraordinary steps to conduct such raids if it didn't have substantial evidence of wrongdoing on the part of its targets," editorialized the *Daily Times*, a suburban Philadelphia paper. "And yet, more than three-and-a-half years later, none of those people have been charged with anything."[41] One other casualty was Weldon's aide Russ Caso. Howard Sklamberg, the lead U.S. Attorney in the Weldon case, charged Caso with failing to file the proper disclosure forms on a job held by his wife. Caso pled guilty and accepted two years of probation, which was two more years than Sklamberg, a Democrat, recommended for Sandy Berger when he prosecuted that case.[42]

Weldon was not the first congressman to involve himself with TWA Flight 800. That honor belonged to James Traficant, a maverick Democrat from Ohio. A member of the House Subcommittee on Aviation, Traficant had been a "strong supporter" of Commander William Donaldson's independent investigation into the TWA 800 disaster. Then, said Donaldson, Traficant had a "sudden and severe change of heart."[43] It coincided precisely with a federal plea deal by Traficant's senior political advisor in 1998. "After Mr. O'Nesti's guilty plea," observed Donaldson in a press release, "Mr. Traficant avoided all contact with Commander Donaldson and proactively attacked the Donaldson investigation."[44] This is not to say that Traficant was innocent of the charges that would eventually land him in a prison for seven years, but he came to see, as did Weldon, that justice in Washington is a notoriously subjective affair.

Chapter: **SIXTEEN**

ENGINE TROUBLE

As the years passed, two realities forced their way into the conversations among TWA 800 researchers. One was the futility of attempting to determine, without a high level insider as guide, *exactly* what happened on the night of July 17, 1996—who fired what from where and why. The second was the vanity of expecting that guide to come forward on his own. Few people knew the dynamics of the shoot-down, and with each passing year, the incentives for them to volunteer what they knew diminished.

As I was coming to see, something as mundane as a pension could go a long way in assuring a lifetime of silence. Jim Kallstrom acknowledged as much himself. In criticizing the investigators who testified in the 2013 documentary *TWA Flight 800*, he groused, "They could have been real men and been whistleblowers back then." He attributed their hesitance to "their government pensions."[1] Kallstrom overlooked a few other disincentives, such as Clinton's Executive Order 13039, the removal of several investigators from the Calverton hangar for challenging the FBI, the public humiliation of Pierre Salinger, and the arrest of Terry Stacey and the Sanderses. More problematic still was the failure of the media to offer whistleblowers a safe harbor.

Despite the many reasons not to speak out, from time to time I would hear from lower-level servicemen who claimed to know something. As I was writing this book, in fact, one "Sailor" e-mailed me the following:

> We were using commercial aircrafts as simulation! We were doing this because there was to be absolutely no live missiles! But when Commander Cook* heard that there was a real missile launched, he got on WISKEY [sic] secured channel and started conversing about the live fire! Commander Cook was in charge of the exercise! USS CARR was the Warfare Commander for the exercise! You double-check that because after the deployment he was sent to Warfare College to teach. My leading petty officer, as he was sitting in the Captain's chair in CIC [combat information center], made it so clear that I say nothing of what I saw or heard because the government could ruin me with my social security number and even kill me. And his words were, "so with that being said, pull the RD390 tapes, close all positional log books, including the bridges, tape them and leave them on the DRT table!" They took a few things to a place called the shred room where we destroy documents using salt water and a shredder! When we ran, we ran to Bermuda where we were not allowed to leave the ship, no phone calls, e-mails secured, and nothing was to be discussed! Everyone that was involved was told in CIC, "This didn't happen!"

---

* Name changed.

I did some checking. The USS *Carr* was, in fact, a guided missile frigate. The RD-390 is a multi-channel tape recorder. The named skipper took command five days before the TWA 800 incident. The previous year the ship underwent extensive combat system upgrades which led to "two highly successful dual missile firing exercises" in early 1996. The ship's official history is oddly silent on where the ship operated between April 1996 and November 1996 when it headed for the Mediterranean.[2] Then too, the USS *Carr* fit the description of the ship Lisa Perry and other witnesses had seen earlier on the evening of July 17: a large (453 feet) military fighting ship, battleship gray, a big globe, lots of equipment, ID number on the front. Of note, the skipper did go on to teach at the U.S. Army War College, not unlike the *Vincennes* captain, Will Rogers, who instructed his fellow officers in San Diego before retiring.

In December 2015, at my prompting, "Sailor" contacted Commander Cook through Facebook.[3] After an exchange of pleasantries, Sailor introduced the subject indirectly by sending Cook a link to an Internet article that blamed the destruction of TWA 800 on a military missile.[4] "I am sorry Capt. [Cook] for the direct, but it troubles me! Please forgive me." Replied Cook in the kind of semi-literate shorthand common on Facebook, "No problem. We were no where [sic] around Ny. And the missles [sic] we fire were in the Puerto Rico Opera area." Sailor prodded gently about the possibility of another Navy vessel being involved, and Cook responded, "The Navy proved there no units around and no one fires a missles [sic] without strict area clearance. Rest assured can not be hidden or allowed."

Not wanting to accuse an individual based on an unverifiable source, no matter how well the source's account held up, I have altered the commander's name. Independent researchers have the freedom to pursue stories over time, but we do not have clout. Clout comes with having a major newsroom as back up—the greater the misdeed, the greater the need for it. In its absence, people like this commander feel no pressure to share much of anything.

Short of a confession from one of the participants in the TWA 800 cover-up, my colleagues and I have had to rely on circumstantial evidence, the more visual the better. The holy grail of this pursuit has been the amateur video of the missile, the one around which Nelson DeMille constructed the plot of his bestseller, *Nightfall*. MSNBC probably aired it briefly that first night, and foreign stations showed it after that, but the FBI appears to have seized all available copies.

Videos about the event have proved helpful if for no other reason than that they keep the story alive. Some of these add information. Others unintentionally show the bankruptcy of the government position. In 2005, Pierre-Emmanuel Luneau-Daurignac produced a helpful documentary on TWA Flight 800 for a major French network. In April of that year I went to Paris to meet with Luneau-Daurignac and several other journalists whose interest in the story remained keen. Retired United Airlines captain Ray Lahr was to join us.

In the early morning hours of April 19, Lahr left his Malibu home for a trip to Los Angeles International Airport, and beyond that to Charles De Gaulle. He arrived sleepless on the morning of April 20. Michel Breistroff met him at the airport in his Jaguar. Some ten years prior, then still in his early fifties, Breistroff retired to better follow the career of his son, also named Michel, who starred on the Harvard hockey team and on the French national team. He loved the boy dearly and was devastated when young Michel died aboard TWA 800. Breistroff has been on a mission ever since.

Michel and Ray met me at my hotel. On the surface, Breistroff has everything going for him—looks, wealth, style. That said, the loss of his beloved son has robbed much of the joy from his life. For his part, Ray Lahr, then a few months shy of his eightieth birthday, was a work of nature. With the death of Commander Donaldson nearly five years earlier, he had emerged as the leader of the ongoing dissident investigation into the demise of TWA Flight 800. His good-natured persistence helped pull the various factions together in their collective effort to keep the case alive. Tireless at eighty, Ray and I would walk for hours around Paris later that day.

At lunchtime, we journeyed to the aptly named Cafe des Delices in Paris's sixth arrondissement. There, we met with the French journalists and Luneau-Daurignac. Breistroff, in fact, had appeared in studio on camera after the showing of Luneau-Daurignac's documentary. He seemed neither optimistic, nor pessimistic, merely determined. As helpful as the journalists were, it struck me that if anyone were able to force this case open it would be the family members like Breistroff. On the first anniversary of the crash, he confronted Kallstrom at a ceremony on Long Island. Breistroff impressed Pat Milton as well. She spent three pages of her book on the confrontation.[5] "All that matters to me is knowing the truth," Breistroff reportedly told Kallstrom. "My life is over. I sit in a chair at night and go to bed at two a.m. When I get up in the morning, it is not daylight for me, but only darkness again. I want to trust you, but there are people higher than you that may be pulling strings."

"Michel," Kallstrom replied, "there is no way in hell that if a Navy missile or any other missile shot this plane down it could ever be hidden from me." By this time, Kallstrom was deeply in denial. The Navy had deceived him left and right. He had sanctioned the fraudulent dog training exercise. With his blessing, the FBI and the CIA were far along in the creation of the zoom climb video and the manufacture of the witness interviews needed to pull it off. Kallstrom's seeming sincerity may have swayed Milton, but it did not move Breistroff. To this day, he is confident he was right: people higher than Kallstrom were pulling strings.

Breistroff is not the only family member who has refused to accept the government's unholy spin. Another parent I have gotten to know along the way is Lisa Michelson, the mother of then nineteen-year-old Yon Rojany. On the afternoon of July 17, 1996, Yon arrived at JFK Airport with a ticket for Rome. Basketball coach Larry Brown had seen Yon play in California and encouraged him to try out for the Italian Basketball League. Yon took his advice. When TWA cancelled Flight 841 to Rome, its agents secured him a seat on Flight 800 before Yon had a chance to call his mom. It didn't matter. As soon as Michelson heard of the Flight 800 crash and saw the images of its burning debris, she intuited that Yon had been on board. She called TWA desperately throughout the night and did not learn of Yon's fate for sure until her niece was able to check the passenger manifest in Paris nearly two days after the plane went down. All that Michelson remembers upon hearing the news is falling to the ground and crying. In the months that followed she called the NTSB almost daily. "They did their best to assure me that it was mechanical failure," Lisa told me in 2003. "I am not able to explain to you specifically why I didn't believe them, but I didn't. Too many things I was told just didn't make sense."[6]

A month before the Paris meeting, Lisa, Ray, and I met in a Santa Monica restaurant with a serious Hollywood player interested in producing a movie about TWA 800. Several other producers had approached Sanders and me over the years. In every case, as in this one, someone higher up in the money chain said no. Among those who contacted us were representatives of controversial director Oliver Stone whose would-be TWA 800 project for ABC in 1998 had come to naught. Our dealings with Stone went nowhere as well.

Family members do not get discouraged that easily. Michelson credits her son Eric—and now her grandchildren—with keeping her going through the ordeal. It is not easy for her to talk about the disaster even today. When asked what it is that she hopes to get by keeping the investigation alive, Michelson answers concisely, "the truth." She adds, "The truth is so easy, so simple. To lie is difficult."[7] This is the same answer that Breistroff gives. The same answer that Don Nibert, father of Cheryl from Montoursville, gives. The same answer that Marge Krukar, brother of Andrew, gives. Whenever I think of sloughing off this case, I think of them. I think of them too when I read anew Kallstrom's gripe that people like Lahr, Sanders, and myself have "increased the pain already inflicted on the victims' families."

Said Kallstrom to Breistroff about anyone who might have ordered a cover-up, "I would like nothing better than to expose them. No matter who the cowards were, I would stand up and tell the whole world about it."[8] Within months, Kallstrom would close the FBI case, sell the CIA's duplicitous video to a credulous media, and block all eyewitness testimony at the NTSB hearing that followed. The man apparently has a sterner constitution than the rest of us. On the tenth anniversary of the crash in July 2006, Michelson got in Kallstrom's face at the memorial service on Long Island. "I can't believe you're still sticking to this story," she said to him. "How can you lie to people's faces?" He dropped his head and said nothing.

The evening of the tenth anniversary, CNN aired its own documentary on the crash called *No Survivors: Why TWA 800 Could Happen Again.*[9] One detail stood out in this otherwise orthodox rehashing of the government position: the treatment of the notorious zoom climb. In CNN's recreation, a noseless aircraft flew not straight up but straight ahead, trending downward. "Only twelve minutes after take off," the CNN narrator claimed, "the center fuel tank blast rips away the bottom of the plane. The cockpit and nose section plunge into the sea. For another half minute or so, the decapitated plane flies on. Then, it loses momentum and begins its deadly drop toward the ocean below."

Incredibly, the zoom climb had *fully* disappeared. Lahr had spent the previous three years battling the CIA and the NTSB to secure the calculations used to determine the crippled plane's vertical climb, and now CNN, with the NTSB's blessing, was telling Lahr there was no zoom climb in the first place. Without it, CNN had to imagine some other optical illusion powerful enough to confuse the witnesses into thinking down was up. "Investigators believe the red lights seen by eyewitnesses could have been an intense fire immediately after the fuel tank erupted," the narrator continued, now beginning to embarrass the network with sheer disinformation.

Among the many nuggets buried in the CIA document cache was one that astonished even the cynics among us: the CIA analysts knew there was no zoom climb and had known this as early as March 1999. In a memo from March 24 of that year an unnamed analyst more or less owned up to the con. The "maximum CIA calculated altitude in the final study was about 14,500 feet," he conceded. He added that the noseless plane's maximum angle of attack was "about 35 degrees," not the seventy or so degrees shown in the video. "This high angle suggests the likelihood that engine compressor stall would occur." From the beginning this is what aviation professionals said would happen when the nose was severed; the remainder of the plane would pitch up, stall, and fall.

This was what the best witnesses reported seeing. The CIA acknowledged this more than a year before the NTSB's final hearing but apparently did not share the news with the NTSB and certainly did not inform the media.[10]

Two months after the debut of CNN's *No Survivors*, Lahr and his Washington-based attorney John Clarke received some judicial good news. In fact, the *National Law Journal* deemed the news unusual enough to capsulize the story on its front page as, "A rare win in fight for TWA crash records."[11] The story related how federal judge Howard Matz found Lahr's evidence "sufficient to permit Plaintiff to proceed based on his claim that the government acted improperly in its investigation of Flight 800 or at least performed in a grossly negligent fashion." Arguing that the "public interest" was at stake in Lahr's pursuit of the truth, Matz allowed him access to seven of the twelve CIA documents he had requested.

In August 2007, a Lahr FOIA suit resulted in an unexpected harvest. A document the FBI sent to him and Clarke detailed a communication that took place six days after the crash. It read as follows: "On Tuesday, July 23, 1996, a representative from the Defense Intelligence Agency (DIA) advised [the FBI] that after a visual analysis of both the videotape as well as a number of still photographs taken from various portions of the tape, the phenomenon captured by [name redacted] appeared to be consistent with the exhaust plume from a MANPAD [Man-portable air-defense] missile."[12]

The video discussed in the FBI document was shot on July 12, 1996, five days *before* the crash. This was not news. Lahr had received a heavily redacted document earlier that told the story of how a fellow and his friend on Long Island were attempting to videotape the sunrise when they saw and recorded "a grey trail of smoke ascending from the horizon at an angle of approximately 75 [degrees]." So compelling was the sight that the fellow made a comment to his friend, heard on the tape, "They must be testing a rocket." Pat Milton discussed the video in her book.

What Milton did not discuss and what the redacted memo did not show was the DIA's involvement. This unredacted version revealed that the FBI took the video seriously enough to bring in the DIA for further analysis, and the DIA found the video image to be consistent with the exhaust plume from a missile. For the record, the DIA is a Department of Defense combat support agency and a serious player in the United States intelligence community. An important component of the DIA is the Missile and Space Intelligence Center (MSIC), an Alabama-based operation charged with gathering intelligence on enemy surface-to-air missiles and short-range ballistic missiles. During a Senate inquiry in May 1999, the FBI's number two man on the investigation, Lewis Schiliro, conceded that MSIC analysts had arrived on the scene in Long Island just two days after the July 17, 1996 crash of TWA Flight 800 and interviewed eyewitnesses along with the FBI.[13]

In September 2007, a month after Lahr received his unexpected surprise in the mail, I got a surprise of my own. A producer at Fox News had a video he thought I should see. I stopped by when I was in New York and picked it up. Wary of being involved at all, the producer would not tell me how he obtained it. Ideally, Fox News would have covered the story that this video generated, but there were forces at work at Fox, just as there were at ABC, that kept the network from exploring the TWA 800 story in any meaningful way.

I did not know exactly what those forces were, but I saw them at work just two months prior. Another Fox staffer enlisted me to be a guest on a segment she was producing for *Hannity's America*. At her request I sent a copy of *Silenced*. As I was doing research in California at time on another book project, she arranged to do a remote interview with me in a San Francisco studio. The interview lasted twenty minutes, and she gave the impression she actually watched *Silenced* and took it seriously. Her questions were intelligent. Unfortunately, the produced segment was not. The give-away came quickly. My on-screen identifier was "conspiracy theorist," never a good sign.

Standing in for the FBI was Pat Milton. In a fair fight, I would have KO'ed Milton in the first round, but I never got a shot. The producer crunched my twenty minutes of interview time down to twenty seconds of TV time. In those twenty seconds, I tried to summarize the eyewitnesses accounts, but it was not time enough to dissuade Sean Hannity from presenting the rehashed misinformation the producer put on the teleprompter. A year after CNN fully flattened out the CIA zoom climb, Fox News resurrected it in all its Orwellian subtlety. Ill-served by his producer, Hannity stated matter-of-factly that what the eyewitnesses actually saw was "really just the aftermath of the explosion," and that was that.[14]

If my producer friend gave me this new infrared video to atone for his network's timidity, he succeeded. The video had been shot immediately after the crash from the U.S. Navy P-3 Orion. There was no mistaking the perspective as the camera occasionally tilted down past the plane's propellers to the smoldering wreckage below. Apparently, a copy had surfaced years earlier as a result of a Freedom of Information Act request. At the time, it did not cause much of a stir. The video simply showed the main debris field, and there was nothing controversial about it. The video more or less confirmed the wreckage pattern as later diagramed. The NTSB witness group, which the FBI thwarted at every opportunity, may well have seen the same edited version. In its 1997 Factual Report, the witness group acknowledged receipt of the video but claimed it "provided no additional information pertinent to the investigation."[15] No future NTSB or FBI report mentioned the video.

The unedited video I received showed something the earlier video obviously had not. Although the videographer focused on the main debris field, he did not stay with it. Five different times he panned the camera off to the northwest, perhaps a mile or two, and there he fixed on a fully separate burning object, one capable of sending great plumes of smoke into the sky. In no subsequent government report was there any mention, let alone clarification, of what that object might have been. A single engine on a 747 of this vintage had a lot of fuel to burn. By weight, it was about twenty times larger than the engine of your average automobile.

When I first told James Sanders of the video, I said the smoking wreckage was northeast of the major debris field. "Hmmm," Sanders responded, "I thought it would have been northwest." He was right. I misspoke. I meant to say northwest, back towards JFK. Sanders was on to something. He was convinced a missile warhead explosion, likely external to the plane, blasted the No. 3 engine off the right wing. This was where the explosive traces were found both on the wing and in the adjoining section of fuselage. We now had a literal smoking gun. (For those who might wish to see the video, it is available online at WND. com embedded in the article, "Stunning New Video of 800 Crash Site" from October 15, 2007.)

If this were an engine, as it certainly appeared to be, the NTSB had refused to acknowledge the same. The NTSB had divided the wreckage into three zones depending on where the various pieces fell. In the red zone, the one closest to JFK, were the seats and overhead bins from rows seventeen through nineteen where the plane first ruptured. These were the same rows on which the mysterious reddish-orange residue was found. In that same zone too were the bodies of the people who had been in those seats, many of them mutilated by the force of the explosion but not burned. In the yellow zone was the forward section of the plane, including the cockpit, first class, and business sections. This part was severed by the blast and plunged relatively intact into the sea.

The final NTSB report from August 2000 put all four engines in the so-called green zone, the swath of the debris field *farthest* from JFK.[16] This was the zone that included the headless two-thirds of the fuselage that sputtered on for some distance before erupting in the fireball that almost all the witnesses observed. According to the NTSB, the green zone wreckage included both wings, the main landing gear, the tail section, the bulk of the center fuel tank, and "all four engines."

The P-3 video, however, showed what appeared to be a smoking engine a mile or more northwest of this zone. Sanders had good reason to suspect it was the No. 3 engine. Early in his investigation, he had secured a copy of a local CBS news broadcast in which the announcer said, "On Monday, the fourth and final engine was located along with small pieces of wreckage found nearest Kennedy Airport, pieces that fell from the plane first."[17] TWA's Terry Stacey had shared with Sanders an early map of the debris field, and that placed only three engines in the green zone—1, 2, and 4. The calculated movement of items between zones alarmed Stacey early on, but retagging engines went well beyond tidying up the data. Then too there was the testimony of Witness 648, a fisherman, who was closer to the crash site than any other. He watched as "the right wing separated from the fuselage." As his FBI 302 documents, "He did not see any engine pods on it."[18]

This wayward engine proved problematic for the NTSB from the beginning. The *Times* matter-of-factly reported fact that the fourth engine was not recovered until August 15, four weeks after the crash and nine days after local CBS news reported it found. Less important than the timing of the find was the location. The local report placed it "nearest Kennedy Airport" as the P-3 video suggested. The *Times* failed to acknowledge anything unusual about the engine's location or its condition. "Some turbine blades were missing," rationalized the *Times*, "but the damage may have been caused by the impact."[19]

The following day the NTSB's Robert Francis assured the public there was "nothing really extraordinary" about any of the engines, the last of which had been taken apart in "an unusually quick" process. The fact that some unnamed "officials" had claimed that the "No. 3 engine" showed "foreign object damage" was not to be taken seriously. That alleged foreign object, Francis insisted, was "part of the engine itself."[20] The *Times* reporting, however, left unclear whether the last engine found was, in fact, the No. 3 engine. Sanders believes it was. He is convinced that the location of the engine was so damaging to the developing government case for a spontaneous fuel tank explosion that the FBI and/or NTSB had to corrupt the debris field charts by eventually placing the recovered engine in the same zone as the others. He submitted a FOIA request to review the salvage documents from this period, a request the FBI has not yet fulfilled.

In addition to Stacey, several other investigators at Calverton complained about the retagging of parts. The most outspoken was the NTSB's Hank Hughes. Chief among the accused was the NTSB's ubiquitous David Mayer. "During the investigation, I personally witnessed Dr. Mayer changing wreckage recovery tags on interior wreckage components without proper authority," said Hughes in a sworn affidavit. "Mayer's changes falsified the factual record of the actual physical locations from which those components were recovered." When Hughes asked Mayer why he was retagging items, he reportedly answered, "I didn't want to confuse the Chairman," meaning NTSB chairman Jim Hall.[21]

Mayer was not the only one monkeying with the evidence. In one of the several meetings held to undo Mayer's mess, investigators working through the International Association of Machinists and Aerospace Workers (IAMAW) learned that Paul Harkins, the Navy's supervisor of salvage, tagged more than one hundred pieces of wreckage without authorization or documentation.[22] The actions of Mayer and Harkins, together with "the FBI's altering, tainting and removing evidence," said Hughes, "acted to undermine the investigation."[23]

Worse, the NTSB brass kept the other parties to the investigation in the dark about the way Mayer had rigged the tag database. In fact, they were reluctant to discuss anything controversial. When he started voicing his dissent prior to the NTSB hearing in August 2000, the IAMAW's Rocky Miller learned that silence was the approved policy. "If you believe in corporate memory," the NTSB's investigator in charge, Al Dickinson, told him, "you won't ask any questions or speak at the public hearing."[24]

The video of smoking wreckage observed from the P-3 should have been enough to reopen the investigation. If nothing else, the NTSB needed to explain why its officials had failed to even mention the source of that smoke plume in any of their public hearings. To prod them into action, I met with one of the *New York Times* reporters who covered the crash and gave him a copy of the video. That he was willing to meet with me testified to his open-mindedness, but nothing came of the meeting. If Fox News was not willing to touch this story, I had no reason to believe the *Times* would, and my suspicions were, as usual, confirmed.

The mid-air break-up of Iranian Airbus 655 had the potential to explain the location of the stray TWA 800 engine. As it happened, some crewmen on the bridge of the USS *Montgomery* near the *Vincennes* watched as a Navy standard missile destroyed this aircraft. There was nothing theoretical about their observations. They saw the first missile explode at or near the left wing of the plane and watched in awe as a section of the wing "with an engine pod still attached" fell to the sea.[25] Although the Navy did not have the opportunity to assess IR 655's debris field in any detail, this engine would have fallen into the zone closest to the airliner's point of departure, much the way the smoking TWA 800 engine appeared to. Not surprisingly, the NTSB and FBI made no reference in any of their reports to the *Vincennes* incident. By journeying to Little Rock in 1992, Admiral Crowe helped assure that the saga of the IR 655 would never be fully told. Jamie Gorelick and Sandy Berger had a harder task. They had to assure that the true story of TWA 800 would never be told at all.

Chapter: SEVENTEEN

BENGHAZI MOMENT

I n early December 1997, two weeks after closing its investigation, the FBI sent a letter to NTSB chairman James Hall telling him its conditions for the upcoming public hearing on TWA Flight 800, the first to be held by the NTSB. Incredibly, these included: "no public discussion or publication of the interviews conducted with witnesses to the crash, no presentation of the video simulation of the crash created for the F.B.I. by the Central Intelligence Agency, and no reference to the search for residue of explosives on the wreckage."[1] Although these exclusions essentially negated any real value the hearings might have had, the *New York Times* reported them deep in an article on a potential Boeing redesign as matter-of-factly as they reported the hearing's date and location.

If the media took no notice of the FBI's power play, Tom Stalcup did. Then working on his Ph.D. in physics at Florida State, Stalcup intuited what was going on. The CIA video troubled him when he watched it two weeks prior, but now the authorities were removing from the discussion any evidence that might challenge that video and the thesis it represented. Working through their fixers, the Clintons reminded the media that only the paranoid would question official orthodoxy. Officials working the TWA 800 case would call Stalcup a conspiracy theorist and worse, but from that first NTSB hearing on, they faced no more relentless a critic than this young physicist.

I first met Stalcup in the spring of 2001. On his own dime, he came to Kansas City to lend his testimony to our documentary *Silenced*. Tall and reserved with a shock of dark hair, Stalcup observed the TWA 800 misdirection through a scientist's eyes. Given the data and his own knowledge base, the CIA video struck him as an affront to the laws of physics, and he was fully capable of explaining why. Although he would go on to launch his own IT company, Stalcup never gave up on TWA 800. More than fifteen years after the crash, he collaborated with former CBS producer Kristina Borjesson on a documentary so compelling even the *New York Times* had to concede it was *not* "crackpot conspiracy theory stuff."[2]

Called simply *TWA Flight 800* and ably directed by Borjesson, the documentary circulated around Washington before its Epix network premiere on July 17, 2013, the seventeenth anniversary of the crash. Most impressively, Stalcup and Borjesson persuaded a half-dozen highly credible whistleblowers from within the investigation to tell their stories on camera. These included (all affiliations circa 1996) the NTSB's Hank Hughes, Bob Young from TWA, ALPA investigator Jim Speer, Suffolk County chief medical examiner Charles Wetli, U.S. Army forensic pathologist Colonel Dennis Shanahan, and Rocky Miller, investigation coordinator for the IAMAW. The producers supplemented the whistleblower testimony with that of numerous family members, witnesses, and experts like Ray Lahr, former NTSB Board member Vernon Grose, EGIS developer David Fine, FBI bomb analyst Bob Heckman, and FBI lab whistleblower Frederic Whitehurst. Many of these people came together to form a group Stalcup called the "TWA 800 project."

Stalcup and Borjesson walked viewers through the complete spectrum of evidence. As they made clear, *all* evidence—witness accounts, explosive residue, splatter patterns, radar data, debris field maps—pointed to a missile attack on the aircraft. Ever the physicist, Stalcup described the radar data as the crash's "smoking gun." He referred here not to the air traffic controller data suggesting a missile strike but a ballistics analysis of the radar immediately post-crash. Stalcup argued that the radar evidence showed the debris exiting the side of a plane at a high velocity, Mach 4 or greater. The NTSB, however, contended that a low-velocity, forward-moving, fuel-air explosion in the fuel wing tank caused the plane to blow apart. If true, this would have been a first. Since the introduction of Jet-A fuel in 1965, no commercial aircraft had ever spontaneously exploded.

The documentary made a more dramatic impact when it discussed the effects of a high-speed explosion on the passengers. Indeed, the producers could have made a second, more gruesome documentary using the evidence gathered by the two pathologists, Wetli and Shanahan. As they and Hughes testified, the force of the blast shattered bodies and sent bone shards flying through the cabin. At least one shard pierced the fuselage like an arrowhead. The image of this was chilling. A low-velocity, fuel-air explosion would have burned the passengers in their seats, but it would not have mutilated them. Said Hughes, "The damage to the seats and the injury to the passengers was random which in my mind indicate a high ordinance detonation not a low speed explosion like a center fuel tank blowing up." When asked where the explosion originated, Hughes answered without hesitation, "external to the aircraft."[3] The strength of the documentary was the human element, especially the testimony of the whistleblowers. They were too numerous and too knowledgeable to ignore. The eyewitnesses added to the video's emotional power.

In addition to those featured in *Silenced*, Stalcup spoke with several who had not previously gone public, including Greek pilot Vassilis Bakounis, who was interviewed in Cyprus. A veteran Olympic Airlines pilot, Bakounis was in the U.S. in 1996 working on his commercial pilot's license. On the night of July 17 he was flying along the south shore of Long Island at about two thousand feet when he saw "a light coming out of the sea." It caught Bakounis's attention. "I followed that light for many seconds before it makes, kind of veers to the right,"[4] said Bakounis using his hands to illustrate the turn. The gesture, in fact, looked like an upside down Nike swoosh. "Then I see an explosion," Bakounis continued, "then its flame was falling down like an umbrella of flames." Bakounis elaborated that the streak of light started "very, very low" and then "climbed past his altitude." The FBI ignored Bakounis. This was not easy to do. Several witnesses reported seeing his plane. He gave an interview to a Greek publication five weeks after the crash. Independent researchers, including one that the FBI was monitoring, translated the interview and put it on their web sites. No matter. The CIA disregarded Bakounis's testimony as well.

Stalcup and Borjesson did a much better job than the CIA or NTSB in aligning witness testimony with the location of TWA 800 at the time of its destruction. Their animation of the disaster tracked three missiles, each exploding in close proximity to the doomed airliner. Politically savvy, the producers avoided saying who fired those missiles or why the authorities undermined the investigation. The informed viewer, however, had to suspect the one navy capable of a missile strike this sophisticated and so close to shore.

In June 2013, a month before the scheduled airing of the video on the crash's seventeenth anniversary, Stalcup and his colleagues petitioned the NTSB to reopen the investigation. They had some high level supporters. One was Vernon Grose. Over the years, Grose had been CNN's go-to guy on aviation safety. He had done more than 170 media interviews on TWA 800 alone. "I am convinced by the evidence that a missile—not the center wing tank explosion—brought it down," said Grose. "It's time to take a fresh look at all the evidence, much of which was withheld by the FBI."[5]

Given the quality of the documentary, the guardians of the TWA 800 orthodoxy knew they had a problem on hand and sent their fixers out to resolve it. These included Peter Goelz and Jim Kallstrom. Soon after the petition was filed both veteran spinmeisters appeared on national TV to reassert the official narrative. Predictably, the pair dismissed their critics in the crudest of absolutes. When CNN's Jake Tapper asked Goelz about Stalcup's argument, Goelz answered, "There is no evidence whatsoever that supports his theory."[6] The next day on Fox News, Kallstrom told Bill Hemmer that the documentary's thesis was "preposterous, pure fiction."[7] Casual viewers had no reason to disbelieve either of them.

The very nearly identical riffs by Goelz and Kallstrom strongly suggest one unseen hand prodding them both. When Tapper raised the issue of the eyewitness testimony, Goelz said, "Almost all of the witnesses say this: 'I heard a sound. I looked up and then I saw a streak of light or firework and an explosion.'" When Hemmer asked about the witnesses, Kallstrom also claimed, "The vast majority of those people looked up when they heard the bang." Kallstrom added, "The plane had already exploded, and [the witnesses] were seeing the plane falling apart." Goelz spun the same yarn. According to him, the witnesses saw only "the last six seconds" of the forty-plus second break-up of the aircraft. "No witness saw the first event forty seconds prior to that," he insisted.

Were I to chart a TWA 800 hierarchy of lies, this orchestrated bunkum would rank near the top. As mentioned earlier, the FBI did not even bother to ask seven of the forty best witnesses about sound. Another nineteen told the FBI they heard nothing at all. In only fourteen of the forty summaries did a witness admit to hearing a sound, and in only three of those did that person report hearing a sound before looking up. In fact, these forty witnesses saw all or most of the entire sequence. That sequence began, as Bakounis affirmed, with "a light coming out of the sea" and ended nearly a minute later with the shattered plane "falling down like an umbrella of flames."

More curious still, before July 2013 the FBI had not endorsed the CIA's bogus sound propagation analysis, nor had the NTSB. The FBI's final summary made no reference to sound. At the final NTSB hearing in August 2000, David Mayer all but rejected the CIA thesis, telling chairman Jim Hall, "Our [witness] analysis is not based on sound." It seems likely that Goelz and Kallstrom resorted to this argument for the same reason the CIA had: it sounded scientific. With it, they could intimidate their interrogators. Kallstrom, in fact, made a caustic remark about the "basic physics" of the crash in setting up his thesis. Try as they might, Tapper or Hemmer were in no position to contradict such authoritative sources, certainly not in the three to five minutes a typical TV segment runs.

Two days after Kallstrom's appearance, I was beamed in from a Kansas City TV studio to talk about the documentary on CNN's *New Day* with Alison Kosik.[8] For balance, CNN enlisted Jim Polk, a "Pulitzer Prize–winning journalist" who had contributed to CNN's 2006 special report on TWA 800. Kosik set up this segment by claiming with much more confidence than the NTSB ever had that "a spark from faulty wiring" caused the plane's center fuel tank to explode. To reinforce the point, she played an interview from the 2006 report with Eastwind pilot David McClaine. "I didn't see any missile at all," said McClaine who had seen the crash from above. In a feint at fairness, Polk told Kosik in studio, "There was a helicopter pilot who says he did see a missile before the explosion." And that was it for the witnesses.

"Jack," asked Kosik, "what do you think happened if it wasn't an internal explosion like [McClaine and his co-pilot] saw?" I might have answered that one of the great scandals of the investigation was that it took nearly three years for the NTSB to interview McClaine and that when its investigators finally did, McClaine demolished the CIA's zoom climb theory. McClaine also told the NTSB he was not necessarily in position to see a missile: "The fuselage and the wing could have blocked that out."

Time being precious, I took another tack. "Well, unlike what Jim says, there were two hundred seventy eyewitnesses to a missile strike," I said, relying here on the FBI count. "Ninety-six of them, this is FBI eyewitnesses, saw it from the horizon ascend all the way up to the plane." Using hand gestures to make my point, I continued, "They all described it the same way: that it was a red tip, a plume trail after it, gray, and then it gets near the plane and it arcs over, zigzags, hits the plane, blows up."

I then explained how the FBI recruited the CIA to create the zoom climb animation that discredited the eyewitnesses. "When the CNN did its animation ten years later—ten years after the crash, they eliminated that zoom climb altogether," I said. "So I ask Jim [Polk] this, why did you eliminate the zoom climb if the CIA—and what was the CIA doing involved in this in the first place?—if the CIA used that to expressly discredit the eyewitnesses?"

This was not a question Polk wanted to hear. "I would agree with you the CIA animation is controversial," said Polk with an eye on the 2013 understatement-of-the-year award. "We did not make [TWA 800] climb in our animation because, frankly, the transponder disappeared on the radar at the time of the explosion. So there's no altitude readout on the rest of the flight and so there's no supporting evidence for the CIA's animation."

No supporting evidence for the CIA's animation? As Polk must have suspected, *all* evidence—starting with McClaine's testimony—showed the zoom climb to be an intentional fraud. As mentioned earlier, even the CIA conceded privately that the 747 could not climb a few hundred feet let alone a few thousand. "It all ended right there," said McClaine of the blast. "And everything went down." Polk had access to McClaine's NTSB testimony but since it did not fit into the approved storyline he simply ignored it. He should not have. The eyewitnesses saw something ascend for as many as thirty seconds. If that something was not a flaming TWA 800, it was surely a missile. Polk and CNN had done enough research to tell the great, untold story of our time, but they apparently lacked the courage to tell it.

After the commercial break, Kosik asked me with a hint of condescension, "if there was an external blast, who shot [TWA 800] down, why would anybody shoot it down, and why would there be this cover up?" Not perfectly sure who shot the plane down, and having only a minute or so to speak, I focused on a subject I knew well. "Let me address the cover-up," I answered. "Five weeks after the crash, the *New York Times* had this headline above the fold right: Prime Evidence that Explosive Device Found in or Destroyed TWA Flight 800. That's a paraphrase, but it's close." The actual headline was this: "Prime Evidence Found That Device Exploded in Cabin of Flight 800." This article ran on August 23, 1996. According to the *Times*, only the FBI's uncertainty about whether the device was a bomb or a missile kept Kallstrom from declaring TWA 800's destruction a crime.

"Above the fold left," I continued, "was 'Clinton Signs Welfare Reform Bill on Eve of Democratic National Convention.' One of those headlines had to go." I pantomimed dropping the right headline from the screen. "This was Bill Clinton's Benghazi moment," I added. "They [the Clintons] just wanted to kick this can down the road until after November so it would not affect the outcome of the election."

The answer was that simple and that obvious. In June 2013 everyone who followed the news knew what I meant by "Benghazi moment." Bill and Hillary Clinton had no more noble a goal in July 1996 than Hillary and Barack Obama had in September 2012 when they lied about Benghazi. In each case, that goal was to get beyond the November elections by whatever means necessary.

Like Obama, the Clintons would not have shared their motives with anyone beyond their most intimate circle, Sandy Berger, say, and maybe Jamie Gorelick and Robert Francis. Political people like Tenet, Panetta, Goelz, and Clarke were savvy enough not to ask too many questions. As to the military officers involved, their Christmas came in July 1996 with an unexpected CYA authorization from the White House. They did not need to know any more than that. More difficult to explain were the actions of Kallstrom, Mayer, Hall, Loeb, Dickinson, and a few other non-political people who obstructed the investigation but had nothing obvious to gain by doing so. Stalcup leaned particularly hard on Mayer whom he fairly accused of "corruption, malfeasance, and possible illegal activity."

Here, I speculate, but the message these actors received, the one that Gorelick would have first articulated at the August 1996 meeting with Kallstrom in Washington, might have gone something like this: "An enemy aircraft attacked TWA 800. As of now, we don't know which enemy. We may never know. The Navy attempted to shoot down the aircraft but failed. If we alert the American people, they will demand retaliation, and that may lead us into a war we don't want and don't need. They will also hesitate to fly, and that could cripple the economy. For reasons of national security, we need your help to put this incident to bed." At the 9/11 hearings, Berger and Clarke elevated the White House's near paralysis to a virtue.

On September 11, 2012, I doubt if Hillary shared the TWA 800 playbook with Obama, but she followed the script, and he followed her lead. Their political futures, at least at this moment, tracked together. That endless night Obama avoided the White House Situation Room much as the Clintons had on the night of July 17, 1996. Where exactly Obama holed up has never been revealed, but spokesman Jay Carney did acknowledge he was in touch with Hillary: "He spoke with the secretary of state at approximately 10 p.m.," said Carney. "He called her to get an update on the situation."[9]

About that same time Hillary released a statement blaming "inflammatory material posted on the Internet" for the attack on the Benghazi consulate. She was referring specifically to the absurd trailer for the would-be film, *The Innocence of Muslims*. Said the secretary piously, she who gave a standing ovation to *The Book of Mormon* on Broadway, "The United States deplores any intentional effort to denigrate the religious beliefs of others. Our commitment to religious tolerance goes back to the very beginning of our nation."[10] Hillary was not confused. She was lying. Shortly after the sending the press release, she informed the president of Egypt. "We know that the attack in Libya had nothing to do with the film. It was a planned attack, not a protest." Later that night, in an e-mail to daughter Chelsea, she pinned the attack on an "Al Qaeda-like group."[11] Her fingerprints were all over the blame-the-video strategy, however, and Obama made sure the media knew it.

That strategy almost came undone five weeks later at a CNN presidential debate famously "moderated" by Candy Crowley.[12] At the pivotal moment in this town hall style debate, Crowley bypassed the audience and asked Obama a question of her own. Obama looked much too well prepared for it. Walking confidently towards Crowley as she asked,

"Does the buck stop with the secretary of state?" Obama had his answer ready. "Secretary Clinton has done an extraordinary job, but she works for me," he said. "I'm the president, and I'm always responsible."

Obama vigorously defended not only his administration's response to the Benghazi crisis but also his own comments in the Rose Garden the day after the attack. "I told the American people and the world that we were going to find out exactly what happened, that this was an act of terror, and I also said we are going to hunt down those who committed this crime," said the president.

This was more than Romney could endure. He knew well that Obama had endorsed Hillary's video fraud in his Rose Garden speech. "While the United States rejects efforts to denigrate the religious beliefs of others," said Obama, "we must all unequivocally oppose the kind of senseless violence that took the lives of these public servants."[13] Like Hillary, he strongly implied that four Americans were killed in a spontaneous outburst devoid of strategy and provoked by the offending video. There was no other way to have interpreted this comment.

"You said in the Rose Garden the day after the attack it was an act of terror? It was not a spontaneous demonstration, is that what you are saying," Romney pressed Obama, telling Crowley he just wanted to get Obama's response on record. After a moment's hesitation, Obama shouted out, "Get the transcript," and the camera panned to Crowley waving a piece of paper. "He did in fact, sir, call…" said Crowley hesitantly to Romney, "so let me call it an act of terror." Obama jumped back in, "Can you say that a little louder, Candy." She obliged, "He did call it an act of terror." So saying, Crowley and CNN preserved the political future of both Barack Obama and Hillary Clinton.

I hesitate to equate what CNN did to me with what the network did to Romney, but the impulse, I suspect, was much the same. Someone at CNN apparently did not like my Benghazi remark. When CNN released the transcript of the show the next day, it jumped from Polk's final comment to Kosik awkwardly saying, "Well, the good thing is—I have to cut you guys off. But the good thing is that there's a documentary about this." I promptly wrote an article for *American Thinker* titled "CNN

Edits Out Comparison of TWA 800 and Benghazi."[14] CNN apparently caught just enough flak to reinsert the missing section. This allowed me to write a follow-up article titled, "What CNN Cut Out of TWA 800 Interview."[15]

On at least one occasion CNN got the TWA 800 story right, even if by accident. Kudos of sorts goes to CNN host Anderson Cooper. On July 17, 2014, Malaysia Airlines Flight 17 was shot down over the Ukraine by a surface-to-air-missile, likely by pro-Russian insurgents and almost assuredly by accident.[16] In discussing the tragedy that evening, Cooper referred back to "July 17, 1996, when TWA Flight 800 was *shot down* off the coast of Long Island in New York [emphasis added]."[17] Cooper had TWA 800 on the brain. He served as host of a CNN special report on the subject, *Witnessed: The Crash of TWA Flight 800*, that would air two days later.[18] Bizarrely, CNN's *Witnessed* split the difference between the CIA's 3,500-foot zoom climb and the perfectly flat trajectory of CNN's *No Survivors*, the 2006 report Jim Polk and I discussed a year earlier. On air, former NTSB Board member John Goglia claimed that TWA 800 "rose and continue[d] to fly for a few thousand feet more ending up in the 16,000 foot range." In the *Witnessed* animation, borrowed from the NTSB, the viewer saw Flight 800 ascend for about 2000 feet in great sweeping loops, then nose over and fall more or less straight down.

To further confuse its viewers, *Witnessed* featured Eastwind pilot Captain David McClaine returning to make the case he had been making from day one. At the moment of the explosion, "[TWA 800] went down, not up," said McClaine. "The wings fell right off the airplane right away. So how is it going to climb, or what if it had no wings?" Never did CNN try to reconcile the CIA's 3500-foot zoom climb with the NTSB's 2000-foot corkscrew or with the flat trajectory of its own creation, let alone with McClaine's eyewitness account.

Although Cooper had told the truth about TWA 800, media watchers knew it had to have been a slip, Freudian or otherwise. To no one's surprise, he confessed his apparent error before the show ended. "I just want to correct something I said regarding the plane crash, earlier I said that today was the anniversary of flight TWA 800, crashing off the coast of Long Island in 1996," Cooper regretted. "I believe I said that it was shot down. Obviously the government said it was a center fuel tank explosion. Although some people indicated they saw a rocket, there was no evidence of that. It was ruled to be a center fuel tank explosion. So I apologize for misspeaking about that anniversary."[19] No evidence? At least not at CNN.

Chapter: EIGHTEEN

PROCRUSTES

Tom Stalcup was not easily put off. Recognizing this, the authorities continued to chip away at his credibility with all the means at their disposal. One was the carcass of TWA 800, then and now on display at the NTSB Training Center in Virginia. Nothing said, "no stone unturned" quite like a painfully reconstructed aircraft. On July 2, 2013, the NTSB staged a media briefing with the plane as prop. Despite her stellar media credentials and her obvious interest in the crash, the NTSB would not allow Kristina Borjesson to attend. In fact, no members of the TWA 800 Project team were invited, not even the relatives of the victims. The only family members invited were those the NTSB could count on to stick to the script. And stick they did. In its account of the briefing, Reuters gave one of those selected family members the final word, "I was convinced by the NTSB findings when the report came out," he said.

"Hearing talk of a movie coming out and reigniting conspiracy theories that we as family members heard about years ago is opening up old wounds."[1]

Stalcup did not give up easily. Two weeks after the briefing, he sent NTSB Chairwoman Deborah Hersman a formal request asking her to correct the misinformation presented at the July 2 briefing as well as the spin from Jim Kallstrom and Peter Goelz. In September of that year Stalcup sent another letter to Hersman detailing David Mayer's perfidy. In that same communication he sent three separate animations showing the discrepancy between the FAA radar evidence and the imagined debris trajectory plotted by the NTSB. In January 2014, Stalcup, Hughes, Young, and eyewitness Joseph Delgado journeyed to the NTSB's Washington offices. The brass sent a few flak catchers down to meet them. No one assigned to review the TWA 800 Project's petition attended the meeting. Later that month, Stalcup sent a follow-up letter summarizing the meeting. He dropped in one little nugget culled from his FOIA requests: an acknowledgement by former CIA Director George Tenet that Mayer "worked closely" with the lead CIA analyst responsible for the zoom climb animation.

Stalcup persisted, and the NTSB continued to stonewall. He requested a presentation by the TWA 800 Project team before the full NTSB Board, which proposal the NTSB general counsel soon rejected. That same month, March 2014, more than twenty family members asked the NTSB to reconsider. Three months later, in June 2014, the board formally denied the family members' request. Once that request was denied, Stalcup and Hughes wrote what they called an "open letter of protest" to the board's general counsel.[2] Attaching an affidavit from Hughes, they hammered home the conflict of interest implicit in having Mayer's subordinates review a petition accusing Mayer of "malfeasance."

On July 2, 2014, a week after Stalcup's open letter, the NTSB coldly rejected his team's request for a re-opening of the investigation. "None of the physical evidence supports the theory that the streak of light observed by some witnesses was a missile," read the one-page release. "The NTSB determined that an explosion of the center wing fuel tank was the probable cause of the accident."[3] The NTSB case was even weaker than the word "probable" suggests. Its experts spent four years desperately trying to find the cause of the explosion other than the obvious, and the best its expert could conclude was that "the source of the ignition for the explosion could not be determined with certainty."[4] An expert on wiring, former NTSB board member Vernon Grose insisted: "There could not be an [internal] ignition source." If there were, he added, the authorities would have grounded 747s—starting with Air Force One—and demanded changes. They did not.[5] In contrast to the NTSB TWA 800 investigation, the Dutch Safety Board took only a year to conclude definitively that the "detonation of a warhead" above the left hand side of MH 17's cockpit destroyed the plane.[6]

"Probable," however, was win enough to inspire Peter Goelz's Twitter equivalent of an end zone dance. "For those involved," he tweeted, "#TWA800 was a tragedy of infinite pain. Shame on the conspiracists who made it a topic of self aggrandizement and gain."[7] The TWA 800 Project tweeted back, "Sir, please explain this 'gain.' The filmmakers lost a huge amount of money making this film." Goelz's line of attack was a common one. Over the years, scores of critics have insisted I was into TWA 800 "only for the money." Let me assure past and future critics that if money were my motivator I would have stayed in advertising.

Among the new findings Stalcup shared with the NTSB—or at least tried to—was a score of FBI witness statements that had somehow been omitted from the official record. He had managed to secure these through FOIA requests. The NTSB conceded the evidence was new but insisted these 302s did not differ substantially from the other seven hundred or so already in the official record. This was more or less correct. Stalcup, however, dug up additional witness information of much more consequence. Attorney John Clarke requested the same information from the CIA and posted it on Ray Lahr's website in September 2015. These memos show in unseemly detail how the CIA sausage-makers cooked up the zoom climb animation. No one who reads them can doubt for a second how fully and deliberately the CIA and its enablers sabotaged the investigation.

On February 28, 1997, CIA analysts presented a comprehensive PowerPoint titled, "A Witness by Witness Account: A Review of the TWA 800 Witness Reports." The audience was unspecified, but it likely included need-to-know representatives from the CIA, the FBI, and MSIC. Each slide showed the CIA interpretation of a single witness summary. Surprisingly, most of the very best ones were there: the man on the bridge, Mike Wire; school administrator Joseph Delgado; helicopter pilots Fritz Meyer and Christian Baur; UA 217 passenger Dwight Brumley; and even Witness 73. Ignorance offered no possible excuse for what these analysts had done. They took the accounts of the most observant witnesses, siphoned out all conflicting details, and presented the residue as fact.

In constructing their presentation, the analysts so simplified and homogenized witness observations they made it difficult to align the CIA summaries with the FBI 302s. The CIA also assigned the witnesses numbers different than the ones the FBI assigned, and that did not help much either. In several cases, however, the detail was specific enough to compare the two. Among the newly found 302s, now unredacted, was that of Charles Le Brun, an assistant fire chief for the Air National Guard (CIA 152).[8] On the evening of July 17, he was heading south by boat in Moneybogue Bay when he saw a flare-like object ascend. Given his location, the FBI reported, "Le Brun knew it originated from the ocean." The object ascended vertically for about fifteen seconds, then burst into a yellow flash slightly larger than the light of the flare. This yellow flash remained illuminated and descended. It then burst into a huge fireball "about twenty times the size of the yellow flash" and fell toward the sea.

In their summary, the CIA analysts acknowledged the fifteen-second ascent "straight up in the sky" and the fireball twenty times the size of the original flash, but they failed to mention the object's climb "from the ocean."[9] Given Le Brun's credentials and his location, as well as the fact that he saw one object go up and another come down, the analysts could not dismiss his testimony with a glib, "observations limited to end event" as they did with others. Instead, they discounted his testimony because the ascending object "was not white as most observations," a pointless caveat in that they discounted all the rising "white" lights as well.

The CIA analysts so liked Mike Wire they designated him witness "1." As stated earlier, they had to fabricate a second interview with Wire to make his testimony work, but once they did, whether Wire knew it or not, he was their guy. The object Wire saw was moving from west to east, as was TWA 800. This gave the analysts enough wiggle room to conclude that Wire's observations were "consistent with aircraft trajectory." In sum, he only saw a crippled TWA 800. More useful still, Wire heard the sound of the blasts at the appropriate time. Of course, the analysts could not explain how a low energy fuel-air explosion could shake a bridge ten miles away, but that was one of the many anomalies they chose to overlook.

FBI Witness 364 (CIA 47) served up another anomaly. This former Marine helicopter crew chief saw an object ascend vertically. He watched for thirty seconds as the object "rose from the east to the west on a steep angle." Concluded the analysts, "Observations consistent with aircraft hypothesis *except for east to west motion*" (italics in original). That was a big "except." This witness saw these objects moving towards each other. In fact, he told the FBI he thought he had seen "a missile hitting the airplane." The analysts simply ignored the collision. Kallstrom ignored the witness's reference to a missile. "No one ever said a missile," he told a congressional committee in July 1997, "none of the witnesses."[10] In fact, several had.

The analysts worked even harder to make the testimony of FBI Witness 550 (CIA 7) fit their narrative. Out fishing that evening, the witness saw what "looked like a smaller plane coming from the northeast on a dead course heading towards the nose of the larger plane." The two objects then "crunched up" before the larger plane blew up and "became a big fireball which then broke into four pieces." The CIA analysts concluded with startling dishonesty that the witness heard a "series of sounds when two planes *passed* each other" (italics added). They then disqualified the witness account because the "sound doesn't work." In a just world, transforming "crunched up" into "passed each other" would be crime enough to earn an orange jump suit.

Witness 73 (CIA 39), she of the upside down Nike swoosh, saw events so clearly the CIA felt compelled to turn her into a drunk. Three days after the crash, she told the FBI that she saw "the front of the air-craft separate from the back." The mapping of the debris field had long since confirmed her observations. This was no secret. The analysts knew how solid was her account. They conceded she saw "two objects," or at least claimed to, and that "the red object hit the aircraft." The best dis-qualifier they could summon was that the red object did "not follow realistic missile trajectory." That was it. Two months after this presenta-tion, someone saw to it that Witness 73 had a new 302 in her file.

Another act of overt fraud involved FBI Witness 32 (CIA 106), Dwight Brumley, a U.S. Navy master chief. At the climactic moment, Brumley was looking out a right side window on US Air 217, a plane heading northeast thousands of feet above TWA 800's path. As recorded on his original 302, Brumley told the FBI he saw a flare like-object mov-ing from "right to left," very nearly perpendicular to the path of TWA 800. According to the CIA analyst, however, Brumley "observed flare ascending which moved *left to right*" (italics added). This supposed flare, the analyst concluded, "matches aircraft trajectory." In other words, what Brumley saw was TWA 800 in crippled flight. He was said to have admitted as much "in a second interview."[11]

As was the case with Witness 73 and the man on the bridge, Brum-ley's second interview was created out of whole cloth. Careless or reckless or both, authorities left Brumley's original 302 filed in the NTSB docket and manufactured a new one with the original date for his CIA file. It was only after the CIA file surfaced that the fraud became obvious. As was true with Witness 73 and Mike Wire, no one spoke to Brumley after the first week of the investigation. "There was never a second interview with me by either the FBI, the CIA or any other government official," Brumley firmly told Tom Stalcup in a recorded interview. "I always maintained that the object moved from my right to left, and I never said otherwise."[12]

The analysts had more trouble still with Delgado, FBI Witness 649 (CIA 47). He too saw two separate objects, but his ascending object was moving in a southwesterly direction, not towards the east, as was TWA 800. This object made a "dramatic correction" at the last moment and exploded in a "white puff" next to the aircraft. The plane then devolved into a ball of fire and fell behind the tree line. The CIA's deconstruction of Delgado's account hurts the brain. The analysts concluded that the ascending object was actually TWA 800 after a second explosion. The fact that this object was going in the wrong direction did not overly trouble the analysts. Nor did Delgado's highly specific drawing of two objects with distinct trajectories. With a bravado born of impunity they concluded Delgado "did not observe *two objects* around the *initial* event" (italics theirs). Like the mythical Greek highwayman Procrustes, who stretched or chopped captives to fit a certain height, the CIA analysts had a one-sized scenario and stretched or slashed the truth to make the witness accounts fit. If anyone objected there was always a Peter Goelz or a Jim Kallstrom ready to shout "conspiracy theorist."

As a quick reminder, Goelz, Jim Hall's man at the NTSB, claimed on national TV the witnesses saw only "the last six seconds" of the forty-plus second break-up of the aircraft. "No witness saw the first event forty seconds prior to that," he insisted. Of course, they did. One of the witnesses just cited saw an ascent of fifteen seconds. Another saw an ascent of thirty seconds. All saw a descending object for another twenty or thirty seconds. As late as February 1997, the CIA analysts were accepting the duration of these sightings. Goelz's "last six seconds" claim has no known provenance.

The CIA presentation did not convince everyone, at least not the representatives from the DIA's Missile and Space Intelligence Center then working with the FBI. In an undated document, likely soon after this February 1997 presentation, the MSIC reps submitted their concerns in writing to the CIA. For one, the reps could "not agree with the CIA conclusion that no witness saw the initial event."[13] They insisted that several witnesses could not "be lightly disregarded" and might possibly "have seen something other than the aircraft." They noted too that several of these witnesses saw an object moving in the opposite direction of TWA 800 prior to the explosions. The testimony of these witnesses could "not be explained as seeing any portion of the aircraft trajectory proposed by the CIA or other sources," said the reps firmly.

What the CIA analysts lacked in integrity they made up for in nerve. Their exchanges with MSIC and other agencies leave the impression that the White House had the agency's back, and everyone knew it. Among equals, these exchanges would have provoked warfare. They were that insulting. Yes, more than 90 percent saw something other than the zoom climb, said the CIA analysts, but what they saw was likely "a fuel related event in the final seconds of the aircraft's descent toward the water." As to the imagined objects heading west toward TWA 800, those sightings too were "likely related to fuel burning." MSIC seemed to sense the power disparity and yielded without much fight. All that the reps could say in return was, "Continue re-interviewing the witnesses."

Despite institutional pressure to yield, one unnamed FBI agent refused to accept the CIA narrative. For simplicity's sake, let us call him Special Agent Lewis Erskine. Erskine was part of the FBI's two-man missile team. According to an internal CIA memo from April 29, 1997, Erskine's FBI partner was "completely convinced" by the CIA analysis. If true, this suggests he had been gotten to. Erskine, however, had "concerns."[14] That was something of an understatement. In April 1997, he sent the CIA a blistering critique of its zoom climb scenario and demanded answers to more than a dozen salient questions. He wanted to know why the analysts failed to account for the eight witnesses who saw an object "hit the aircraft" or the numerous witnesses who saw the object move from east to west, the opposite direction of TWA 800. In all, Erskine cited some thirty "problem witnesses" whose accounts did not square with the "agency scenario." With some precision, he also challenged the aerodynamics of the CIA's zoom climb.

The CIA analyst, likely Randolph Tauss, responded with his usual obfuscations, but he made one surprising concession, namely that he had no physical proof a zoom climb after the initial "pitch up" of the aircraft. No one denied the plane might have appeared to pitch up after the nose was blown off. Ray Lahr described the phenomenon as "putting two people on one side of a teeter totter." As witness Lisa Perry saw it, "The tail section fell backward." For Joseph Delgado, the plane "arched upward." But not a single witness saw the 747 ascend after this initial convulsion. The CIA analyst did not contest this point. "Whatever happens after these first few seconds," he responded to Erskine, "is not understood by the CIA and would require extensive modeling of the aircraft beyond the CIA capabilities." A point that bears repeating is that two years later, in a March 1999 memo, a CIA analyst would privately concede that the "maximum calculated altitude" for TWA 800 post-explosion was 14,500 feet.[15] Publicly, the agency said nothing to correct the record. All this said, the FBI went ahead and showed the CIA's zoom climb video to the nation seven months after the CIA conceded to Erskine that it had no supportive data.

The reader will recall that in November 1997 Kallstrom claimed he "looked throughout the government" to find the people best able to analyze "all the known data about Flight 800 in conjunction with the eyewitness reports."[16] He allegedly found those people at the CIA, but on this point the chief analyst demurred. That assignment, he admitted, was "beyond the CIA capabilities."

Erskine raised one more concern unvoiced in any other official document—the "possible 'missile self destruct/proximity' theory." He chided the analyst for claiming that the apparent lack of physical evidence disproved the missile theory. He reminded the analyst that a missile blast triggered by a proximity fuse "would likely leave little or no evidence of a hit on the aircraft." In his response, the CIA analyst referred only to the damage a "portable SAM" would have caused. Refusing to even consider the possibility of a naval misfire, he implied that since a shoulder-fired missile could not have wreaked such catastrophic damage, a mechanical failure must have.

In his conclusion, Erskine hit the CIA hard. He recommended that "the Agency withdraw its conclusions" until it could meet several conditions, any one of which would unravel the CIA scenario. These included the integration of radar data, the validation of key witnesses, and the reconciliation of the thirty "problem witnesses" with the zoom climb scenario. The CIA analyst did not seem overly worried. He knew that Tenet and Kallstrom had already signed off on his analysis. "CIA will continue to look at problematic witnesses," he responded, "but we believe we have adequately explained all of them within the agency scenario." The analyst got to work quickly. The very day he sent this memo, April 29, 1997, Witness 73's new 302 magically appeared in her file.

At Kallstrom's direction, the FBI did proceed to re-interview witnesses. At the congressional hearing in July 1997, he claimed that his agents interviewed "most of [the witnesses] more than once."[17] That was just one lie out of many that day, but the FBI did record about thirty additional interviews with witnesses. Of course, some of these interviews were provably apocryphal. That did not stop Kallstrom from testifying in July 1997 that the second interviews, when combined with the CIA's "sophisticated analysis," would soon provide a "clear understanding of these critical eyewitness observations."[18]

On reading statements such as this, I find myself feeling sorry for Kallstrom. He helped construct a case he knew to be fraudulent, and he had to sense just how fragile the construction was. If it collapsed, the CIA analysts could run and hide. The NTSB bureaucrats could plead ignorance. The Clintons could seek executive privilege, and he alone would have to answer to the victims' mothers and fathers, brothers and sisters, sons and daughters. Nothing the courts might throw at him would wound that deeply.

TCR 00:21·02·15

Five days before TWA 800's demise, an amateur videographer captured an apparent missile test in progress off the coast of Long Island. Although not visible in this still, the video also captured burning debris falling from the sky. *Federal Bureau of Investigation*

Chapter: NINETEEN

THE SMOKING GUN

No one ever expected *the* video to show up, least of all in a batch of miscellaneous FBI documents secured through a FOIA request. I refer here to the video of the missile strike that MSNBC reportedly aired on the night of July 17, 1996, the one around which Nelson DeMille wrote his novel, *Night Fall*. But then one day, nineteen years after James Sanders began his lonely quest for the truth, a Las Vegas postman delivered a video to his house that had all the appearances of being "the" video.

The video came with no explanation as to what it was. A skeptic by nature, Sanders watched it through and could not believe what he was seeing. The light seemed right. The place seemed right. The Long Island accent of the videographer seemed right. There was a new moon hovering over the Atlantic Ocean, and yes, when Sanders checked, there was a new moon on the night of July 17. And as to what was happening out at sea, there was no denying that seemed right too. For Sanders, this video had the potential not only to vindicate his efforts, but also to erase the criminal stain on his and Elizabeth's records. Sanders made copies and sent one to me. By this time, I was well into the research on this book, which was good. Had I not been, I might have failed to understand what I was seeing.

After days of waiting, a neatly packaged jump drive arrived at my office. I inserted the drive in my Mac, opened up the document, and hoped that my computer would be able to show the video. Everything worked. The view seemed to be from a deck not far from the ocean. That was good. My best correspondent on this subject, the 747 pilot who watched the video over and over in a Hong Kong Hospital bed, said it was shot from a deck, but he also said there was a party going on. There was no party here. It was just a guy and his buddy trying to master what seemed to be a new video camera.

Then, sure enough, a smoke trail emerged from the horizon zigzagging its way up at about a seventy-five degree angle in an east to west direction. "It must be a rocket or something going up," said the one fellow matter-of-factly. "Uh, oh," I said to myself. This may not be what we hoped it was. I remembered the document that Ray Lahr had received years earlier about the existence of a video shot at dawn on July 12, 1996, by a fellow on Long Island trying to capture the sunrise. According to that document, he reportedly said, "They must be testing a rocket." That quote was much too close to what the fellow actually said on the video to be a coincidence. The light was deceptive. I could not tell whether it was dusk or dawn. So I found a helpful web site called "Moon Page." I loaded in the date, the time, and the time zone. I then compared the morning moon on July 12 to the evening moon on July 17. No question. Yes, each moon was new, but the July 12 moon was waning exactly as was the moon in the video. The July 17 moon was waxing.

Before calling Sanders with the news, I looked carefully at the video and the assembled stills. Yes, he would be disappointed, but this video had powerful evidentiary value of its own. It was amateurish but clearly genuine. All the agencies were aware of it. As mentioned earlier, the Defense Intelligence Agency had advised the FBI on July 23, 1996, that the imagery captured on the video "appeared to be consistent with the exhaust plume from a MANPAD." The video, however, showed much more than an exhaust plume going up. It showed something coming down. As Sanders and I now understood, by July 23, just six days after the crash, the authorities were already pulling their punches.

In fact, the CIA started talking down the possibility of a missile strike of any sort within days of the crash, if not hours. In a July 20 memo, an analyst reported "no evidence of a missile" in the radar data.[1] That same memo argued that the aircraft was beyond the range of virtually all shoulder-fired missiles. In no memo was there any mention of a possible naval misfire even though one memo acknowledged the Navy was reportedly "conducting an exercise in the area."[2] The analyst mentioned this only because he was interested in seeing if any of the ships had raw radar video recordings to share.

As noted earlier, a July 30 CIA memo warned that the FBI was preparing a report pointing to a missile strike. After interviewing 144 witnesses, "mainly professionals," the FBI agents involved were convinced a shoulder-fired missile destroyed TWA 800. That same CIA memo held another surprise. After TWA 800 went down, the FBI received reports from four other witnesses claiming to have seen "a similar surface-to-air something" launched on July 7. "If true," said the CIA analyst, "the FBI would now have witnesses reporting seeing something race towards the sky on the 7th, 12th and 17th."[3] Assuming these sightings to be genuine, the analyst reviewed the various reasons as to why a terrorist with a shoulder-fired missile might have wanted to shoot off a missile on three separate occasions, each five days apart. There was no talk of the Navy.

As with virtually all evidence that threatened the government scenario, the authorities eventually discounted the July 12 video. An internal memo from October 21, 1996, spoke of how the CIA came to this conclusion. According to the analyst, officials from still another intelligence agency, the National Imagery and Mapping Agency (NIMA), "believed, at least initially," that the ascending plume in the July 12 video "might be a MANPAD smoke trail." Upon further review, however, they concluded, "The trail appears to have most likely been a contrail from a very far away aircraft."

The deception was that easy—at least until someone either carelessly or craftily sent Sanders the July 12 video. To be sure, the camera work on this video makes analysis difficult. The action appears to be farther out to sea than was TWA 800's, and the cameraman, unaware of what he was seeing, continued to readjust the lens and scan the horizon. That said, the video's irregular, ascending smoke trail does not resemble any aircraft contrail I have ever seen. It is too thick, dark, and irregular. In fact, it almost perfectly matches the direction and angle of attack of the smoke trail that Joseph Delgado sketched for investigators.

The video shows a secondary action, however, that betrays the deceit at the heart of the NIMA analysis: very near the point where the smoke trail ends, flaming debris falls out of the sky. In none of the CIA memos was the falling debris mentioned. This added detail renders the idea of a terrorist missile even more preposterous. The ascending object—or another one unseen—appears to have hit something and destroyed it. The target object might have been a drone, a test missile, or possibly even a terrorist plane packed with explosives as envisioned in the Bojinka plot. On close examination, the smoke trail left by the falling debris seems to intersect the vestiges of the ascending trail. This makes sense. The target object continued east as it fell. The Delgado drawing captured this same phenomenon with TWA 800. If there was a climatic explosion on July 12, the cameraman missed it, but, then again, the target of this apparent missile would not have had a fuel tank nearly as large as that of a 747.

On July 17, 1996, a Long Island woman by the name of Linda Kabot shed some unwitting light on the possible nature of the target. That evening Kabot was taking photographs at a fundraising party for her boss, Vincent Cannuscio, the Republican Town Supervisor of Southampton. The event was held outdoors, at Docker's, an East Quogue restaurant with a deck that overlooks Shinnecock Bay. Kabot was facing north with her back to the ocean a few blocks away when she snapped one photo with the potential to rewrite history. At the time, however, she did not notice anything unusual.

A few days later, Kabot picked up the developed photos. In one, she saw what the *New York Times* described as a "long cylindrical object high in the sky," its left end tilted downward, its right end "brightly lighted."⁴ Good citizen that she was, Kabot called the FBI. At this stage, just days after the disaster, the FBI was still serious about seeking the truth. Agents interviewed her and other guests at the event, took the negatives, but left Kabot with the original. The *Times* did not use the word "drone" in its August 26 coverage of the Kabot photo, but a drone was likely what Kabot captured on film. The ever-incurious *Times* never mentioned Kabot or the photo again.

Witness 150, Lisa Perry, had likely seen the same object. In an interview on July 23, 1996, she told the FBI she saw an "unusual object traveling at high speed north to south." She described it as "cylindrical, tubular, and bullet shaped" with no wings, no vapor trail, and a slight upward trajectory.⁵ She followed the object for several seconds when she saw it approach a "large commercial airliner" traveling at roughly the same altitude. Although she saw no collision, she described the break-up of the aircraft with impressive accuracy.

The media ignored Perry's testimony and allowed the Kabot photo to fade from memory. On November 18, 1997, however, the FBI resurrected the photo in its closing summary of the case. For analysis the FBI had turned the photo over to an entity it called the "CIA National Imagery and Mapping Administration (NIMA)." Upon reading this I did a double take. Nowhere in my research on NIMA did I get the impression NIMA was affiliated with the CIA. This was the same bunch that insisted the smoke trail in the July 12 video was an airplane contrail. Here, they were advising the FBI that the object in the photo was "not a missile" and "not a drone."

The reason drones were ruled out smacked of tautology: "No drone exercises conducted near Long Island July 17, 1996." Nearly a year before this press conference, the stubborn NTSB witness group had requested to see the Kabot photo and the FBI's analysis of the same. In its Factual Report from October 1997, the Witness Group noted that the requested material "has not been received."[6] No matter. In its case-closing press conference, the FBI assured America the Kabot photo was one of many things that were not what they appeared to be:

- The apparent drone in the Kabot photo was determined to be "an aircraft" of indeterminate type.
- The apparent missile trail on a July 17 photo taken by a woman named Heidi Kreiger was determined to be "debris on the film surface."
- The apparent missile on Dick Russell's radar tape was determined to be "a ghost of Jet Express 18 which was at a different location."
- The apparent missile residue on the seat cushions, the testing of which led to the indictment of the Sanderses, was determined to be glue, a "chlorinated polymeric material, commonly used as contact adhesive."
- The apparent PETN and RDX found inside and outside the fuselage were determined to be the sloppy after effects of a "canine explosives training aboard the victim aircraft."
- The witness observations, once thought "overwhelming" proof of a missile strike, were determined to be a collective optical illusion thanks to the "brilliant and professional" work of the CIA.
- "The vast majority" of the witness observations were determined to be "consistent" with the CIA analysis, although admittedly there remained "a few" that could "not be fully explained."

These were just the anomalies that the FBI breezily explained away in its final summary. There were, of course, many more.

- The FBI determined that there was no strategic retagging of airplane parts, including engine No. 3, given that "the logged recovery location of all debris from the wings and the cabin structure was verified."
- The summary made no mention of the serious charges brought against David Mayer and others for changing tags.
- The summary made no mention of the P-3 video.
- As to the reported "foreign object damage" to engine No. 3, the FBI summary added no new information.
- "The [cockpit voice recorder] review disclosed no evidence of a criminal act," no evidence of anything for that matter. Ditto the flight data recorder. Said the NTSB's John Goglia earlier, "The data was missing and it's unexplainable, it's just missing." The FBI was as silent as the CVR on this issue.
- The "infrared sensor information from a U.S. satellite" that allegedly helped the CIA establish the zoom climb scenario went unmentioned.
- Unmentioned was the large mystery ship fleeing the scene at up to thirty-five knots, the one suspicious vessel the FBI inexplicably failed to identify.
- Unmentioned was the sound propagation analysis around which the CIA based its analysis. In fact, the word "sound" does not appear in the FBI summary.
- Unmentioned were the "116 pieces of debris" FBI lab director Donald Kerr said were sent to the FBI lab in Washington for further testing.
- The FBI claimed "there were no missile firing [sic] for two years prior to July 17, 1996, in the Whiskey 105-106-107 areas," which meant the July 12 video could not have shown an ascending missile, nor could the July 7 witnesses have seen one.

- Finally, there was no mention of the July 12 video. To acknowledge this video would have been to concede the very real possibility that there had been a "missile firing" just five days prior to the destruction of TWA 800.

There was one other bit of evidence that the FBI chose not to discuss. This was the fax Long Island resident Dede Muma received from an employee at San Diego's Teledyne Ryan Aeronautical in May 1997. The employee, Eric Hittinger, had intended to send the fax to his superior on assignment at Calverton but transposed the last two numbers. As fate would have it, the fax went to Muma. She in turn forwarded it to the *Southampton Press*.[7] The *Press* ran the illustration shown in the fax through the highly authoritative Jane's Information Services, and Jane's determined the object pictured to be a Teledyne Ryan BQM-34 Firebee I, a target drone about 23 feet long capable of flying more than 700 miles an hour.

Although the FBI would not talk to the *Press*, Hittinger did. He said the FBI had contacted Teledyne Ryan to identify pieces of wreckage that looked like parts of a drone. He faxed the illustration to help his superior on the scene at Calverton make the identification. When the *Press* caught up with Hittinger in July 1997, he assured the reporter the part in question did not belong to a Firebee and that "it was all put to bed some time ago." Accuracy in Media's Reed Irvine talked to the Teledyne employee on the scene, Walt Hamilton. According to Irvine, Hamilton said the part did, in fact, look like a Teledyne Ryan product. He requested the drawings to make sure it wasn't. "If it wasn't from a Firebee," wrote Irvine, "it must have been from another drone, evidence the FBI hid and the NTSB has destroyed."[8]

Authorities had an incentive to discount the Kabot photo and the Muma fax. In its summary the FBI acknowledged that three submarines—the USS *Wyoming*, the USS *Trepang*, and the USS *Albuquerque*—were in the "immediate vicinity of the crash site." So too, said the FBI, were an Aegis cruiser and a U.S. Navy P-3 Orion. The P-3, in fact, just happened to be flying about seven thousand feet above TWA 800 when the plane was blown out of the sky. Were there a drone or target missile in the mix, the U.S. Navy would have had all the "combatants" needed for a Cooperative Engagement Capability (CEC) missile test.

In 1996, the Navy was in the process of introducing this enormously complex system. The CEC was created to integrate the information coming from each of the combatant's sensors—range, bearing, elevation, Doppler updates etc.—and feed the integrated picture back to the individual combatants. In the CEC live-fire tests, which began as early as 1994 in Puerto Rico, drones played the role of "unknown assumed enemy." The P-3's role was to relay data among the various units involved.

In July 1996, this information was not classified. If curious, the FBI—or the media—could have reviewed a comprehensive article in the November 1995 *John Hopkins APL Technical Digest* titled simply, "The Cooperative Engagement Capability." One color illustration captured an actual test off the Virginia coast in 1994 when the various ships in the USS *Dwight D. Eisenhower* battlegroup successfully cued and tracked a tactical ballistic missile. In the middle of the illustration, relaying information among the vessels, was the P-3.[9]

The P-3 should have given the game away. The authorities could explain away the hundreds of missile sightings on July 17, the radar track of a missile, the photo of a drone, the photo of a smoke trail, the missile sightings on July 12 and July 17, even the location of ships and submarines. There was no denying, however, that right in the middle of the mix, exactly where one would expect to find a surveillance aircraft in a missile test, was the P-3. Its transponder "broken," the plane was flying within a mile or so of what was said to be the first spontaneous mid-air explosion in the era of Jet-A fuel. This was either most freakish coincidence in the history of aviation or the proverbial "smoking gun." If the media needed to confirm their suspicions, they should have asked the Navy brass why the P-3 was sent on a meaningless sub-hunting exercise hundreds of mile away while the terrorists who allegedly shot down TWA 800 were still at large. Finally, the media might have asked Jim Kallstrom how FBI investigators overlooked so obvious a lead.

I do not presume to know the exact details of what happened the night of July 17, 1996, but the evidence for a missile test gone awry overwhelms the dispassionate observer. With Ramzi Yousef on trial in New York, with serious people worried about the threat to attack America with flying bombs, with the Atlanta Olympics just two days away, with Saddam Hussein celebrating Iraq's Independence Day, it made sense for the Navy to test its cooperative engagement capabilities in the Atlantic, arguably even in the crowded air space around New York. The probable tests on July 7 and July 12 caused no stir. It seems likely that the Navy increased the degree of difficulty on July 17, perhaps in response to a genuine threat. If the participants had merely cued and tracked as they did in the earlier test off the Virginia coast, two hundred thirty people would not have died that night. As was true with the *Vincennes* in 1988, something went wrong.

Based on available evidence, it appears that at least two missiles detonated near TWA 800 in quick order, one at the No. 3 engine on the right side, and the second and fatal blast, according to the IAMAW, at "the lower left side of the aircraft." If there were a drone in the mix, it seems to have been destroyed.

Several very good witnesses named the right wing as the site of one explosion, including Witness 73 and fisherman William Gallagher who "saw something hit the right side of the plane."[10] As the *New York Times* reported, investigators found traces of PETN on the right wing within five days of the crash and confirmed traces of PETN inside the fuselage near the right wing. ALPA's Jim Speer had a section of the right wing tested for nitrates, and when it tested positive the FBI shut the test down. The No. 3 engine appeared to have been the first object blown off the aircraft.

The IAMAW, the most forthright participant in the NTSB investigation, spoke openly of the left side blast. Although restrained in its language, the union's final report had the ring of truth about it: "A high pressure event breached the fuselage and the fuselage unzipped due to the event. The explosion [of the center fuel tank] was a result of this event." In layman's terms, a blast—"outside of the aircraft in close proximity to the aircraft"—ripped open the center fuel tank and caused the fuel to vaporize and explode.

Yes, the center fuel tank did blow up. The IAMAW confirmed as much. No one ever said otherwise. The IAMAW, however, did not shy from rejecting the official NTSB position on the fuel tank's role in the plane's destruction: "We have not been a party to any evidence, wreckage or tests that could conclude that the [center fuel tank] explosion was and is the primary contributor to this accident."[11] As of August 14, 1996, the *New York Times* was reporting much the same, specifically that "the center fuel tank caught fire as many as 24 seconds after the initial blast that split apart the plane."[12]

For its part, the NTSB could offer no evidence to rebut the IAMAW case for an external blast save for an absence of "physical evidence." In the light of what is now known about the corruption of the investigation, this argument carries no weight. The one honest member of the FBI missile team noted that a missile triggered by a proximity fuse "would likely leave little or no evidence of a hit on the aircraft." Then too, as the NTSB conceded in its final report, "Some areas of fuselage skin and [center fuel tank] are missing."[13] Why doubt that officials who distorted witness observations, rearranged the debris field, and reinterpreted *all* data and visual imagery to fit their preferred scenario would have qualms about making physical evidence go "missing." According to the NTSB's Hank Hughes, who openly protested the "disappearance of parts from the hangar," this evidence did not go missing by accident.

Accidents can happen. This was a huge one, a tragic one. But the larger wrong, the moral wrong, the uncorrected wrong began *after* the plane's destruction. The Navy could not have—and would not have— concealed its responsibility unless authorized to do so. Nor would the FBI and CIA have intervened on their own initiative. These authorizations could only have come from the White House. This was the rare White House in American history, perhaps the only one, reckless enough to have authorized a cover-up this bold.

Much about the government's performance in the TWA 800 investigation surprises, but none of it shocks. Governments inevitably fail the people. Our founders knew this. They constructed a constitution that accounted for the weaknesses of human nature. As a corrective, they passed the First Amendment. "Our citizens may be deceived for awhile, and have been deceived," wrote Thomas Jefferson in 1799, "but as long as the presses can be protected, we may trust to them for light."[14] Two centuries later, Jefferson's trust in the press was thoroughly betrayed.

In his review of Stalcup and Borjesson's *TWA Flight 800*, the *Times*' Neil Genzlinger wondered whether there was a government agency with the credibility to reopen the investigation, especially given how "poorly" the agencies in question came off in the documentary. In an unwitting bit of institutional self-criticism, Genzlinger concluded, "It's hard to imagine any entity that would command the authority that could put the Flight 800 case to rest."[15] The readers of that article—or this book—have to ask, "How about the *New York Times*?"

NOTES

ONE: THE BREACH

1. Transcript, 9/11 Commission Hearing, CNN, March 24, 2004, http://www.cnn.com/TRANSCRIPTS/0403/24/nfcnn.01.html.

2. TWA Flight 800, NTSB docket materials, DCA-96-MA070, August 2000, Exhibit 4A, appendix B.

3. Ibid.

4. NTSB Aircraft Accident Report, *In-flight breakup over the Atlantic Ocean, Trans World Airlines Flight 800 Boeing 747-131, N93119, near East Moriches, New York, July 17, 1996* (Washington, DC: Diane Publishing, 2000), 232, http://bit.ly/1LqLGsX.

5. Hillary Rodham Clinton's White House Schedules, *New York Times*, March 20, 2008, http://projects.nytimes.com/clinton-schedules.

6. Transcript, *Witnessed: The Crash of TWA Flight 800*, CNN, July 19, 2014, http://transcripts.cnn.com/TRANSCRIPTS/1407/19/csr.01.html.

7. Richard Clarke, *Against All Enemies* (New York: Simon & Schuster, 2004), 121.

8.　Phone interview with Robert Patterson, July 15, 2004 (est.) and follow-up in person interview, Newport Beach, California, October 15, 2006.

9.　NTSB docket materials, Exhibit 4A, appendix M.

10.　Transcript, *Witnessed*.

11.　Robert Woodward, *The Choice: How Clinton Won* (New York: Touchstone, 1997), 421.

12.　Ibid., 367.

13.　Evan Thomas et al., *Back from the Dead: How Clinton Survived the Republican Revolution* (New York: The Atlantic Monthly Press, 1997), 79.

14.　Patricia Milton, *In the Blink of an Eye: The FBI Investigation of TWA Flight 800* (New York: Random House, 1999), 7.

TWO: CONSPIRACY THEORIST

1.　Loren Fleckenstein, "New Data Show Missile May Have Nailed TWA 800," *Press-Enterprise*, March 10, 1997.

2.　FBI press release, December 5, 1997.

3.　FBI New York Office Press Release, November 18, 1997, http://www.lchr.org/a/11/j/fbitwa.htm.

4.　NTSB Hearing, August 22, 2000, https://en.wikisource.org/wiki/Portal:TWA_Flight_800_investigation/Day1.

5.　Transcript, "Jim Kallstrom's Take on the Plane," March 20, 2014, http://www.rushlimbaugh.com/daily/2014/03/20/jim_kallstrom_s_take_on_the_plane.

6.　Patricia Milton, *In the Blink of an Eye: The FBI Investigation of TWA Flight 800* (New York: Random House, 1999), 353.

7.　William Langewiesche, "Dead End Story," *New York Times*, September 26, 1999, https://www.nytimes.com/books/99/09/26/reviews/990926.26langewt.html.

THREE: THE BEST PEOPLE

1.　"Top 10 Stories of 1996," CNN.com, http://www.cnn.com/EVENTS/1996/year.in.review/.

2.　Whittaker Chambers, *Witness* (Washington, DC: Regnery, 2014), 793.

3.　George Johnson, "Pierre, Is That A Masonic Flag on the Moon?" *New York Times*, November 24, 1996, http://www.nytimes.com/1996/11/24/weekinreview/pierre-is-that-a-masonic-flag-on-the-moon.html.

4. Jeffrey Reid, "'Pierre Salinger Syndrome' and the TWA 800 Conspiracies," CNN.com, July 17, 2006, http://www.cnn.com/2006/US/07/12/twa. conspiracy/.

5. Phone interviews with Dick Russell, the most recent and detailed on July 25, 2015.

6. Phone interview with Jim Holtsclaw, July 28, 2015.

7. Affidavit, James Allan Holtsclaw, October 25, 2002, http://twa800.com/lahr/affidavits/j-james-holtsclaw.pdf.

8. "What Happened to TWA Flight 800," CNN.com, July 19, 2015, http://www.cnn.com/US/9607/19/twa.investigation/index.html?_s=PM:US.

9. Christine Negroni, *Deadly Departure: Why the Experts Failed to Prevent the TWA Flight 800 Disaster and How It Could Happen Again* (New York: HarperCollins, 2000), 138–39.

10. Affidavit of Richard Russell, January 2, 2003, http://twa800.com/lahr/affidavits/m-richard-russell.pdf.

11. The e-mail was published by CNN.com in August 1996, http://www.cnn.com/US/9611/08/twa.update/email.html.

12. Jocelyn Noveck, "Pierre Salinger's TWA Flight 800 Missile News Conference," Associated Press, November 8, 1996, http://www.welfarestate.com/twa800/pierre.htm.

FOUR: THE VIDEO

1. Thomas Jefferson letter to Charles Yancey, 1816, http://famguardian.org/Subjects/Politics/thomasjefferson/jeff1350.htm.

2. Unless specified otherwise, all the quotes that follow can be found in Jack Cashill and James Sanders, *Silenced*, 2001.

3. FBI New York Office Press Release, "FBI: No criminal evidence behind TWA 800 crash," November 18, 1997, http://www.cnn.com/US/9711/18/twa.fbi.presser/.

4. TWA Flight 800, NTSB docket materials, DCA-96-MA070, August 2000, Exhibit 4A, appendix B.

FIVE: THE MAN ON THE BRIDGE

1. Jack Cashill and James Sanders, *Silenced* (2001).

2. TWA Flight 800, NTSB docket materials, DCA-96-MA070, August 2000, Exhibit 4A, appendix FF.

3. NTSB Aircraft Accident Report, *In-flight breakup over the Atlantic Ocean, Trans World Airlines Flight 800 Boeing 747-131, N93119, near*

East Moriches, New York, July 17, 1996 (Washington, DC: Diane Publishing, 2000), 236, http://bit.ly/1LqLGsX.

4. "Navy Aircraft Testing May Have Caused Earthquake-Like Sonic Boom Felt from New Jersey to Long Island," NBC New York, January 27, 2016, http://www.nbcnewyork.com/news/local/Earthquake-Sonic-Boom-Shaking-New-Jersey-New-York-Connecticut-Long-Island-Tri-State-Shaking-NY-CT-NJ-366886661.html.

5. NTSB docket materials, Exhibit 4A, appendix Z.

6. David Hendrix, "Witnesses Boost Missile Theory," *Press-Enterprise*, October 20, 1997, cached at http://whatreallyhappened.com/RANCHO/CRASH/TWA/AUDIO.html.

7. Letter from George Tenet to Jim Hall, March 15, 1999, cached at TWA Flight 800: The Impossible Zoom Climb, raylahr.entryhost.com, "CIA records released to Tom Stalcup," records 76–100.

8. Randolph M. Tauss, "The Crash of TWA Flight 800," https://www.cia.gov/offices-of-cia/public-affairs/entertainment-industry-liaison/twaflight.pdf.

9. Executive Order 12333—United States intelligence activities, Federal Register, December 4, 1981, http://www.archives.gov/federal-register/codification/executive-order/12333.html.

10. FBI New York Office Press Release, November 18, 1997.

11. CIA documents cached at TWA Flight 800: The Impossible Zoom Climb, raylahr.entryhost.com, "CIA records released to Tom Stalcup," records 51–75.

SIX: INTELLIGENCE MEDAL OF MERIT

1. Randolph M. Tauss, "The Crash of TWA Flight 800," https://www.cia.gov/offices-of-cia/public-affairs/entertainment-industry-liaison/twaflight.pdf.

2. TWA Flight 800, NTSB docket materials, DCA-96-MA070, August 2000, Exhibit 4A, appendix B.

3. Ibid.

4. Ibid., appendix C.

5. Ibid.

6. Ibid.

7. Ibid.

8. Ibid.

9. Ibid.

10. Ibid., appendix D.
11. Ibid.
12. Ibid.
13. Ibid.
14. Ibid.
15. Ibid.
16. Ibid.
17. Ibid.
18. Ibid., appendix E.
19. Ibid.
20. Ibid.
21. Ibid.
22. Ibid.
23. Ibid.
24. Ibid.
25. Ibid.
26. Ibid., appendix F.
27. Ibid.
28. Ibid.
29. Ibid.
30. Ibid.
31. Ibid., appendix G.
32. Ibid.
33. Ibid.
34. Ibid.
35. Ibid.
36. Ibid., appendix H.
37. Ibid., appendix B.
38. Ibid., appendix H.
39. Ibid.
40. Tauss, "The Crash of TWA Flight 800."
41. Ibid.
42. NTSB docket materials, Exhibit 4A, appendix B.
43. "Affidavit of Mr. Dwight Brumley," TWA800.com, http://twa800.com/lahr/affidavits/p-dwight-brumley.pdf.
44. Ibid.

SEVEN: THE GOOD BUREAUCRAT

1. Bob Woodward, *The Last of the President's Men* (New York: Simon & Schuster, 2015), e-book, chapter 22.

2. Al Kamen, "Route to NTSB Runs Through Tennessee," *Washington Post*, May 28, 1993, cached at High Beam Research, http://www.highbeam.com/doc/1P2-948549.html.

3. Phone interview with Vernon Grose, October 23, 2015.

4. Patricia Milton, *In the Blink of an Eye: The FBI Investigation of TWA Flight 800* (New York: Random House, 1999), 131.

5. Christine Negroni, *Deadly Departure: Why the Experts Failed to Prevent the TWA Flight 800 Disaster and How It Could Happen Again* (New York: HarperCollins, 2000), 85.

6. Phone interview with Vernon Grose, October 23, 2105 and follow-up e-mail exchange on November 9, 2015.

7. TWA Flight 800 Investigation/ Day 2–3, Wikisource, https://en.wikisource.org/wiki/Portal:TWA_Flight_800_investigation/Day2-3.

8. NTSB Witness Group Factual Report, Docket No. SA-516, Exhibit No. 4A, October 16, 1997, http://twa800.com/4a/exhibit4a.html.

9. Megyn Kelly Reports, Fox News, June 19, 2013, https://www.youtube.com/watch?v=Qg0vN1j_Q0A.

10. NTSB Aircraft Accident Report, *In-flight breakup over the Atlantic Ocean, Trans World Airlines Flight 800 Boeing 747-131, N93119, near East Moriches, New York*, July 17, 1996 (Washington, DC: Diane Publishing, 2000), 255, http://bit.ly/1LqLGsX.

11. As shown in *Silenced*.

12. TWA Flight 800, NTSB docket materials, DCA-96-MA070, August 2000, Exhibit 4A, appendix G.

13. Ibid., appendix D.

14. Ibid., appendix C. All Perry material can be found here.

15. Ibid., appendix H.

16. Ibid., appendix N.

17. Ibid., appendix O.

18. *The Washington Times*, Tuesday, August 15, 2000, cached at Associated Retired Aviation Professionals: The Flight 800 Investigation, http://twa800.com/images/times-8-15-00.gif.

19. David Hendrix, "Witnesses Boost Missile Theory," *Press-Enterprise*, October 20, 1997, cached at http://whatreallyhappened.com/RANCHO/CRASH/TWA/AUDIO.html

20. NTSB docket materials, Exhibit 4A, appendix FF.

21. "Conspiracy Inoculation," *New York Times*, November 19, 1997, http://www.nytimes.com/1997/11/19/opinion/conspiracy-inoculation.html.
22. "After the Crash," *New York Times*, July 19, 1996, http://www.nytimes.com/1996/07/19/opinion/after-the-crash.html.
23. "FBI: No criminal evidence behind TWA 800 crash," CNN.com, November 18, 1997, http://www.cnn.com/US/9711/18/twa.fbi.presser/.
24. Randolph M. Tauss, "The Crash of TWA Flight 800," https://www.cia.gov/offices-of-cia/public-affairs/entertainment-industry-liaison/twaflight.pdf.

EIGHT: RESPONSIBLE JOURNALISM

1. E-mail to author, circa June 20, 2001.
2. Al Kamen, "Bombshell from Lawrence Livermore," *Washington Post*, March 28, 1994, http://www.washingtonpost.com/pb/archive/politics/1994/03/28/bombshell-from-lawrence-livermore/bbec0be8-84a0-47b8-a725-e6013e1c4024/?resType=accessibility.
3. Lawrie Mifflin, "Media Talk; ABC News at Odds With Parent Network," *New York Times*, October 26, 1998, http://www.nytimes.com/1998/10/26/business/media-talk-abc-news-at-odds-with-parent-network.html.
4. Kristina Borjesson, *Into the Buzzsaw: Leading Journalists Expose the Myth of a Free Press* (New York: Prometheus Books, 2004), 323.
5. E-mail to the author, November 9, 2015.
6. Borjesson, *Into the Buzzsaw*, 325.
7. Transcript, CNN The Point with Greta Van Susteren, July 17, 2001, http://www.cnn.com/TRANSCRIPTS/0107/17/tpt.00.html.
8. Reed Irvine and Cliff Kincaid, "Advice to CNN, Part II," Accuracy in Media, August 17, 2001, http://www.aim.org/media-monitor/advice-to-cnn-part-ii/.
9. Reed Irvine, "CNN Has Two Black Eyes," Accuracy in Media, August 3, 2001, http://www.aim.org/publications/weekly_column/2001/08/03.html.

NINE: SEPTEMBER 11

1. For more detail, see Jack Cashill, "What Does Leon Panetta Know About TWA 800," January 8, 2009, WND.com, http://www.cashill.com/twa800/what_does_leon_panetta.htm.
2. Phone interview with Thomas Young, November 11, 2015.

3.   Reed Irvine, "The 'Bombing' of TWA 800," Accuracy in Media, September 19, 2001, http://www.aim.org/aim-column/the-bombing-of-twa-800/.

4.   Transcript, CBS News Special Report, September 11, 2001, cached at http://pastebin.ca/raw/1965515.

5.   Transcript, "Larry King Live," September 11, 2001, cached at Associated Retired Aviation Professionals: The Flight 800 Investigation, http://twa800.com/news/kerry-9-11-01.htm.

6.   CNBC News Transcripts, *Hardball with Chris Matthews*, September 24, 2001, cached at Associated Retired Aviation Professionals: The Flight 800 Investigation, http://twa800.com/news/kerry-transcript-9-24-01.htm.

7.   Walter Robinson and Glen Johnson, "Airlines Fought Security Changes," *Boston Globe*, September 20, 2001, cached at http://www.webguild.com/sentinel/airlines_fought.htm.

8.   Letter cached at Associated Retired Aviation Professionals: The Flight 800 Investigation, http://twa800.com/news/mundo-9-25-01.htm.

9.   Phone interview with Thomas Young, November 11, 2015.

10. Nelson DeMille, *Night Fall* (New York: Grand Central Publishing, 2004). The incidents that DeMille relates are condensed from the book's foreword.

TEN: FIT TO PRINT

1.   N. R. Kleinfield, "The Crash of Flight 800," *New York Times*, July 18, 1996, http://www.nytimes.com/1996/07/18/nyregion/crash-flight-800-overview-twa-jetliner-leaving-new-york-for-paris-crashes.html.

2.   "Explosion Aboard T.W.A. Flight 800," *New York Times*, July 19, 1996, http://www.nytimes.com/1996/07/19/nyregion/explosion-aboard-twa-flight-800-remarks-by-clinton-about-the-crash-of-flight-800.html.

3.   President Bill Clinton, January 26, 1998, video cached at Miller Center of Public Affairs, University of Virginia, http://www.bing.com/videos/search?q=i+did+not+have+sexual+relations+with+that+woman%2c+miss+lewinsky.+%E2%80%9D&view=detail&mid=146486F89583EEE7CD33146486F89583EEE7CD33&FORM=VIRE7.

4.   David Johnston, "Explosion Aboard T.W.A. Flight 800: The Theories," *New York Times*, July 19, 1996, http://www.nytimes.com/1996/07/19/nyregion/explosion-aboard-twa-flight-800-theories-multitude-ideas-but-little-evidence.html.

5. Matthew Purdy, "Investigators Suspect Explosive Device as Likeliest Cause for Crash of Flight 800," *New York Times*, July 19, 1996, http://partners.nytimes.com/library/national/960719explosion-aboard-t.html.

6. CIA documents cached at TWA Flight 800: The Impossible Zoom Climb, raylahr.entryhost.com, "CIA records released to Tom Stalcup," records 26–50.

7. David Johnston, "The Crash of Flight 800: The Possibilities," *New York Times*, July 21, 1996, http://www.nytimes.com/1996/07/21/nyregion/crash-flight-800-possibilities-tips-leads-theories-are-flooding.html.

8. CIA documents cached at TWA Flight 800: The Impossible Zoom Climb, raylahr.entryhost.com, "CIA records released to Tom Stalcup," records 26–50.

9. Matthew Purdy, "No Evidence of Explosive So Far in Crash Inquiry," *New York Times*, July 24, 1996, http://www.nytimes.com/1996/07/24/nyregion/no-evidence-of-explosive-so-far-in-crash-inquiry.html.

10. "The Fate of Flight 800; The President's Remarks at Kennedy to the Families of the Crash Victims," *New York Times*, July 26, 1996, http://www.nytimes.com/1996/07/26/nyregion/fate-flight-800-president-s-remarks-kennedy-families-crash-victims.html.

11. Matthew Wald, "The Fate of Flight 800: The Data," *New York Times*, July 26, 1996, http://www.nytimes.com/1996/07/26/nyregion/fate-flight-800-data-record-quick-destruction-briefest-sound-then-silence.html.

12. Matthew Purdy, "The Fate of Flight 800: The Flight Data," *New York Times*, July 27, 1996, http://www.nytimes.com/1996/07/27/nyregion/fate-flight-800-flight-data-backing-bomb-theory-devices-stopped unison.html.

13. "Mr. Clinton Moves on Air Security," *New York Times*, July 26, 1996, http://www.nytimes.com/1996/07/26/opinion/mr-clinton-moves-on-air-security.html.

14. Joe Sexton, "The Fate of Flight 800: The Investigation," *New York Times*, July 28, 1996, http://www.nytimes.com/1996/07/28/nyregion/fate-flight-800-investigation-while-cause-crash-sought-parallel-criminal-inquiry.html.

15. CIA documents cached at TWA Flight 800: The Impossible Zoom Climb, raylahr.entryhost.com, "CIA records released to Tom Stalcup," records 26–50.

16. Taylor Branch, *The Clinton Tapes: Wrestling History in the White House* (New York: Simon & Schuster, 2010), 371.

17. Ibid., 372.

18.　Ibid.

19.　Byron York, "The Facts About Clinton and Terrorism," *National Review*, September 11, 2006, http://www.nationalreview.com/article/218683/facts-about-clinton-and-terrorism-byron-york.

20.　Kevin Ready and Cap Parlier, *TWA 800: Accident or Incident* (Prescott, AZ: Saint Gaudens Press, 1998).

21.　Transcript, "TWA Flight 800: No Survivors," CNN.com, June 31, 2013, http://www.cnn.com/TRANSCRIPTS/1306/21/acd.02.html.

22.　Branch, *The Clinton Tapes*, 371.

23.　David Johnston and Tim Weiner, "Seizing the Crime Issue, Clinton Blurs Party Lines," *New York Times*, August 1, 1996, http://www.nytimes.com/1996/08/01/us/seizing-the-crime-issue-clinton-blurs-party-lines.html.

24.　Don Van Natta, "Fuel Tank's Condition Makes Malfunction Seem Less Likely," *New York Times*, August 14, 1996, http://www.nytimes.com/1996/08/14/nyregion/fuel-tank-s-condition-makes-malfunction-seem-less-likely.html.

25.　TWA Flight 800, NTSB docket materials, DCA-96-MA070, August 2000, Exhibit 4A, appendix C.

26.　Dan Barry, "F.B.I. Says 2 Labs Found Traces Of Explosive on T.W.A. Jetliner," *New York Times*, August 24, 1996, http://www.nytimes.com/1996/08/24/nyregion/fbi-says-2-labs-found-traces-of-explosive-on-twa-jetliner.html.

27.　Don Van Natta, "Prime Evidence Found That Device Exploded in Cabin of TWA 800," *New York Times*, August 23, 1996, http://www.nytimes.com/1996/08/23/nyregion/prime-evidence-found-that-device-exploded-in-cabin-of-flight-800.html.

28.　Jocelyn Noveck, "Pierre Salinger Claims Navy Missile Shot Down TWA Flight 800," Associated Press, November 8, 1996, cached at http://www.welfarestate.com/twa800/pierre.htm.

29.　Patricia Milton, *In the Blink of an Eye: The FBI Investigation of TWA Flight 800* (New York: Random House, 1999), 227.

30.　Don Van Natta, "Small Pieces of T.W.A. Jet's Wreckage Intrigue Investigators," *New York Times*, August 9, 1996, http://www.nytimes.com/1996/08/09/nyregion/small-pieces-of-twa-jet-s-wreckage-intrigue-investigators.html.

31.　Barry, "F.B.I. Says 2 Labs Found Traces Of Explosive on T.W.A. Jetliner."

32.　Harold Trimm, *Forensics the Easy Way* (Hauppauge, NY: Barron's Educational Series, 2005), 151.

33. Tom Stalcup and Kristina Borjesson, *TWA Flight 800* (TWA 800 Project, LLC, 2013).

34. David Johnston, "At F.B.I. Lab, A Scientific Mission and a Challenge of Its Methods, *New York Times*, August 3, 1996, http://www.nytimes. com/1996/08/03/nyregion/at-fbi-lab-a-scientific-mission-and-a-challenge-of-its-methods.html.

35. Dick Morris, *Behind the Oval Office: Winning the Presidency in the Nineties* (New York: Random House, 1997), 33.

36. Francis X. Clines, "Clinton Signs Bill Cutting Welfare; States in New Role," *New York Times*, August 23, 1996, http://www.nytimes. com/1996/08/23/us/clinton-signs-bill-cutting-welfare-states-in-new-role. html.

37. Barry, "F.B.I. Says 2 Labs Found Traces Of Explosive on T.W.A. Jetliner."

38. Christine Negroni, *Deadly Departure: Why the Experts Failed to Prevent the TWA Flight 800 Disaster and How It Could Happen Again* (New York: HarperCollins, 2000), 185.

39. Ibid.

ELEVEN: BLACK HOLE

1. Bill Clinton, *My Life* (New York: Random House, 2004), 334.

2. Richard Clarke, *Against All Enemies* (New York: Simon & Schuster, 2004), 123–24.

3. Hillary Clinton, *Living History* (New York: Scribner, 2003), 363.

4. Louis Freeh, *My FBI: Bringing Down The Mafia, Investigating Bill Clinton, and Fighting the War on Terror* (New York: St. Martin's Press, 2005), 291.

5. Dick Morris, *Off with Their Heads: Traitors, Crooks, and Obstructionists in American Politics, Media, and Business* (New York: Harper Collins, 2003), 106.

6. Good Morning America, June 19, 2013, https://www.youtube.com/ watch?v=2wPZGZXmIEk.

7. Transcript, "TWA Flight 800: No Survivors," CNN.com, June 31, 2013, http://www.cnn.com/TRANSCRIPTS/1306/21/acd.02.html.

8. Special Report of the Select Committee on Intelligence, United States Senate, January 4, 1995 to October 3, 1996, published January 22, 1997, http://www.intelligence.senate.gov/publications/committee-activities-special-report-select-committee-intelligence-january-4-1995.

9. CIA documents cached at TWA Flight 800: The Impossible Zoom Climb, raylahr.entryhost.com, "CIA records released to Tom Stalcup," records 51–75.

10. CIA documents cached at TWA Flight 800: The Impossible Zoom Climb, raylahr.entryhost.com, "CIA records released to Tom Stalcup," records 1–10.

11. Clarke, *Against All Enemies*, 121.

12. Ibid., 122.

13. CIA documents cached at TWA Flight 800: The Impossible Zoom Climb, raylahr.entryhost.com, "CIA records released to Tom Stalcup," records 26–50.

14. Clarke, *Against All Enemies*, 122.

15. Ibid., 124.

16. Ibid., 125.

17. Patricia Milton, *In the Blink of an Eye: The FBI Investigation of TWA Flight 800* (New York: Random House, 1999), 282.

18. Clarke, *Against All Enemies*, 126.

19. Ibid.

20. "Clarke's Take on Terror," *60 Minutes*, CBS, March 19, 2004, http://www.cbsnews.com/news/clarkes-take-on-terror/.

TWELVE: DOG DAYS

1. Don Van Natta, "More Traces of Explosive in Flight 800," *New York Times*, August 31, 1996, http://www.nytimes.com/1996/08/31/nyregion/more-traces-of-explosive-in-flight-800.html.

2. "TWA Flight 800 Crash Investigation," C-SPAN, May 10, 1999, http://www.c-span.org/video/?123165-1/twa-flight-800-crash-investigation.

3. Patricia Milton, *In the Blink of an Eye: The FBI Investigation of TWA Flight 800* (New York: Random House, 1999), 262.

4. As interviewed for *Silenced*.

5. Tom Stalcup and Kristina Borjesson, *TWA Flight 800* (TWA 800 Project, LLC, 2013).

6. "TWA Flight 800 Crash Investigation," C-SPAN, May 10, 1999.

7. Stalcup and Borjesson, *TWA Flight 800*.

8. As interviewed for *Silenced*.

9. Ibid.

10. Phone interview with Gene York, June 8, 2015.

11. Matthew Wald, "New Focus on Malfunctions In Inquiry on T.W.A. Crash," *New York Times*, September 19, 1996, http://www.nytimes. com/1996/09/19/nyregion/new-focus-on-malfunctions-in-inquiry-on-twa-crash.html.

12. Milton, *In the Blink of an Eye*, 229.

13. Matthew Purdy, "Bomb Security Test On Jet May Explain Trace of Explosives," *New York Times*, September 21, 1996, http://www.nytimes. com/1996/09/21/nyregion/bomb-security-test-on-jet-may-explain-trace-of-explosives.html.

14. Ibid.

15. Don Van Natta, "Setback in T.W.A. Crash Inquiry Adds Urgency to the Search for Evidence of a Bomb," *New York Times*, September 22, 1996, http://www. nytimes.com/1996/09/22/nyregion/setback-in-twa-crash-inquiry-adds-urgency-to-the-search-for-evidence-of-a-bomb.html?pagewanted=all.

16. Ibid.

17. Milton, *In the Blink of an Eye*, 231.

18. Letter to Rep. James Traficant from Jim Kallstrom in response to Traficant's questions, September 5, 1997, http://www.apfn.org/thewinds/flight800.pdf.

19. The gate assignment from June 10, 1996 is listed as Appendix VII in Peter Lance: *Triple Cross: How bin Laden's Master Spy Penetrated the CIA, the Green Berets, and the FBI—and Why Patrick Fitzgerald Failed to Stop Him* (New York: HarperCollins, 2006), 567.

20. This was reported by Dave Hendrix of the Riverside *Press-Enterprise* and published as a chapter, "St. Louis Canine Scheme," in James Sanders' book, *Altered Evidence* (Philadelphia, PA: Offset Paperbacks, 1999). Tom Shoemaker and Kay Pennington also did original research on the story as reported in the December 1988 and January 1999 *TWA Case Files Newsletter*.

21. Ibid.

22. Transcript, Hearing before the Subcommittee on Aviation, July 10, 1997, http://commdocs.house.gov/committees/Trans/hpw105-33.000/hpw105-33_0f.htm.

23. Christine Negroni, *Deadly Departure: Why the Experts Failed to Prevent the TWA Flight 800 Disaster and How It Could Happen Again* (New York: HarperCollins, 2000), 185.

24. Ibid., 186.

25. Transcript, Hearing before the Subcommittee on Aviation.

26. Milton, *In the Blink of an Eye*, 231–32.

27. Phone interview with Herman Burnett, August 2001.
28. Todd Purdum, "Clinton Signs a Wide-Ranging Measure on Airport Security," *New York Times*, October 10, 1996, http://www.nytimes.com/1996/10/10/us/clinton-signs-a-wide-ranging-measure-on-airport-security.html.

THIRTEEN: LOST AT SEA

1. CIA documents cached at TWA Flight 800: The Impossible Zoom Climb, raylahr.entryhost.com, "CIA records released to Tom Stalcup," records 26–50.
2. Robert Patterson, *Dereliction of Duty: The Eyewitness Account of How Bill Clinton Compromised America's National Security* (Washington, DC: Regnery, 2003), 139.
3. FBI NO/FORN memo 1995, Appendix XI, in Peter Lance: *Triple Cross: How bin Laden's Master Spy Penetrated the CIA, the Green Berets, and the FBI—and Why Patrick Fitzgerald Failed to Stop Him* (New York: HarperCollins, 2006), 576.
4. Ibid.
5. Patricia Milton, *In the Blink of an Eye: The FBI Investigation of TWA Flight 800* (New York: Random House, 1999), 6.
6. John Barry and Roger Charles, "Sea of Lies," *Newsweek*, July 12, 1992, http://www.newsweek.com/sea-lies-200118.
7. Michael Gordon, "Cover-Up Denied in Downing Of Iranian Passenger Jet in '88," *New York Times*, July 22, 1992, http://www.nytimes.com/1992/07/22/world/cover-up-denied-in-downing-of-iranian-passenger-jet-in-88.html.
8. David Evans, "Crowe Endorsement Of Clinton Raises More Than Eyebrows," *Chicago Tribune*, September 25, 1992, http://articles.chicagotribune.com/1992-09-25/news/9203270346_1_crowe-iranian-territorial-waters-clinton-campaign.
9. William Crowe, "Clinton's Vietnam Era Compatriots at Oxford; Divisive and Peripheral," *New York Times*, October 13, 1992, http://www.nytimes.com/1992/10/13/opinion/l-clinton-s-vietnam-era-compatriots-at-oxford-divisive-and-peripheral-350092.html.
10. Andrew Revkin, "Conspiracy Theories Rife On Demise of Flight 800," *New York Times*, September 17, 1996, http://www.nytimes.com/1996/09/17/nyregion/conspiracy-theories-rife-on-demise-of-flight-800.html.

11. Jocelyn Noveck, "Pierre Salinger's TWA Flight 800 Missile News Conference," Associated Press, November 8, 1996, http://www.welfarestate.com/twa800/pierre.htm.

12. Milton, *In the Blink of an Eye*, 89.

13. Ibid., 91.

14. TWA Flight 800, NTSB docket materials, DCA-96-MA070, August 2000, Exhibit 4A, appendix M.

15. Milton, *In the Blink of an Eye*, 153.

16. Matthew Purdy, "Despite Many Denials, T.W.A. Missile Rumor Is Back," *New York Times*, November 9, 1996, http://www.nytimes.com/1996/11/09/nyregion/despite-many-denials-twa-missile-rumor-is-back.html.

17. NTSB docket materials, Exhibit 4A, appendix M.

18. Kristina Borjesson, *Into the Buzzsaw: Leading Journalists Expose the Myth of a Free Press* (New York: Prometheus Books, 2004), 291.

19. E-mail exchange and follow-up interview, November 15, 2010.

20. Noveck, "Pierre Salinger's TWA Flight 800 Missile News Conference."

21. Milton, *In the Blink of an Eye*, 150–52.

22. Purdy, "Despite Many Denials, T.W.A. Missile Rumor Is Back."

23. Letter from Alice Rowe and Lisa Perry to Cmdr. Donaldson, October 17, 1998, http://twa800.com/pages/perry.htm.

24. FBI New York Office Press Release, "FBI: No criminal evidence behind TWA 800 crash," November 18, 1997, http://www.cnn.com/US/9711/18/twa.fbi.presser/.

25. E-mail communications with Allen Strasser, August 2008, for more detail see Jack Cashill, "Pilot Sheds New Light on TWA 800 Scandal," August 7, 2008, WND.com, http://www.cashill.com/twa800/pilot_sheds.htm.

26. Milton, *In the Blink of an Eye*, 186.

27. E-mail communications, June 2013, for more detail see Jack Cashill, "Did Navy Sub Missile Hit TWA 800?" WND.com, June 21, 2013, http://www.wnd.com/2013/06/did-navy-sub-missile-hit-twa-800/.

28. NTSB Aircraft Accident Report, *In-flight breakup over the Atlantic Ocean, Trans World Airlines Flight 800 Boeing 747-131, N93119, near East Moriches, New York, July 17, 1996* (Washington, DC: Diane Publishing, 2000), 88–89, http://bit.ly/1LqLGsX.

29. Reed Irvine, "Navy Vessels on Classified Maneuvers," AIM Report, September 1999, http://www.aim.org/publications/aim_report/1999/09a.htm.

30.   Letter from Lewis Schiliro to Rep. James Traficant, July 27, 1997, http://
      twa800.com/letters/fbi.htm.

31.   "Erroneous Airspeed Indications Cited in Boeing 757 Control Loss,"
      Accident Prevention, October 1999, http://flightsafety.org/ap/ap_oct99.
      pdf.

32.   Christine Negroni, *Deadly Departure: Why the Experts Failed to Prevent
      the TWA Flight 800 Disaster and How It Could Happen Again* (New
      York: HarperCollins, 2000), 93.

33.   Jerry Markon et al., "Divers Wait as Devices Scan Ocean," *Newsday*,
      July 22, 1996, cached at http://whatreallyhappened.com/RANCHO/
      CRASH/TWA/PING/ping.html.

34.   Negroni, *Deadly Departure*, 117.

35.   Ibid., 170.

36.   "The Fate of Flight 800: The President's Remarks at Kennedy to the
      Families of the Crash Victims," *New York Times*, July 26, 1996, http://
      www.nytimes.com/1996/07/26/nyregion/fate-flight-800-president-s-
      remarks-kennedy-families-crash-victims.html.

37.   Group Chairman's Factual Report of Investigation Cockpit Voice
      Recorder, October 20, 1997, Associated Retired Aviation Professionals:
      The Flight 800 Investigation, http://www.twa800.com/ntsb/8-15-00/
      docket/Ex_12A.pdf.

38.   CVR transcript TWA Flight 800, Aviation Safety Network, http://
      aviation-safety.net/investigation/cvr/transcripts/cvr_tw800.php.

39.   CIA documents cached at TWA Flight 800: The Impossible Zoom Climb,
      raylahr.entryhost.com, "CIA records released to Tom Stalcup," records
      26–50.

40.   "Executive Order 13039—Exclusion of the Naval Special Warfare
      Development Group From the Federal Labor-Management Relations
      Program," March 11, 1997, The American Presidency Project, http://
      www.presidency.ucsb.edu/ws/?pid=53855.

41.   Matthew Purdy, "Missile Theory Rebutted in T.W.A. Flight 800 Crash,"
      New York Times, March 12, 1997, http://www.nytimes.com/1997/03/12/
      nyregion/missile-theory-rebutted-in-twa-flight-800-crash.html.

42.   Transcript, *Witnessed*.

43.   As interviewed for *Silenced*.

FOURTEEN: MR. SMITH GOES TO WASHINGTON

1.   Bob Woodward, "How Mark Felt Became 'Deep Throat,'" *Washington
      Post*, June 20, 2005, https://www.washingtonpost.com/politics/how-
      mark-felt-became-deep-throat/2012/06/04/gJQAlpARIV_story.html.

2. Robert Davey, "High-Ranking Military Officers, Independent Investigators, Pilots, and Eyewitnesses Believe a Missile Destroyed TWA Flight 800," *Village Voice*, July 21, 1998, http://www.villagevoice.com/news/high-ranking-military-officers-independent-investigators-pilots-and-eyewitnesses-believe-a-missle-destroyed-twa-flight-800-6424009.

3. Mark Hosenball, "Re-Creating Flight 800's Final Seconds," *Newsweek*, November 30, 1997, http://www.newsweek.com/re-creating-flight-800s-final-seconds-170906.

4. Videotaped interview with Don Nibert, August 30, 2001.

5. CIA documents cached at TWA Flight 800: The Impossible Zoom Climb, raylahr.entryhost.com, "CIA records released to Tom Stalcup," records 51–75.

6. Ibid.

7. Brian Knowlton, "Boeing to Buy McDonnell Douglas," *New York Times*, December 16, 1996, http://www.nytimes.com/1996/12/16/news/16iht-merge.t_0.html.

8. Ralph Nader, Letter on Boeing McDonnell Douglas Merger, December 23, 1996, http://www.cptech.org/at/boeing/dec231996.html.

9. John Broder, "Office Depot And Staples Merger Halted," *New York Times*, July 1, 1997, http://www.nytimes.com/1997/07/01/business/office-depot-and-staples-merger-halted.html.

10. Boeing press release, November 18, 1997, now cached at http://whatreallyhappened.com/RANCHO/CRASH/TWA/CIAVIDEO/boeing.html.

FIFTEEN: THE FIXERS

1. Mark Hosenball, "Desperately Seeking the Next Willie Horton," *Newsweek*, June 2, 1996, http://www.newsweek.com/desperately-seeking-next-willie-horton-178768.

2. Jerry Gray, "Politics: The Democrats; Clinton Tells U.S. Athletes, 'I Want You to Mop Up'," *New York Times*, July 20, 1996, http://www.nytimes.com/1996/07/20/us/politics-the-democrat-clinton-tells-us-athletes-i-want-you-to-mop-up.html.

3. Patricia Milton, *In the Blink of an Eye: The FBI Investigation of TWA Flight 800* (New York: Random House, 1999), 226.

4. David Johnston, "No. 2 Official at Justice Dept. Leaving After 3 Years There," *New York Times*, January 15, 1997, http://www.nytimes.com/1997/01/15/us/no-2-official-at-justice-dept-leaving-after-3-years-there.html.

5. Michelle Cottle, "Nice work if you can get it: how Fannie Mae became Washington's biggest power player," *Washington Monthly*, June 1, 1998, http://www.thefreelibrary.com/Nice+work+if+you+can+get+it:+how+Fannie+Mae+became+Washington's...-a020789484.

6. Tim Weiner, "Nominations Have Made C.I.A. Chief Odd Man Out," *New York Times*, December 6, 1996, http://www.nytimes.com/1996/12/06/us/nominations-have-made-cia-chief-odd-man-out.html.

7. CIA documents cached at TWA Flight 800: The Impossible Zoom Climb, raylahr.entryhost.com, "CIA records released to Tom Stalcup," records 26–50.

8. Ibid., records 51–75.

9. Tim Weiner, "For 'the Ultimate Staff Guy,' a Time to Reap the Rewards of Being Loyal," *New York Times*, March 20, 1997, http://www.nytimes.com/1997/03/20/us/for-the-ultimate-staff-guy-a-time-to-reap-the-rewards-of-being-loyal.html.

10. Selwyn Raab, "F.B.I. Agent Won't Testify At Mafia Figure's Hearing," *New York Times*, May 18, 1996, http://www.nytimes.com/1996/05/18/nyregion/fbi-agent-won-t-testify-at-mafia-figure-s-hearing.html.

11. Letter from Kallstrom's office to Louis Freeh, April 10, 1996, Appendix V in Peter Lance, *Triple Cross: How bin Laden's Master Spy Penetrated the CIA, the Green Berets, and the FBI—and Why Patrick Fitzgerald Failed to Stop Him* (New York: HarperCollins, 2006), 553.

12. Dennis Fitzgerald, *Informants and Undercover Investigations: A Practical Guide to Law, Policy, and Procedure* (Boca Raton, FL: CRC Press, 2007), 230.

13. Michael Brick, "Agent Accused in Mob Murders Seeks Immunity," *New York Daily News*, April 11, 2006, http://z14.invisionfree.com/GangstersInc/ar/t754.htm.

14. "Goelz Named to Top Administrative Post at NTSB," NTSB Press Release, December 4, 1997, http://www.ntsb.gov/news/press-releases/Pages/Goelz_Named_to_Top_Administrative_Post_at_NTSB;_Finch_to_Head_Government_Public_and_Family_Affairs_Office.aspx.

15. Jeff Gerth and Stephen Labaton, "Ex-Clinton Aide Is Linked to Big Chinese Project," *New York Times*, March 6, 1997, https://www.nytimes.com/books/97/12/14/home/030697hubbell.html.

16. Jeff Gerth and Stephen Labaton, "Payment to an Ex-Clinton Aide Is Linked to Big Chinese Project," *New York Times*, March 6, 1997, http://www.nytimes.com/1997/03/06/us/payment-to-an-ex-clinton-aide-is-linked-to-big-chinese-project.html.

17. Ibid.

18. "Fannie Mae Head to Quit," *New York Times*, January 11, 2003, http://www.nytimes.com/2003/01/11/business/fannie-mae-head-to-quit.html.

19. Chris Neefus, "Former Clinton Official Paid $26 Million by Fannie Mae Before Taxpayer Bailout Now on Obama Shortlist to Run FBI," cnsnews.com, http://www.cnsnews.com/news/article/former-clinton-official-paid-26-million-fannie-mae-taxpayer-bailout-now-obama-shortlist.

20. David Rosenbaum, "For Members of Panel, Past Work Becomes an Issue in the Present," *New York Times*, April 14, 2004, http://www.nytimes.com/2004/04/14/us/threats-responses-commissioners-for-members-panel-past-work-becomes-issue.html.

21. "Sandy Berger's Theft of Classified Documents: Unanswered Questions," Staff Report, U.S. House of Representatives, Committee on Oversight and Government Reform, https://fas.org/irp/congress/2007_rpt/berger.pdf.

22. Ibid.

23. Richard Clarke, *Against All Enemies* (New York: Simon & Schuster, 2004), 106.

24. "Transcript: Wednesday's 9/11 Commission Hearings," March 24, 2004, *Washington Post*, http://www.washingtonpost.com/wp-dyn/articles/A20349-2004Mar24.html.

25. "Text of Condoleezza Rice statement," *USA Today*, April 8, 2004, http://usatoday30.usatoday.com/news/washington/2004-04-08-rice-transcript_x.htm.

26. Rosenbaum, "For Members of Panel, Past Work Becomes an Issue in the Present."

27. Memo from Jamie Gorelick to Louis Freeh and others, April 14, 2005, http://www.justice.gov/sites/default/files/ag/legacy/2004/04/14/1995_gorelick_memo.pdf.

28. "Gorelick's Wall," *Wall Street Journal*, April 15, 2004, http://www.wsj.com/articles/SB108198447949083135.

29. Eric Lichtblau, "A Kerry Adviser Leaves the Race Over Documents," *New York Times*, July 21, 2014, http://www.nytimes.com/2004/07/21/us/a-kerry-adviser-leaves-the-race-over-documents.html.

30. Eric Lichtblau, "Clinton Aide Pleads Guilty to Taking Secret Papers," *New York Times*, April 2, 2005, http://www.nytimes.com/2005/04/02/politics/clinton-aide-pleads-guilty-to-taking-secret-papers.html?_r=0.

31. Ibid.

32. Ibid.

33. Carol Loennig, "Berger is Fined for Smuggling Classified Papers," *Washington Post*, September 9, 2005, http://www.washingtonpost.com/wp-dyn/content/article/2005/09/08/AR2005090801711.html.

34. "Campaign Finance in American Politics," http://www.campaignmoney.com/.

35. William Bender, "Weldon blasts Sestak's ties with fired CIA senior analyst," *Delco Times*, April 23, 2006, http://alt.politics.bush.narkive.com/RiRbW1Pp/weldon-blasts-sestak-s-ties-with-fired-cia-senior-analyst.

36. Weldon Congressional Campaign press release, "Sestak's Secretary works for Sandy Berger," May 10, 2006, http://www.abledangerblog.com/2006/05/sestaks-press-secretary-works-for.html.

37. Transcript, William Jefferson Clinton on FOX News Sunday, September 24, 2006, http://www.foxnews.com/story/2006/09/26/transcript-william-jefferson-clinton-on-fox-news-sunday.html.

38. Greg Gordon, "Congressman in tight race for re-election comes under federal investigation," McClatchy Newspapers, October 13, 2006, http://www.mcclatchydc.com/incoming/article24458383.html.

39. Kate Zernike, "In Pennsylvania, Questions About War Erode a Traditional Republican Advantage," *New York Times*, October 15, 2006, http://www.nytimes.com/2006/10/15/us/politics/15weldon.html?_r=0.

40. Brian Naylor, "FBI Investigates Pennsylvania Republican Weldon," NPR, October 20, 2006, http://www.npr.org/templates/story/story.php?storyId=6352043.

41. "It's time feds bring Weldon matter to close," *Delco Times*, August 4, 2009, http://www.delcotimes.com/general-news/20090804/editorial-its-time-feds-bring-weldon-matter-to-close.

42. Christopher Matthews, "Sklamberg Leaves D.C. U.S. Attorney's Office for FDA," Main Justice, May 20, 2010, http://www.mainjustice.com/2010/05/20/sklamberg-leaves-d-c-u-s-attorneys-office-for-the-fda/.

43. Press Release, "Donaldson Exposes Traficant's Duplicity on TWA Flight 800," May 24, 1999, cached at Associated Retired Aviation Professionals: The Flight 800 Investigation, http://twa800.com/news/prtraficant.htm.

44. Ibid.

SIXTEEN: ENGINE TROUBLE

1. Megyn Kelly Reports, Fox News, June 19, 2013, https://www.youtube.com/watch?v=Qg0vN1j_Q0A.

2. USS *Carr*, http://navysite.de/ffg/FFG52.HTM#co.

3. Conversation captured in an e-mail exchange, December 9, 2015.

4. Michael Rivero, "Was TWA 800 Shot Down By a Military Missile?" http://whatreallyhappened.com/RANCHO/CRASH/TWA/twa. php#axzz3yZczrqdK

5. Patricia Milton, *In the Blink of an Eye: The FBI Investigation of TWA Flight 800* (New York: Random House, 1999), 329–31.

6. "TWA Flight 800: A Mother's Letter," June 19, 2003, WND.com, http:// www.wnd.com/2003/06/19368/.

7. Phone interview with Lisa Michelson, June 28, 2015.

8. Milton, *In the Blink of an Eye*, 331.

9. Transcript, "TWA Flight 800: No Survivors," CNN.com, June 31, 2013, http://www.cnn.com/TRANSCRIPTS/1306/21/acd.02.html.

10. CIA documents cached at TWA Flight 800: The Impossible Zoom Climb, raylahr.entryhost.com, "CIA records released to Tom Stalcup," records 76–101.

11. *National Law Journal*, September 18, 2006, cached at TWA Flight 800: The Impossible Zoom Climb, http://raylahr.entryhost.com/9-18-06-National-Law-Journal.pdf.

12. See "Twa Flight 800: The Impossible Zoom Climb," http://raylahr. entryhost.com.

13. TWA Flight 800, NTSB docket materials, DCA-96-MA070, August 2000, "TWA Flight 800 Crash Investigation," C-SPAN, May 10, 1999, http://www.c-span.org/video/?123165-1/twa-flight-800-crash-investigation.

14. *Hannity's America*, Fox News, July 29, 1997.

15. NTSB Witness Group Factual Report, October 16, 1997, cached at Associated Retired Aviation Professionals: The Flight 800 Investigation, http://twa800.com/4a/exhibit4a.html.

16. NTSB Aircraft Accident Report, *In-flight breakup over the Atlantic Ocean, Trans World Airlines Flight 800 Boeing 747-131, N93119, near East Moriches, New York, July 17, 1996* (Washington, DC: Diane Publishing, 2000), 74.

17. CBS News 2, August 5, 1996.

18. TWA Flight 800, NTSB docket materials, DCA-96-MA070, August 2000, Exhibit 4A, appendix H.

19. Matthew Wald, "Nothing 'Extraordinary' Is Found in 747's Engines," *New York Times*, August 17, 1996, http://www.nytimes.com/1996/08/17/nyregion/nothing-extraordinary-is-found-in-747-s-engines.html.

20. Ibid.

21. Affidavit of Henry Hughes, cached at The TWA 800 Project, https:// twa800project.files.wordpress.com/2014/06/affidavit-of-hank-hughes. pdf.

22. "Analysis and Recommendations Regarding T.W.A. Flight 800," submitted by R. T. Miller, https://twa800.sites.usa.gov/files/twa800/ DCA96MA070/50470.pdf.

23. Affidavit of Henry Hughes.

24. As interviewed in Tom Stalcup and Kristina Borjesson, *TWA Flight 800* (TWA 800 Project, LLC, 2013).

25. John Barry and Roger Charles, "Sea of Lies," *Newsweek*, July 12, 1992, http://www.newsweek.com/sea-lies-200118.

SEVENTEEN: BENGHAZI MOMENT

1. Matthew Wald, "Boeing Says Vapor Threat Requires a Tank Redesign," *New York Times*, December 10, 1997, http://www.nytimes. com/1997/12/10/nyregion/boeing-says-vapor-threat-requires-a-tank-redesign.html.

2. Neil Genzlinger, "Leaving No Survivors but Many Questions," *New York Times*, July 16, 2013, http://www.nytimes.com/2013/07/17/arts/ television/twa-flight-800-examines-a-1996-tragedy.html?_r=0.

3. As interviewed in Tom Stalcup and Kristina Borjesson, *TWA Flight 800* (TWA 800 Project, LLC, 2013).

4. Ibid.

5. "Risk Management Expert Calls for New Investigation into Cause of TWA Flight 800 Crash," PRweb, July 8, 2013, http://www.prweb.com/ releases/2013/7/prweb10903410.htm.

6. "The Situation Room," CNN, June 20, 2013, https://www.youtube.com/ watch?v=Pd95PkWbkn8.

7. "Former FBI investigator defends probe into TWA 800 crash," Fox News, June 20, 2013, http://video.foxnews.com/v/2494702166001/former-fbi-investigator-defends-probe-into-twa-800-crash/?#sp=show-clips.

8. Transcript, CNN Newsroom, June 22, 2013, http://edition.cnn.com/ TRANSCRIPTS/1306/22/cnr.02.html.

9. Fred Lucas, "WH: Obama Called Hillary on Night of Benghazi Attack— More Than Six Hours After It Started," cnsnews.com, February 20, 2013, http://cnsnews.com/news/article/wh-obama-called-hillary-night-benghazi-attack-more-six-hours-after-it-started.

10. Donovan Slack, "Hillary Clinton condemns Benghazi attack," *Politico,* September 12, 2012, http://www.politico.com/blogs/politico44/2012/09/hillary-clinton-condemns-benghazi-attack-135265.

11. Brendan Bordelon, "Benghazi Committee Bombshell: Clinton Knew 'Attack Had Nothing to Do with the Film,'" *National Review,* October 22, 2015, http://www.nationalreview.com/article/425933/benghazi-committee-emails-hillary-clinton-lied-video-excuse.

12. "Second Presidential Debate: Libya," CBS News, October 16, 2012, http://www.cbsnews.com/videos/second-presidential-debate-libya/.

13. "President Obama Speaks on the Attack on Benghazi," whitehouse.gov, September 12, 2102, https://www.whitehouse.gov/photos-and-video/video/2012/09/12/president-obama-speaks-attack-benghazi.

14. Jack Cashill, "CNN Edits Out Comparison of TWA 800 and Benghazi," *American Thinker,* June 26, 2013, http://www.americanthinker.com/articles/2013/06/cnn_edits_out_comparison_of_twa_800_and_benghazi.html.

15. Jack Cashill, "What CNN Cut Out of TWA 800 Interview," *American Thinker,* June 27, 2013, http://www.cashill.com/twa800/what_cnn_cut_out.htm.

16. Andrew Kramer and Dan Bilefsky, "Malaysia Airlines Crash Investigators May Have Found Missile Clues in Ukraine," *New York Times,* August 11, 2015, http://www.nytimes.com/2015/08/12/world/europe/malaysia-airlines-crash-mh17-ukraine-missile.html?_r=0.

17. "Malaysia Flight Crashes With 295 On Board," CNN Breaking News, July 17, 2014, https://www.youtube.com/watch?v=UFLb49pPSe4.

18. Transcript, *Witnessed.*

19. "Malaysia Flight Crashes With 295 On Board," CNN Breaking News, July 17, 2014, https://www.youtube.com/watch?v=BUqbteKLkzg.

EIGHTEEN: PROCRUSTES

1. Susan Cornwell, "Safety investigators stand by cause of TWA Flight 800 Crash," Reuters, July 2, 2013, http://www.reuters.com/article/2013/07/03/us-usa-flight-probe-idUSBRE96201120130703.

2. Letter to David Tochen, June 26, 2014, The TWA 800 Project, https://twa800project.files.wordpress.com/2014/06/stalcup-hughes-to-tochen-final.pdf. This letter documents the Project's history of petitioning the NTSB.

3. "NTSB Stands By Investigation of 1996 Crash of TWA Flight 800," NTSB, http://twa800.sites.usa.gov/.

4. NTSB Aircraft Accident Report, *In-flight breakup over the Atlantic Ocean, Trans World Airlines Flight 800*, xvi.

5. Phone interview with Vernon Grose, October 23, 2015.

6. "MH17 Crash," Dutch Safety Board, October 2015, http://cdn.onder zoeksraad.nl/documents/report-mh17-crash-en.pdf.

7. "NTSB Refuses to Reopen TWA Flight 800 Crash Probe," NBC News, July 2, 2014, http://www.nbcnews.com/news/us-news/ntsb-refuses-reopen-twa-flight-800-crash-probe-n147051.

8. CIA documents cached at TWA Flight 800: The Impossible Zoom Climb, raylahr.entryhost.com, "CIA records released to Tom Stalcup," records 1–10.

9. Ibid. All other CIA interpretations of the FBI 302s can be found at this location.

10. Transcript, Hearing before the Subcommittee on Aviation, July 10, 1997.

11. Document cached at TWA Flight 800: The Impossible Zoom Climb, raylahr.entryhost.com/"CIA records released to Tom Stalcup," Court Ordered releases, CIA: May 13, 2008.

12. Brumley interview as seen in Tom Stalcup's Rebuttal of CIA Video About TWA Flight 800, https://www.youtube.com/watch?v=IyluFVxqBlo.

13. CIA documents cached at TWA Flight 800: The Impossible Zoom Climb, raylahr.entryhost.com, "CIA records released to Tom Stalcup," records 26–50.

14. Document cached at TWA Flight 800: The Impossible Zoom Climb, raylahr.entryhost.com/"CIA records released to Tom Stalcup," Court Ordered releases, CIA: May 13, 2008, 8–13.

15. CIA documents cached at TWA Flight 800: The Impossible Zoom Climb, raylahr.entryhost.com, "CIA records released to Tom Stalcup," records 76–101.

16. FBI New York Office Press Release, November 18, 1997, http://www.lchr.org/a/11/j/fbitwa.htm.

17. Transcript, Hearing before the Subcommittee on Aviation, July 10, 1997.

18. Ibid.

NINETEEN: THE SMOKING GUN

1. CIA documents cached at TWA Flight 800: The Impossible Zoom Climb, raylahr.entryhost.com, "CIA records released to Tom Stalcup," records 26–50.

2. Ibid.

3. Ibid.

4. Dan Barry, "Is That a Missile? Snapshot on Night of Air Crash Turns Hot," *New York Times*, August 26, 1996, http://www.nytimes.com/1996/08/26/nyregion/is-that-a-missile-snapshot-on-night-of-air-crash-turns-hot.html.

5. TWA Flight 800, NTSB docket materials, DCA-96-MA070, August 2000, Exhibit 4A, appendix C.

6. NTSB Witness Group Factual Report, October 16, 1997.

7. Michael Pitcher, "Fax Gives Glimpse of Crash Investigation," *Southampton Press*, July 24, 1997, http://archive.southamptonpress.com/shpress/1997-3/97072408.htm.

8. Reed Irvine, "NTSB Destroys Incriminating Evidence," Accuracy In Media, December 14, 2001, http://www.aim.org/publications/weekly_column/2001/12/14.html.

9. "The Cooperative Engagement Capability," *John Hopkins APL Technical Digest*, November 1995. The illustration of the P-3 is on page 3of the *Digest*. http://www.jhuapl.edu/techdigest/td/td1604/APLteam.pdf.

10. David Hendrix, "Witnesses Boost Missile Theory," *Press-Enterprise*, October 20, 1997, cached at http://whatreallyhappened.com/RANCHO/CRASH/TWA/AUDIO.html.

11. International Association of Machinists and Aerospace Workers, "Analysis and Recommendations Regarding T.W.A. Flight 800," https://twa800.sites.usa.gov/files/twa800/DCA96MA070/50470.pdf. See also http://twa800.com/iamaw/iamaw_submission.pdf.

12. Don Van Natta, "Fuel Tank's Condition Makes Malfunction Seem Less Likely," *New York Times*, August 14, 1996, http://www.nytimes.com/1996/08/14/nyregion/fuel-tank-s-condition-makes-malfunction-seem-less-likely.html.

13. NTSB Aircraft Accident Report, *In-flight breakup over the Atlantic Ocean, Trans World Airlines Flight 8Boeing 747-131, N93119, near East Moriches, New York, July 17, 1996* (Washington, DC: Diane Publishing, 2000), 273, http://bit.ly/1LqLGsX.

14. Thomas Jefferson to Archibald Stuart, 1799, http://famguardian.org/Subjects/Politics/thomasjefferson/jeff1600.htm.

15. Neil Genzlinger, "Leaving No Survivors but Many Questions," *New York Times*, July 16, 2013, http://www.nytimes.com/2013/07/17/arts/television/twa-flight-800-examines-a-1996-tragedy.html?_r=0.

INDEX